Ready-to-Use

WRITING
PROFICIENCY
LESSONS &
ACTIVITIES

4th Grade Level

Carol H. Behrman

**THE CENTER FOR APPLIED
RESEARCH IN EDUCATION**
Paramus, New Jersey 07652

Library of Congress Cataloging-in-Publication Data

Behrman, Carol H.
    Ready-to-use writing proficiency lessons & activities : fourth grade level / by Carol H. Behrman.
      p. cm.
    ISBN 0-13-042012-3
    1. English language—Composition and exercises—Study and teaching (Elementary)
  2. Language arts (Elementary) 3. Activity programs in education. I. Title.

    LB1576.B4265 2002
    372.62'3'044—dc21
                                                 2002028723

Acquisitions Editor: *Bernice Golden*
Production Editor: *Tom Curtin*
Interior Design/Page Layout: *Dimitra Coroneos*

© 2002 by The Center for Applied Research in Education

Printed in the United States of America

10 9 8 7 6 5 4 3 2 1

ISBN 0-13-042012-3

ATTENTION: CORPORATIONS AND SCHOOLS

The Center for Applied Research in Education books are available at quantity discounts with bulk purchase for educational, business, or sales promotional use. For information, please write to: Prentice Hall Special Sales, 240 Frisch Court, Paramus, NJ 07652. Please supply: title of book, ISBN, quantity, how the book will be used, date needed.

THE CENTER FOR APPLIED RESEARCH IN EDUCATION
Paramus, New Jersey 07652

http://www.phdirect.com

DEDICATION

ABOUT THE AUTHOR

Carol H. Behrman was born in Brooklyn, New York, graduated from City College of New York, and attended Columbia University's Teachers' College, where she majored in education. She married Edward Behrman, an accountant, and moved to Fair Lawn, New Jersey, where they raised three children. They currently reside in Sarasota, Florida. For many years, Mrs. Behrman taught grades five through eight at the Glen Ridge Middle School in New Jersey, where she created a program utilizing a writing process that combined language arts with word-processing instruction. She has written nineteen books, fiction and nonfiction, for children and young adults, and has conducted numerous workshops on the writing process for students, teachers, and aspiring writers. She has served as writer-in-residence at Chautauqua Institution and has been an adjunct lecturer at Seton Hall and New York University's Writing Center.

Mrs. Behrman is also the author of *Writing Skills Problem Solver* (2000), *Writing Activities for Every Month of the School Year* (1997), *Write! Write! Write!* (1995), and *Hooked on Writing!* (1990), all published by The Center for Applied Research in Education.

ABOUT THIS WRITING TESTPREP TEACHING RESOURCE

Activities

Ready-to-Use Writing Proficiency Lessons & Activities gives classroom teachers and reading specialists a powerful and effective tool for addressing writing standards and competencies at the fourth-grade level. This resource offers a variety of easy-to-use, reproducible activity sheets that provide review and application of the basic language skills as well as extensive practice in producing the types of writing called for in the standardized tests. The activities are grouped into the following ten sections:

- **Section 1:** The 26 activities in "Choosing the Right Word" help students select the most appropriate word when they write. Homonyms, verbs, adjectives, sensory words, and similes are introduced in these pages.

- **Section 2:** The 23 activities in "Making Mechanics and Usage Work for You" provide a review of capitalization, punctuation, pronoun usage, plurals, and spelling. After completing these activities, students will be more confident in these troublesome areas.

- **Section 3:** "Writing Sentences" contains 23 activities that teach the students basic strategies (and more) for writing interesting and effective sentences. Here, the students learn to work with subjects and predicates. Then, besides reviewing fragments and run-ons, students combine simple sentences into compound and complex sentences.

- **Section 4:** The 21 activities in "Writing Paragraphs" teach students how to develop a well-constructed paragraph. Activities on writing effective topic sentences and strong concluding sentences, as well as developing the topic efficiently and relevantly, are featured here. Students also write paragraphs following the steps in the writing process.

- **Section 5:** Your students will organize their ideas through brainstorming, clustering, or outlining after they finish the 20 activities in "Essay-Writing Techniques." Introducing the topic in an interesting way, using related examples, staying on the subject, and concluding the essay in a meaningful way are all covered here.

- **Section 6:** The "nuts and bolts" of how to write in order to convey information effectively are covered in "Writing Informative Essays." Students develop eight essays by completing 24 activities that employ the writing process.

- **Section 7:** Students will write more convincingly after they practice the essentials covered in "Writing Persuasive Essays." Eight essays, developed by completing the 24 activities, emphasize the strengths of the writing process.

- **Section 8:** Eight narrative and descriptive essays are the focus of the 24 activities in "Writing Narrative/Descriptive Essays." Here, students will work on various topics as their stepping-off points for this type of writing.

- **Section 9:** Whether a letter's purpose is to inform or to persuade, the "Writing Letters" section provides students with 21 activities that review the purposes and components of a letter.

- **Section 10:** The 27 activities in the concluding section, "Writing Stories," spark students' imaginations. Here, your young authors will develop the skills to write interesting and memorable realistic, fantasy, and mystery stories.

Teacher Preparation and Lessons

Teacher lesson plans and suggestions for direct instruction precede each section of activities. When appropriate, answer keys for the various activities are also provided. The activities in Sections 1-3 can be used—either as part of a larger language arts program or specifically for test preparation—to introduce, review, and reinforce basic language skills with individual students, small groups, or the entire class, as appropriate. Students should be encouraged to apply these skills as they complete the writing activities in Sections 4-10. You may wish to select skills pages and assign them before students complete a specific writing assignment and before they complete the Practice Test.

Practice Tests and Standardized Assessment

The Practice Tests at the end of Sections 1-3 can be used as a pretest and/or as a posttest to assess basic language skills. Distribute a Practice Test and Answer Sheet to each student. Point out the importance of reading and following directions carefully, especially when taking standardized tests. Make sure students understand the formats of these practice test items. You may wish to copy one of the items on the chalkboard and model how to follow directions in order to complete it properly. Tell students that it is important to read all the choices before selecting an answer. Demonstrate how to darken the circles on the Answer Sheet.

The Practice Tests at the end of Sections 4-10 take students through the writing process for producing a passage based on a prompt. A checklist at the beginning of each test reminds students which skills and techniques are required for each type of writing. Many of these skills and techniques are also listed on the scoring guide accompanying each test. These scoring guides were created to assist you in assessing students' writing on the test. Students may find it helpful to use the scoring guides to assess their own writing and/or to assess the sample student writing passages provided with the tests. Until students are familiar with the process, you may wish to work with a simplified version of the guides or with one section at a time. Make sure that when students assign a score to a writing passage, they are able to support their decision with evidence. Scores for the sample writing passages and a rationale for each one are provided at the end of the Teacher Preparation pages for each section.

A good indicator of what is required on standardized writing tests at the fourth-grade level is the National Assessment of Educational Progress (NAEP) writing test. Information on the NAEP can be found at *www.NAGB.org* or at *www.nces.ed.gov/nationsreportcard*. In this resource, information on standardized testing and on scoring rubrics for the NAEP as well as for the states of Pennsylvania, Oregon, Illinois, and Idaho appears at the beginning of Sections 5-10. The scoring guides accompanying the writing practice tests were adapted from the New Jersey state test. You may wish to compare these guidelines with those for your individual state when scoring students' writing samples.

Writing Proficiency Lessons & Activities are also available from the publisher at the Eighth-Grade Level and the Tenth-Grade Level. The lessons, activities, and sample test items in all three grade-level volumes are invaluable tools for helping students to master basic language and writing skills in preparation for taking standardized tests as well as to develop a sound foundation for becoming proficient writers throughout their lives.

CONTENTS

SECTION 2
MAKING MECHANICS AND USAGE WORK FOR YOU   41

SECTION 3
WRITING SENTENCES   77

PRACTICE TEST: WRITING SENTENCES   110

SECTION 4
WRITING PARAGRAPHS   117

SECTION 5
ESSAY-WRITING TECHNIQUES   147

SECTION 9
WRITING LETTERS   277

SECTION 10
WRITING STORIES   307

APPENDIX
PREPARING YOUR STUDENTS FOR
STANDARDIZED PROFICIENCY TESTS 345

CHOOSING
THE RIGHT WORD

Teacher Preparation and Lessons

Activities 1-1 through 1-4 are designed to enlarge students' vocabularies and make their writing more precise. Activities 1-5 through 1-18 concentrate on using the parts of speech correctly. Activities 1-19 and 1-20 focus on words often confused. Activities 1-21 through 1-26 help students improve their usage of literal and figurative language. You may wish to use the PRACTICE TEST at the end of the section as a pretest and/or as a posttest. Answer keys for this section can be found on pages 5-8.

ACTIVITIES 1-1 and 1-2 review **synonyms** and **antonyms**. To teach synonyms, write the following paragraph on the board: *Andy is a big guy. He wears a big shirt size. His hands and feet are big. He has big muscles, too.* Elicit that the repetition of *big* makes this paragraph boring. Ask what other words with the same or similar meaning could be used instead of *big (large, enormous, huge, gigantic)*. Remind students that words with the same or similar meanings are called *synonyms*. On the board, make a list of synonyms for *big*. Then rewrite the paragraph using some of the synonyms. Distribute **Activity 1-1 Synonyms.** Discuss the introductory material together. When students have completed this activity, have each altered sentence read aloud by several students to demonstrate the variety of synonyms they have substituted for the underlined words. Introduce *antonyms* by writing the following pairs of words on the board: *young/old; top/bottom*. Elicit that these are opposites, called antonyms. Distribute **Activity 1-2 Antonyms** and read the boxed material together. When students have completed the activity, list students' antonyms for each item on the board. **NOTE:** You may wish to have students use a children's thesaurus to complete Activities 1-1 and 1-2.

ACTIVITIES 1-3 and 1-4 introduce **homonyms.** Write and say the following words: *to, two, too*. Have the class say them. Elicit that these are *homonyms*, words that sound the same but have different spellings and meanings. Then write the words *pair, plain, principal*, and *weak*. Elicit and write a homonym for each word. Tell students that the context of a sentence will determine which homonym to use. Distribute **Activity 1-3 Homonyms (Part One).** Read the boxed material and have students complete the activity. Follow a similar procedure with **Activity 1-4 Homonyms (Part Two).** Use sample words *find, hour, heard*, and *your*.

ACTIVITY 1-5 teaches **common and proper nouns.** Explain that common nouns name any person, place, or thing. Write on the board *girl, country, state*, and *month*, and use each word in a sentence. Then ask students to name a specific girl, a specific country, a specific state, and a specific month. Write each one with an initial capital letter. Circle the capital letters and point out that proper nouns name specific people, places, and things. You may wish to complete **Activity 1-5 Common and Proper Nouns** together.

ACTIVITIES **1-6 through 1-10** concentrate on **verbs.** Tell students that there are two kinds of verbs: action verbs and linking verbs. To teach **action verbs,** write the word *run* on the board. Elicit more specific words that also mean *run.* Answers such as *sprint* and *jog* will probably be given. Emphasize that using precise or exact action verbs such as *sprint* and *jog* will make their writing more interesting. Distribute **Activity 1-6 Action Verbs.** Discuss the introductory material together. Make sure students understand the directions.

Activity 1-7 introduces **linking verbs.** Write the following sentence on the board: *Jeremiah looked happy during the party.* Tell students that *looked* is a linking verb that connects the subject, *Jeremiah,* to the adjective *happy.* Write the following linking verbs on the board: *appear, are, become, feel, is, seem, smell, sound, taste, was,* and *were,* and have each one used in a sentence. Distribute **Activity 1-7 Linking Verbs.** Read the definition and examples and have students complete the page. When they have finished Part A, help them underline or draw arrows between the two words connected by the linking verbs.

Activity 1-8 introduces **main verbs** and **helping verbs.** Write the following sentence on the board: *Kim had walked a mile before the storm began.* Read it aloud and underline the verbs *had walked.* Point out that *walked* is the main verb and *had* is a helping verb. Explain that helping verbs come before the main verb and show the time of the action. Point out that *had* shows action in the past. List these helping and main verbs: *is walking, are walking, was walking, were walking, have walked, has walked,* and *had walked.* Review the introductory material at the top of **Activity 1-8 Main Verbs and Helping Verbs.** Have students complete the page.

Activities 1-9 and 1-10 teach **irregular verbs.** Write the headings *Present, Past,* and *Past (along with has, have, and had)* on the board. Write the forms of *talk* under the headings as an example of a regular verb. Then write the forms of *begin* as an example of an irregular verb under the headings. Compare the two verb formations. Distribute **Activity 1-9 Irregular Verbs (Part One).** Read the introductory material and have students complete the activity with a partner. Later, distribute **Activity 1-10 Irregular Verbs (Part Two).** If possible, have the students complete the activity independently.

ACTIVITIES **1-11 through 1-16** review **adjectives.** Remind students that adjectives describe, or modify, nouns or pronouns. They tell *what kind, how many,* or *which one.* Write the words *big dog, many dogs,* and *that dog* on the board. Tell students that the words *big, many,* and *that* are adjectives that help to describe *dog.* The adjective's purpose is to describe the noun or pronoun and to make the sentence more interesting. Review the introductory material at the top of **Activity 1-11 Adjectives.** Make sure students understand the directions.

Introduce the next activity by writing this sentence on the board: *The runner, tired and thirsty, finished the marathon.* Point out that the words *tired* and *thirsty* are adjectives that are **placed** *after* **the noun** they describe *(runner).* Distribute **Activity 1-12 Placement of Adjectives.** Review the introductory material. Complete the first item with students to make sure they understand the directions.

Begin **Activity 1-13 Proper Adjectives** by defining and showing examples of **proper adjectives** such as *Spanish, Mexican,* and *American* used in sentences. Distribute the page and read the introductory material. You may wish to complete the activity with students. Emphasize that proper adjectives are capitalized.

Begin **Activity 1-14 Comparison Adjectives** by distributing the activity. Discuss the three rules for forming comparison adjectives. Have students complete the activity.

Distribute **Activity 1-15 Adding Adjectives.** Read the directions and have students complete the activity. Ask students to read their new sentences.

Begin **Activity 1-16 Articles** by writing on the board: *A man waved to us. An orange was on the table. The apple was left there.* Point out articles *a, an,* and *the* and their function in the sentence. Distribute the page, read the introductory material in the box, and read the directions. Have students complete the activity.

ACTIVITIES 1-17 and 1-18 cover **adverbs.** Tell students that when they write, they use adverbs to tell *when, where,* and *how.* On the board, write these sentences with words in parentheses: *I never* spoke to her. (**when**); Regina walked *there.* (**where**); and They handled it *roughly.* (**how**). Point out how an adverb answers one of these three questions: *When? Where?* and *How?* Distribute **Activity 1-17 Adverbs (Part One).** Read the introductory material together and have students complete the page.

After distributing **Activity 1-18 Adverbs (Part Two),** read the directions and complete the first two items together. Have students complete the activity on their own.

ACTIVITIES 1-19 and 1-20 teach **words often confused.** Distribute **Activity 1-19 Words Often Confused (Part One)** and read the words and definitions together. Have students complete the page with a partner. To introduce Activity 1-20, write: *The Saguaro Cactus is found in the desert. Apple pie is a delicious dessert.* Read the sentences aloud and underline *desert* and *dessert.* Point out that these two words are spelled similarly, have different meanings, and are pronounced differently. Pronounce the words (di zurt', dez' ert). Tell students that when they write, they should watch out for these and other words that are often confused. Distribute **Activity 1-20 Words Often Confused (Part Two).** Read the preliminary material together and have students complete the page.

ACTIVITIES 1-21 through 1-23 deal with improving the students' usage of **literal and figurative language.** Discuss how human beings are sensory beings. Our five senses—touch, sight, taste, sound, and smell—are the doors through which we perceive the world. They are also the tools that a good writer uses to gain entry into the reader's world. Becoming comfortable and familiar with a variety of sensory words will enable the student writer to turn out prose that is vivid and interesting. To begin, elicit the names of the five senses and write them on the board.

Next, write these sentences on the board: *After the flash of lightning and boom of thunder, the tree crashed to the ground. The sour, pungent smoke stung his eye.* Ask students to underline or circle the sensory words in these sentences and identify which sense is involved. Point out that some words can appeal to more than one sense. Distribute **Activity 1-21 Sensory Words (Part One).** Read the introductory material and the directions together. Have students complete the page.

Distribute **Activity 1-22 Sensory Words (Part Two).** Have students complete their lists and then share them with each other.

Distribute **Activity 1-23 Sensory Words (Part Three).** Have students rewrite each sentence using sensory words, and then share their sentences with each other.

ACTIVITIES 1-24 through 1-26 teach **similes and metaphors.** Explain that similes are comparisons using words such as *like* or *as.* Point out that in a poem by a famous poet named Robert Burns, he compares love to a *red, red, rose* and to a *sweet melody played in tune.* Point out that to describe something by comparing it to something else helps the reader picture what they are reading. It also creates more interesting writing. Then write: *These flowers are as red as* _____. Ask the students to complete the line. Write several of their suggestions on the board. Most of the similes suggested by students will probably be short, one-word comparisons. Encourage them to come up with longer ones, such as *as red as my face when I arrived in class twenty minutes late*. Write some of these on the board. Follow the same procedure with the following: *as cold as, as frightened as, as happy as*. Distribute **Activity 1-24 Similes (Part One).** Read the boxed material and directions aloud. When students have completed the similes, have several read aloud.

Distribute **Activity 1-25 Similes (Part Two).** Read the directions and the poem aloud. Students may wish to share their similes when they have finished the page.

Begin **Activity 1-26 Metaphors** by explaining that these are comparisons, but differ from similes because they do not use comparison words such as *like* or *as*. You may wish to read aloud "Fog" by Carl Sandburg and discuss the metaphor in the poem. (comparison of fog to a cat) Explain that in a metaphor, one thing is spoken of as if it were another thing. Discuss the metaphors in the following: *The moon is a silver dollar; the boy is a jumping bean; the sunset is a crimson fire.* Distribute the activity. Read the introductory material and the directions aloud. When students are finished, have them write metaphors of their own.

ANSWER KEY

1–1. SYNONYMS
These are some possible answers.

1. cheerful, joyful
2. ceased, halted
3. cold, icy
4. terror, panic
5. dragged, hauled
6. giggling, chuckling
7. odd, unusual, weird
8. connect, attach

1–2. ANTONYMS
These are some possible answers.

1. sad, unhappy
2. short
3. cold, icy, frigid
4. first
5. good
6. slow
7. best
8. same
9. back, rear
10. dirty
11. old
12. sweet
13. cheap, inexpensive
14. crooked
15. early
16. inside
17. awake
18. wrong, left
19. day
20. hard

1–3. HOMONYMS (PART ONE)

1. plane
2. plain
3. plane
4. principal
5. principles
6. week
7. weak
8. right
9. write
10. right

1–4. HOMONYMS (PART TWO)

1. herd
2. hare
3. hour
4. heard
5. Our
6. hair
7. peace
8. piece

1–5. COMMON NOUNS AND PROPER NOUNS

1. Henry (P), musician (C)
2. Mr. Jenks (P), flute (C)
3. Kerry (P), car (C)
4. Minnesota (P), family (C)
5. California (P), valleys (C)
6. Canadians (P), hockey (C)
7. Grace (P), computers (C)
8. Bob (P), captain (C)
9. Mr. Landers (P), teacher (C)
10. Mount Washington (P), hikers (C)
11. Neil Armstrong (P), astronaut (C)
12. Geraldine (P), babies (C)

1–6. ACTION VERBS

1. strolled
2. sprinted
3. crashed
4. roamed
5. cluttered
6. basked in
7. gazed at
8. yanked
9. caressed
10. glanced
11. gasped
12. erupted

1–7. LINKING VERBS

1. were
2. taste
3. was
4. appear
5. are
6. sounds
7. look
8. was
9. became
10. smell

1–8. MAIN VERBS AND HELPING VERBS

1. had started (started)
2. is eating (eating)
3. was circling (circling)
4. are planning (planning)
5. has landed (landed)
6. were going (going)
7. have waited (waited)
8. has walked (walked)

1–9. IRREGULAR VERBS (PART ONE)

1. swam
2. rung
3. begun
4. brought
5. thought
6. made
7. swam
8. said
9. made
10. began
11. sang
12. made

1–10. IRREGULAR VERBS (PART TWO)

1. become
2. seen
3. came
4. seen
5. went
6. ran
7. gone
8. became
9. run
10. threw
11. saw
12. thrown

1–11. ADJECTIVES

1. great (adj.), quarterback (noun)
2. many (adj.), games (noun)
3. best (adj.), season (noun)
4. happy (adj.), players (noun)
5. shiny, golden (adjs.), bracelet (noun)
6. best (adj.), friends (noun)

1–12. PLACEMENT OF ADJECTIVES

1. frightening (adj.), nightmare (noun)
2. tired (adj.), Ann (noun)
3. long (adj.), day (noun)
4. stern, sharp (adjs.), Mr. Grant (noun)
5. loud, angry (adjs.), voice (noun)
6. ashamed (adj.), Ann (noun)
7. curious (adj.), friends (noun)

1–13. PROPER ADJECTIVES

Answers will vary. These are possible answers.

1. American
2. Chinese
3. Italian
4. April, May
5. Native American
6. French
7. Scottish
8. Canadian
9. Hawaiian
10. Japanese
11. Boston
12. Spanish

1–14. COMPARSION ADJECTIVES

1. taller
2. most handsome
3. better
4. best
5. most honest
6. scarier
7. hardest
8. better
9. bigger
10. hairiest

1–15. ADDING ADJECTIVES

Answers will vary.

1–16. ARTICLES

1. A, a
2. The, the
3. An, a, the
4. the
5. the
6. The, the
7. the
8. The
9. the
10. A
11. the
12. an

1–17. ADVERBS (PART ONE)

1. very (how)
2. usually (when)
3. quietly (how)
4. carefully (how)
5. always (when)
6. briefly (how)
7. below (where)
8. never (when)
9. there (where)
10. really (how)

1–18. ADVERBS (PART TWO)

Answers will vary.

1–19. WORDS OFTEN CONFUSED (PART ONE)

1. whose
2. it's
3. who's
4. their
5. their
6. its
7. they're
8. your
9. You're

1–20. WORDS OFTEN CONFUSED (PART TWO)

Part A

1. lose
2. loose
3. quiet
4. quite
5. desert
6. dessert
7. than
8. then

Part B

I am quite happy with pie for dessert rather than ice cream.

1–21. SENSORY WORDS (PART ONE)

1. black (sight)
2. salty (taste)
3. soft (touch)
4. roared (sound)
5. Spicy (smell)
6. Salty (taste, smell)
7. whispered (sound)
8. hot (taste, touch)
9. brown (sight)
10. rang (sound)
11. hard (touch)
12. sharp (touch, sight)
13. shouts (sound)
14. scratched (sight, sound)

1–22. SENSORY WORDS (PART TWO)

Answers will vary.

1–23. SENSORY WORDS (PART THREE)

Answers will vary.

1–24. SIMILES (PART ONE)

Answers will vary.

1–25. SIMILES (PART TWO)

Part A

The three similes are: *Like the noon-time sky on a sunny day, As blue as the sparkling mountain lake, As blue as the flowered wallpaper in my baby brother's room.*

Part B *Answers will vary.*

1–26. METAPHORS

1. wind≠howling coyote
2. grandfather≠big, shaggy bear
3. teacher≠walking encyclopedia
4. room≠refrigerator
5. city street≠oven
6. Aunt Tessa≠clown
7. coach≠dog (barked orders)
8. blanket≠snow
9. sand≠carpet
10. ocean≠lion (roar)

Name _____ Date _____

1–1. SYNONYMS

Using synonyms can make your writing more interesting.

A synonym is a word that has the same or nearly the same meaning as another word. Instead of using the same word over and over, substituting synonyms for it will add variety and interest to your writing. The words *nice, agreeable, good-natured,* and *pleasant* are all synonyms that can be used to describe someone or something you like.

DIRECTIONS: Rewrite the sentences below using a synonym for each underlined word.

1. Rose is a very <u>happy</u> girl. _____

_____

2. The loud noise coming from the garage <u>stopped</u>. _____

_____

3. It was a <u>chilly</u> night in October. _____

_____

4. Lisa was filled with <u>fear</u> when she heard the weird noises. _____

_____

5. The boys <u>pulled</u> the canoe out of the water. _____

_____

6. We all began <u>laughing</u> when we saw his costume. _____

_____

7. My aunt sometimes wears <u>strange</u> clothes. _____

_____

8. The next step is to <u>join</u> the two pieces together. _____

_____

1–2. ANTONYMS

Here is the definition of antonyms and some examples.

An **antonym** is a word that means the opposite of another word. *Tall* is the opposite (or antonym) of *short*. *Tiny* is an antonym of *huge*.

DIRECTIONS: Write an antonym for each word.

1. happy _____

2. tall _____

3. hot _____

4. last _____

5. bad _____

6. fast _____

7. worst _____

8. different _____

9. front _____

10. clean _____

11. young _____

12. sour _____

13. expensive _____

14. straight _____

15. late _____

16. outside _____

17. asleep _____

18. right _____

19. night _____

20. soft _____

Name _____ Date _____

1–3. HOMONYMS (PART ONE)

Here is the definition of homonyms and some examples.

> *Homonyms* are words that sound alike but have different meanings. They are often spelled differently, too. When you write, make sure you are using the correct homonym. Here are some examples of *homonyms:*
>
> 1. *Plain* can mean "not fancy," "clear," or "a flat area of land." (Jessica wears plain dresses. The answer is plain to see. The beasts roamed the plain.) A *plane* is an airplane. A *plane* is also a tool. (The plane landed at the airport. The carpenter used a plane to smooth the board.)
>
> 2. A *principal* is the head of a school. It also means "main" or "most important." (Mrs. Jenkins is our new principal. Coffee is the principal crop of Brazil.) A rule of conduct is a *principle.* (Because he follows strict principles of behavior, many people like him.)
>
> 3. *Weak* means "not strong." (A weightlifter is not physically weak!) A *week* is seven consecutive days. (Helen's birthday is next week.)
>
> 4. *Right* means "correct" or the direction that is opposite of left. (Use your right hand.) *Write* means to form words with a pen or pencil. (Can you write me a poem?)

DIRECTIONS: Underline the correct homonym in each sentence.

1. One (plain, plane) was left on the airport's runway.

2. He asked for a (plain, plane) ice cream cone since he did not like sprinkles.

3. The carpenter put his (plain, plane) away in the toolbox.

4. When will you meet the school's new (principal, principle)?

5. Is that behavior against his (principals, principles)?

6. Will you be having your meeting this (weak, week)?

7. Regular exercise can prevent muscles from becoming (weak, week).

8. Use the door to the (right, write) to exit the building.

9. I'll (right, write) Uncle Jim a letter tonight.

10. Sheila gave the (right, write) answer.

11

1–4. Homonyms (PART TWO)

Make sure you are using the correct homonym when you write.

> Homonyms are words that sound alike but have different meanings and spellings.
>
> 1. *Heard* is a form of the verb *hear*. (I *heard* you were going to that school.)
>   A *herd* is a group of animals. (The *herd* of cattle was in the pasture.)
>
> 2. An *hour* is sixty minutes. (Were you there for more than an *hour*?)
>   *Our* is a possessive pronoun. (Did you see *our* new house?)
>
> 3. *Hair* is a skin covering. (She tied her *hair* in a ponytail.)
>   A *hare* is a rabbit. (Did the *hare* outrun the turtle?)
>
> 4. *Peace* is the opposite of war. (After the war ended, *peace* returned.)
>   A *piece* is a part of something. (Would you like a *piece* of cake?)

DIRECTIONS: Underline the correct homonym in each sentence.

1. Sal photographed the (herd, heard) of animals in the wilderness.

2. One (hair, hare) chased the other across the field.

3. She will be on stage in an (hour, our).

4. Have you (heard, herd) what we're going to do after the show?

5. (Our, Hour) best chance to catch a toad is to wait here.

6. Liz likes to wear her (hare, hair) in a French braid.

7. The treaty signaled the beginning of (peace, piece).

8. He cut off a (peace, piece) of string for us.

© 2002 by The Center for Applied Research in Education

1–5. COMMON NOUNS AND PROPER NOUNS

Here are the definitions of common and proper nouns and some examples of both.

> 1. A common noun is the general name of any person, place, thing, or idea. Do not capitalize a common noun. Examples of common nouns are *sailor, store, football,* and *happiness.*
>
> 2. A proper noun is the specific name for a person, place, or thing. Capitalize proper nouns. Examples of proper nouns include *Superman, Israel,* and *December.*

DIRECTIONS: Each sentence contains one proper noun and one common noun. Write the letter P above the proper nouns and the letter C above the common nouns.

1. Henry is the best musician.

2. Mr. Jenks purchased the flute yesterday.

3. Please start the older car now, Kerry.

4. The family will soon visit Minnesota.

5. She loves to explore valleys in California.

6. Many Canadians enjoy playing and watching hockey.

7. Grace knows a lot about these newer computers.

8. Do you know that Bob is our new captain?

9. Mr. Landers, our teacher, found it there.

10. Hikers continue to climb Mount Washington.

11. We interviewed the famous astronaut, Neil Armstrong.

12. How many babies has Geraldine photographed?

1–6. ACTION VERBS

Try to use vivid action verbs when you write.

An action verb tells what a subject does, did, or will do. Using vivid or specific action verbs will help make your writing more interesting. Examples of vivid action verbs include *grab, hurl,* and *peek.*

A. DIRECTIONS: Circle the more exact, or vivid, action verb in each sentence.

1. A young couple (strolled, walked) along the lake.

2. Some of the baseball players (ran, sprinted) toward the dugout.

3. Which police officer (broke, crashed) through the door to save the child?

4. The animals (walked, roamed) across the plain.

5. Jere (packed, cluttered) his room with old toys.

6. All the performers (enjoyed, basked in) the applause.

7. They (saw, gazed at) the beautiful sunset last night.

8. Doctor DeSoto (yanked, pulled) out Mr. Fox's tooth.

9. She (touched, caressed) her infant after the delicate operation.

10. Nobody even (looked, glanced) in his direction.

11. After the recovery, the heroic diver (breathed, gasped) for air.

12. Lava (erupted, gushed) from the volcano during the night.

B. DIRECTIONS: Write a sentence about your favorite story character. Use at least one vivid action verb in your sentence.

_____

_____

_____

1–7. LINKING VERBS

Here is the definition of a linking verb and some examples.

> A linking verb connects the subject of a sentence to a noun or an adjective in the predicate. Examples of linking verbs include *appear, are, become, feel, is, look, seem, smell, sound, taste, was,* and *were.* Some of these linking verbs also can be used as action verbs. Compare the meaning of *look* in these sentences: *It **looks** good. Don't **look** down.* In which sentence is *look* a linking verb? In which sentence is *look* an action verb?

A. DIRECTIONS: Circle the linking verb in each sentence.

1. They were teens at that time.

2. Tangerines taste very good.

3. The water's temperature was quite refreshing.

4. The workers appear happy now.

5. These foods are good sources of protein.

6. This explanation sounds correct.

7. You look different in this picture.

8. I was a member of the school's art committee.

9. Two players became professionals after that season.

10. Those roses smell like perfume.

B. DIRECTIONS: Write a sentence about the weather. Use at least one linking verb in your sentence.

_____

_____

_____

1–8. MAIN VERBS AND HELPING VERBS

Here is the definition of main verbs and helping verbs and some examples.

Sometimes sentences contain a **main verb** and a **helping verb**. The helping verb helps show the time of the action. Forms of *be* (*am, is, are, was, were*) and *have* (*has, have, had*) are the most common helping verbs. With forms of *be*, *-ing* is often added to the main verb. With forms of *have*, *-ed* is usually added to the main verb. A verb that can be used as a helping verb can also be used without another verb as the main verb. (*We have twenty fish.*)

A. DIRECTIONS: Underline the main and helping verb in each sentence. Then write the main verb on the line after the sentence.

1. The car had started this morning.   _____

2. Now she is eating her lunch.   _____

3. The butterfly was circling the flower.   _____

4. They are planning to visit in May.   _____

5. The airplane has landed on time.   _____

6. Mom and Dad were going out.   _____

7. I have waited over an hour for you.   _____

8. Jack has walked many miles.   _____

B. DIRECTIONS: Write a sentence with a main verb and a helping verb.

_____

_____

_____

© 2002 by The Center for Applied Research in Education

Name _____   Date _____

1–9. IRREGULAR VERBS (PART ONE)

Here is the definition of an irregular verb and some examples.

Irregular verbs do *not* add the ending *-ed* to form the past tense. Instead, they end in irregular ways. Here are some examples of irregular verbs:

PRESENT	PAST	PAST (used with *has, have,* or *had*)
begin	began	begun
bring	brought	brought
make	made	made
ring	rang	rung
say	said	said
sing	sang	sung
swim	swam	swum
think	thought	thought

DIRECTIONS: Circle the irregular main verb in each sentence.

1. He swam in the deep lake last summer.

2. The bell had rung by that time.

3. Most of the work had begun by that time.

4. He brought the carriage to the woman's house.

5. I thought you were there by the pool.

6. The fans made that television character popular.

7. All of the team members swam in the lake.

8. Is that what he said when he was a small boy?

9. How was the dam made?

10. They began the operation just after eight o'clock.

11. The rock star sang at the benefit concert.

12. Our outfielders made some great catches in yesterday's game.

1–10. IRREGULAR VERBS (PART TWO)

Remember to use the correct forms of irregular verbs when you write.

Here are some more irregular verbs. Study this chart to help you learn these irregular verbs.

PRESENT	PAST	PAST (used with *has, have,* and *had*)
become	became	become
come	came	come
go	went	gone
run	ran	run
see	saw	seen
throw	threw	thrown

DIRECTIONS: On the line within each sentence, write the correct form of the irregular verb in parentheses.

1. What has _____ of my old house? (**become**)

2. The umpire had _____ that the runner was out. (**see**)

3. My dad _____ home late for dinner last night. (**come**)

4. The movie was not _____ by the family. (**see**)

5. We _____ with your neighbor to the graduation. (**go**)

6. Ricky _____ when he saw the people who needed help. (**run**)

7. Have you ever _____ to the Bronx Zoo? (**go**)

8. My best friend as a child _____ a movie star. (**become**)

9. You had _____ your best race at that track meet. (**run**)

10. I _____ the ball back to the pitcher. (**throw**)

11. You said you _____ the man leave the building? (**see**)

12. They had _____ the paper into the basket. (**throw**)

© 2002 by The Center for Applied Research in Education

© 2002 by The Center for Applied Research in Education

Name _____   Date _____

1–11. ADJECTIVES

Adjectives help a writer paint "word pictures."

An adjective modifies or describes a noun or a pronoun. It answers one of these questions: *What kind? How many? Which one?*

1. The scientist wore a *long white* coat. The two adjectives, *long* and *white*, both answer the question *what kind* and modify the noun *coat*.

2. There were *several* fans at the *baseball* game. The adjective *several* answers the question *how many* and modifies the noun *fans*. *Baseball* is also used as an adjective. It answers the question *what kind* and modifies the noun *game*.

3. I did well on *that* test. The adjective *that* answers the question *which one* and modifies the noun *test*.

DIRECTIONS: After each sentence, list the adjective (or adjectives) and the noun that is modified.

1. Bob was a great quarterback.

   Adjective: _____   Noun: _____

2. He won many games for the team.

   Adjective: _____   Noun: _____

3. This year was the best season ever.

   Adjective: _____   Noun: _____

4. They were all happy players.

   Adjective: _____   Noun: _____

5. Jeni bought a shiny, golden bracelet.

   Adjectives: _____   Noun: _____

6. Her best friends came to her party.

   Adjective: _____   Noun: _____

1–12. PLACEMENT OF ADJECTIVES

Here are some ideas about the placement of adjectives.

1. An adjective usually appears *before* the noun it modifies. In the sentence "There was a *round* table." the adjective *round* modifies the noun *table*.

2. An adjective can also be placed *after* the noun it modifies. In the sentence "The winner, *tired* and *happy*, received his medal." the adjectives *tired* and *happy* modify the noun *winner*.

DIRECTIONS: After each sentence, list the adjective (or adjectives) and the noun that is modified.

1. Ann had a nightmare that was frightening.

   Adjective: _____   Noun: _____

2. Ann was tired all morning.

   Adjective: _____   Noun: _____

3. The day was long.

   Adjective: _____   Noun: _____

4. Mr. Grant, stern and sharp, scolded her.

   Adjectives: _____   Noun: _____

5. His voice was loud and angry.

   Adjective: _____   Noun: _____

6. Ann was ashamed.

   Adjective: _____   Noun: _____

7. Her friends were curious.

   Adjective: _____   Noun: _____

1–13. PROPER ADJECTIVES

Here is the definition of proper adjectives and some examples.

A proper adjective is an adjective formed from a proper noun. Proper adjectives begin with a capital letter. The following three sentences have proper adjectives:

1. *My mother makes a wonderful* Irish *stew.* The proper adjective *Irish* modifies, or describes, the noun *stew.*

2. *The* Italian *tenor sang a song from an opera.* The proper adjective *Italian* modifies the noun *tenor.*

3. *The cook opened a can of* Boston *baked beans.* The proper adjective *Boston* modifies the noun *baked beans.*

DIRECTIONS: Fill in each blank with a proper adjective. Remember to begin the adjective with a capital letter.

1. The boy held a (an) _____ flag in the parade.

2. My family went to a (an) _____ restaurant last night.

3. The _____ ambassador was on television last week.

4. _____ showers bring _____ flowers.

5. I read a book by a (an) _____ writer.

6. She wore her hair in a (an) _____ braid.

7. They visited a (an) _____ village.

8. We stopped at the _____ border.

9. The Simpsons took a (an) _____ vacation.

10. Dad watched a (an) _____ movie with subtitles.

11. Please open that can of _____ baked beans.

12. *Amigo* is a (an) _____ word.

1–14. COMPARISON ADJECTIVES

Here are a few tips to remember about comparison adjectives.

1. Adjectives usually show comparison by adding *-er* (when comparing two things) and *-est* (when comparing more than two things.) Examples include the following:

big	bigger	biggest
happy	happier	happiest
grand	grander	grandest

2. Some adjectives show comparison with the words *more* (for comparing two things) and *most* (for comparing more than two things). Examples include the following:

honest	more honest	most honest
terrible	more terrible	most terrible

3. A few irregular comparison adjectives do not follow these rules. Examples include the following:

good	better	best
bad	worse	worst
many	more	most

DIRECTIONS: Fill in the blank space with the appropriate comparison adjective.

1. Mr. Forrester is _____ than his brother. (**tall**)

2. Seth is the _____ boy in his class. (**handsome**)

3. This picture is _____ than the other one. (**good**)

4. This is the _____ party I ever attended. (**good**)

5. He is the _____ president we have had. (**honest**)

6. My Halloween costume is _____ than yours. (**scary**)

7. This test is the _____ one I have taken this year. (**hard**)

8. One Olympic medal is good, but two medals are even _____. (**good**)

9. Your school building is _____ than mine. (**big**)

10. That is the _____ dog I have ever seen. (**hairy**)

1–15. ADDING ADJECTIVES

Here are some ideas about how and when to add adjectives.

1. Adjectives help writers paint "word pictures." These adjectives make sentences more lively, clear, and interesting.

2. Here is a sentence that could use some adjectives: *The man walked down the street.* Now see how the use of some adjectives makes the sentence more interesting. *The tall, friendly man walked down the crowded street.*

DIRECTIONS: Make the following seven sentences more interesting and specific by adding adjectives. Write the new, improved sentences on the lines provided.

1. The girl walked along the beach.

   _____

   _____

2. She wore a dress and carried a bag.

   _____

   _____

3. Three boys were tossing a ball in the water.

   _____

   _____

4. A family sat nearby on a blanket.

   _____

   _____

5. Their children were eating sandwiches.

   _____

   _____

6. A boy was holding a balloon.

   _____

   _____

7. The waves washed over their feet.

   _____

   _____

1–16. ARTICLES

Here is the definition of an article, and some rules and examples.

Articles are special adjectives. Articles are *a, an,* and *the.*

1. The article *a* refers to any member of a group. It is used before a noun that begins with a consonant sound. (Words such as *team* and *radio* can be described by the article *a* since both begin with a consonant sound.)

2. The article *an* also refers to any member of a group. It is used before a word beginning with a vowel sound. (The words *umpire* and *easel* can be described by the article *an* since both start with a vowel sound.)

3. The article *the* refers to a specific member of a group. (*The speech* refers to a specific or particular speech, not just any speech.)

DIRECTIONS: Circle the article (or articles) in each sentence.

1. A penny saved is a penny earned.

2. The early bird catches the worm.

3. An apple a day keeps the doctor away.

4. Too many cooks spoil the broth.

5. Laughter is the best medicine.

6. The first step is the hardest.

7. When in Rome, do as the Romans do.

8. The best things in life are free.

9. Absence makes the heart grow fonder.

10. A chain is only as strong as its weakest link.

11. Necessity is the mother of invention.

12. You can't teach an old dog new tricks.

© 2002 by The Center for Applied Research in Education

Name _____ Date _____

1–17. Adverbs (part one)

Here is the definition of an adverb and some examples.

An adverb tells more about a *verb*, an *adjective*, or another *adverb*.

1. Most adverbs answer the questions *When, Where,* or *How.*

    Then I answered her. (when)

    He left his CD *here*. (where)

    The man spoke *loudly*. (how)

2. Adverbs often end in *-ly*. Examples include *slowly, briskly,* and *truthfully*.

3. Three common adverbs that do not end in *-ly* are *always, very,* and *well*.

DIRECTIONS: Underline the adverb in each sentence. Then, on the line provided, tell whether the adverb answers the question *When, Where,* or *How.*

1. He was a very fast runner. _____

2. They will usually run around the neighborhood. _____

3. The readers quietly turned the pages. _____

4. My mother carefully took the turkey out of the oven. _____

5. I always try to eat nutritional foods. _____

6. Some of the researchers worked briefly on the project. _____

7. Did you see the fish below? _____

8. I will never forget that moment at the concert. _____

9. The man found the package there. _____

10. I really love this song! _____

1–18. Adverbs (part two)

DIRECTIONS: Add one or more adverbs to each sentence. Then rewrite the sentence on the lines. *Remember:* Adverbs tell more about verbs, adjectives, and other adverbs.

1. Mario ran to his room.

   _____

   _____

2. The bird flew to its nest.

   _____

   _____

3. The hungry boy ate the hamburger.

   _____

   _____

4. The band played.

   _____

   _____

5. The baby cried.

   _____

   _____

6. Our teacher spoke.

   _____

   _____

7. A car stopped.

   _____

   _____

8. Each student studied.

   _____

   _____

1–19. Words Often Confused (part one)

Here are some more words that writers often confuse.

Read the definitions of these words often confused. Notice how they are spelled. Use the meaning of the sentence to decide which word to use when you write.

The pronoun *its* means "belonging to it." (*The rabbit scratched its ear.*)
The contraction *it's* stands for *it is.* (*It's pouring rain outside.*)

The pronoun *whose* means "belonging to whom." (*Whose jacket is it?*)
The word *who's* is a contraction for *who is.* (*Who's calling me?*)

The pronoun *your* shows ownership. (*Is this your new bicycle?*)
The contraction *you're* stands for *you are.* (*You're going to be late.*)

The pronoun *their* means "belonging to them." (*The children washed their hands.*)
The contraction *they're* stands for *they are.* (*They're taking a trip to California.*)

The word *there* means "at or in that place." (*Would you like the table over there?*)

DIRECTIONS: Write the correct word on the line to complete each sentence.

1. "Grandfather, _____ car are you driving?" she asked. (**whose, who's**)

2. Mom said _____ the correct thing to do. (**its, it's**)

3. The speaker _____ next won the award. (**who's, whose**)

4. The hikers on the trip carried _____ own backpacks. (**they're, their**)

5. Jesse and Kim always ride _____ bikes to the park. (**there, their**)

6. The moose raised _____ head when we passed by. (**it's, its**)

7. Mom and Dad said _____ going to be late. (**they're, there**)

8. Who is _____ favorite sports player? (**you're, your**)

9. The coach said, "_____ up next!" (**Your, You're**)

1–20. WORDS OFTEN CONFUSED (PART TWO)

Here are more words that writers often confuse.

Words often confused are not always spelled alike. Sometimes they are not pronounced alike. It is important to know the meanings of these words, how to spell them, and how to say them. Then you might not confuse them when you write.

A *desert* (dez'ert) is a dry, sandy place. (*It is hot in the desert.*)

A *dessert* (di zurt') is food eaten at the end of a meal. (*Tom likes apples for dessert.*)

To *lose* (lōōz) means "to no longer have." (*I'm careful not to lose my money.*)

The word *loose* (lōōs) means "not tight." (*Marisa's belt felt loose.*)

The word *quite* (kwīte) means "very." (*My aunt looked quite happy at her birthday party.*)

The word *quiet* (kwī'ĕt) means "silent." (*It is quiet in the country.*)

The word *then* (then) refers to sequence or time. (*We ate dinner and then went walking.*)

The word *than* (than) is used to compare. (*Adam is taller than his brother.*)

A. DIRECTIONS: Write the correct word on the line to complete each sentence.

1. Hold on tightly to your bag or you will _____ it. (**lose, loose**)

2. The wheel on the bicycle will fall off if it is too_____. (**lose, loose**)

3. It is always _____ in the library. (**quiet, quite**)

4. Russell is _____ happy with his new pet. (**quite, quiet**)

5. Camels are found in the _____. (**desert, dessert**)

6. A fruit salad is a healthy _____. (**desert, dessert**)

7. Our new car is bigger _____ the old one. (**than, then**)

8. Do your homework and _____ go out to play. (**than, then**)

B. DIRECTIONS: Rewrite this sentence correctly on the lines below.

      I am quiet happy with pie for desert rather then ice cream.

_____

_____

© 2002 by The Center for Applied Research in Education

1–21. SENSORY WORDS (PART ONE)

Try to use sensory words when you write.

> Writers use sensory words to make their sentences come alive. These words appeal to our five senses—touch, sight, taste, sound, and smell. Examples of sensory words include the following:
>
> I *grasped* the handrail. (*grasped* . . . touch)
> He *spotted* the squirrel up in the tree. (*spotted* . . . sight)
> The *cold* drink quenched my thirst. (*cold* . . . taste)
> His coach *shouted* to the referee. (*shouted* . . . sound)
> She was wearing a *fragrant* perfume. (*fragrant* . . . smell)

DIRECTIONS: Underline the sensory word in each sentence. Then write which sense (touch, sight, taste, sound, smell) is appealed to. **Example:** The cat *jumped* into the air. (*sight*)

1. Russell has black hair. _____

2. The potatoes are salty. _____

3. My puppy's fur is soft. _____

4. The lion roared. _____

5. Spicy smells came from the kitchen. _____

6. Salty breezes came from the Pacific Ocean. _____

7. Marta whispered the secret to her friend. _____

8. The soup is too hot. _____

9. My brother has brown eyes. _____

10. The church bells rang. _____

11. The turtle's shell is hard. _____

12. Be careful with that sharp knife. _____

13. Listen to the shouts of the fans. _____

14. The cat scratched at the door. _____

1–22. SENSORY WORDS (PART TWO)

DIRECTIONS: Each of the five senses (taste, touch, sight, sound, and smell) has its special box below. Fill up the boxes with as many sensory words as you can. Some words can be used for more than one sense. For example, *sharp* could refer to touch or taste. Each box already has a few sensory words to get you started.

TASTE: salty, nutty, hot

TOUCH: hot, icy, soft

SIGHT: green, dark

SOUND: bang, screech

SMELL: sour, spicy

Name _____   **Date** _____

1–23. SENSORY WORDS (PART THREE)

DIRECTIONS: Make each sentence more vivid by adding at least one sensory word to it. Write your new sentences on the lines.

1. The kids had a snack after school. _____

   _____

2. Joe hit the ball with his bat. _____

   _____

3. Jesse cut the meat with the knife. _____

   _____

4. My mom hung the curtains above the window. _____

   _____

5. The car sped down the street. _____

   _____

6. Maria took the shoe off. _____

   _____

7. The letter arrived in an envelope. _____

   _____

8. Luis carried the grocery bag home. _____

   _____

9. My brother put the garbage in the bag. _____

   _____

10. We stepped on the rocks in the stream. _____

   _____

1–24. SIMILES (PART ONE)

Here is the definition of a simile and some examples.

A simile is a comparison between two unlike things. A simile uses the words *like* or *as* in the comparison. Here are a few examples of similes: *Her happy tears flowed like a waterfall.* (Her tears are compared to a waterfall.) *He is as tall as the Empire State Building.* (His height is compared to the height of the Empire State Building.)

DIRECTIONS: Complete the following similes using some words of your choice.

1. as green as _____

2. as scary as _____

3. as noisy as _____

4. as speedy as _____

5. as sweet as _____

6. as tiny as _____

7. The difficult test was just like _____.

8. He plays the guitar like _____.

9. The smoothness of the baby's face is like _____.

10. The wet ground is like _____.

11. My uncle's new car is like _____.

12. Our whirlpool is like_____.

1–25. SIMILES (PART TWO)

A. DIRECTIONS: Underline the similes in the following poem:

> "My mother's eyes are deep, deep blue,
> Like the noon-time sky on a sunny day;
> As blue as the sparkling mountain lake
> Where we swim on summer afternoons;
> As blue as the flowered wallpaper
> In my baby brother's room."

B. DIRECTIONS: Complete the following lines with interesting similes of your choice.

1. Alysa's face was as white as _____.

2. My little brother was as quiet as _____.

3. I was so scared that my heart pounded like _____.

4. That place is as scary as _____.

5. The officer's voice is like _____.

6. That test is as easy as_____.

7. That flock of birds is like _____.

8. My friend is as faithful as _____.

9. I met a man who was as funny as_____.

10. Jeremy swims like _____.

11. This material is as soft as _____.

12. Marla's hair is as dark as _____.

1–26. METAPHORS

Use metaphors and similes to help readers "picture" what you write.

Like a simile, a metaphor is a comparison between two unlike things. However, metaphors do *not* use *like* or *as*. Examples of *metaphors* include the following: *The stars are diamonds in the sky.* (The stars are compared to diamonds.) *All the world's a stage.* (The world is compared to a stage.) *That cloud is a puff of cotton.* (The cloud is compared to cotton.)

DIRECTIONS: Underline the two nouns (or noun phrases) compared by the metaphor in each sentence. If one of the nouns is not mentioned, write it after the sentence.

1. The wind was a howling coyote.

2. My grandfather is a big, shaggy bear of a man.

3. Our teacher is a walking encyclopedia.

4. My room at night is a refrigerator.

5. The city street was an oven on that hot August day.

6. My Aunt Tessa is a clown.

7. The coach barked orders to the third baseman.

8. A blanket of snow lay over the meadow.

9. The wet sand is a soft velvet carpet.

10. Patti listened to the roar of the ocean.

© 2002 by The Center for Applied Research in Education

FOURTH-GRADE LEVEL

CHOOSING THE RIGHT WORD

PRACTICE TEST

PRACTICE TEST: CHOOSING THE RIGHT WORD

DIRECTIONS: Read each question and the sentence that goes with it. Use the Answer Sheet to darken the letter of the choice that best answers each question. If the answer does not appear, darken the letter E.

1. Which is the <u>homonym</u> in this sentence? *The plane landed at the airport.*

    (A) The   (B) plane   (C) landed   (D) airport   (E) None

2. Which is the <u>adjective</u> in this sentence? *He always liked friendly people.*

    (A) He   (B) always   (C) liked   (D) people   (E) None

3. Which word is a <u>proper adjective</u>? *He loved to eat Irish stew.*

    (A) He   (B) Irish   (C) loved   (D) eat   (E) None

4. Which word is an <u>adverb</u>? *She never eats junk food between meals.*

    (A) She   (B) never   (C) junk   (D) meals   (E) None

5. Which is the <u>sensory word</u> in this sentence? *Millie enjoys spicy foods.*

    (A) Millie   (B) enjoys   (C) spicy   (D) foods   (E) None

6. Which form of <u>throw</u> completes this sentence correctly? *Have you ever _____ a football?*

    (A) throw   (B) throwed   (C) threw   (D) thrown   (E) None

7. What are the two <u>articles</u> in this sentence? *He went to get an ice cream cone at the deli.*

    (A) He, went   (B) get, an   (C) at, the   (D) ice cream   (E) None

8. Name the <u>adverb</u> in this sentence. *Will he get his money now?*

    (A) Will   (B) get   (C) his   (D) now   (E) None

© 2002 by The Center for Applied Research in Education

9. The <u>sensory word</u> in this sentence appeals to which sense? *Chocolate was delicious.*

   (A) sight   (B) taste   (C) sound   (D) touch   (E) None

10. What is the <u>simile</u> in this sentence? *He was as meek as a lamb.*

    (A) He was   (B) was as meek   (C) was as meek as   (D) as meek as a lamb
    (E) None

11. What is the <u>main verb</u> in this sentence? *Walt has taken his test.*

    (A) Walt   (B) has taken   (C) taken   (D) his   (E) None

12. What is the <u>verb</u> in this sentence? *The trees are blowing in the wind.*

    (A) trees are   (B) are blowing   (C) in the   (D) the wind (E) None

13. What is the <u>linking verb</u> in this sentence? *The sun feels warm.*

    (A) The   (B) sun   (C) feels   (D) warm   (E) None

14. What is the <u>common noun</u> in this sentence? *Mary loved to go to the movies.*

    (A) Mary   (B) loved   (C) to go   (D) movies   (E) None

15. Which word is incorrect in this sentence? *Harry waited for desert.*

    (A) Harry   (B) waited   (C) for   (D) desert   (E) None

Choosing the Right Word

PRACTICE TEST: ANSWER SHEET

Darken the circle above the letter that best answers the question.

1. ◯ ◯ ◯ ◯ ◯
   A B C D E

2. ◯ ◯ ◯ ◯ ◯
   A B C D E

3. ◯ ◯ ◯ ◯ ◯
   A B C D E

4. ◯ ◯ ◯ ◯ ◯
   A B C D E

5. ◯ ◯ ◯ ◯ ◯
   A B C D E

6. ◯ ◯ ◯ ◯ ◯
   A B C D E

7. ◯ ◯ ◯ ◯ ◯
   A B C D E

8. ◯ ◯ ◯ ◯ ◯
   A B C D E

9. ◯ ◯ ◯ ◯ ◯
   A B C D E

10. ◯ ◯ ◯ ◯ ◯
    A B C D E

11. ◯ ◯ ◯ ◯ ◯
    A B C D E

12. ◯ ◯ ◯ ◯ ◯
    A B C D E

13. ◯ ◯ ◯ ◯ ◯
    A B C D E

14. ◯ ◯ ◯ ◯ ◯
    A B C D E

15. ◯ ◯ ◯ ◯ ◯
    A B C D E

Choosing the Right Word

KEY TO PRACTICE TEST

1. ● B
2. ● E
3. ● B
4. ● B
5. ● C
6. ● D
7. ● E
8. ● D

9. ● B
10. ● D
11. ● C
12. ● B
13. ● C
14. ● D
15. ● D

MAKING MECHANICS AND USAGE WORK FOR YOU

Teacher Preparation and Lessons

The activities in Section 2 cover a wide variety of common mechanics and usage skills. Having a solid foundation in these skills will help students become proficient writers. The concluding activity assesses your students' knowledge of the skills covered. You may wish to use this **PRACTICE TEST** as a pretest and/or posttest. Answer keys can be found on pages 44-48.

ACTIVITIES 2-1 and 2-2 are designed to help students develop a working knowledge of rules for **capitalization**. Write the following sentence on the board and read it aloud. *My uncle, A. A. Ross, took a trip up the Mississippi River on the Fourth of July and bought a Chinese lantern at Best Goods.* Point out the capital letters that begin the sentence, the names and initials of people, proper nouns and adjectives, geographic features, and holidays. Distribute **Activity 2-1 Capital Letters (Part One)** and read the rules together. Ask students to tell which rule applies to each capital letter in the sentence. Then have students complete the page independently or with a partner. Follow the same procedure with **Activity 2-2 Capital Letters (Part Two),** using this sample sentence: *The librarian said, "On the first Monday in October, Principal Smith will read 'A New Beginning' from Stories of the Gold Rush."*

ACTIVITY 2-3 addresses rules for **abbreviations**. If possible, display the following lists: two-letter abbreviations for the fifty states, days of the week, months of the year, and titles of people. Point out that states' abbreviations are not followed by commas. Then distribute **Activity 2-3 Abbreviations.** Read the rules at the top and complete the page with students. Make sure they are familiar with abbreviations for their own city or town, street, and state.

ACTIVITY 2-4 reviews the formation of **compound words**. Write the words *book, mark,* and *store* as well as this sentence on the board: *He bought a _____ at the _____.* Have students use the words to form compounds that will complete the sentence (*bookmark, bookstore*). Remind them that the meaning of a compound word is different from the meaning of each word that comprises it. Distribute **Activity 2-4 Compound Words** and have students complete the page independently.

ACTIVITIES 2-5, 2-6, and 2-7 teach correct **pronoun** usage. Explain that pronouns take the place of nouns and can serve as subjects or objects of a sentence. They can also show possession. Some pronouns help to point out a specific person, place, or thing. Others are used to ask a question. For both **Activity 2-5 Subject, Object, and Possessive Pronouns** and **Activity 2-6 Demonstrative and Interrogative Pronouns,** read the information in the box and complete item 1 together before students complete the page. Distribute **Activity 2-7 Choosing the Correct Pronoun** for additional practice. Point out to students that using pronouns correctly can help them improve their writing.

ACTIVITIES 2-8 and 2-9 teach correct usage of **prefixes** and **suffixes**. Prefixes are word parts that can be added to the beginning of base words (words that stand alone as a meaningful unit). Write these words on the board: *preview, nonsense, disappear*. Identify the prefixes *pre-, non-,* and *dis-* and the base words *view, sense,* and *appear*. Discuss the meaning of each base word and its prefix. Distribute **Activity 2-8 Prefixes** and read the definitions together. Have students complete the page. To introduce the activity on suffixes, write *like/likable, hope/hopeful, friend/friendly*. Explain that suffixes are word parts added at the end of base words. Point out that adding a suffix changes the word's part of speech. Discuss the meanings of each word pair. Have students complete **Activity 2-9 Suffixes** independently.

ACTIVITIES 2-10 through 2-12 teach usage of **apostrophes** and **hyphens**. Write these words on the board: *girl's/girls', do not/don't,* and *twenty-five*. Circle the apostrophes and the hyphen. Point out the importance of using these punctuation marks correctly. Distribute **Activity 2-10 Apostrophes and Contractions** and read the rules for forming contractions together. Have students complete the page independently. Before distributing **Activity 2-11 Apostrophes and Possessive Nouns,** write the words *dog's, women's,* and *dogs'* on the board and have students use each one in a sentence. Explain that to show possession, 's is added to singular nouns and to plural nouns that do not end in *s*. An apostrophe alone is added to plural nouns that end in *s*. Distribute the page and read the rules together. Distribute **Activity 2-12 Hyphens.** Complete the page together.

ACTIVITY 2-13 reviews how to **punctuate sentences**. Write the following four sentences on the board: *1. Put the cat down. 2. We won! 3. I saw a cat. 4. Where is it?* Explain that each sentence type requires its own end mark. Sentence 1 is an imperative sentence (gives a command) and requires a period. Sentence 2 is exclamatory and requires an exclamation mark. Sentence 3 is declarative (makes a statement) and requires a period. Sentence 4 is a question and requires a question mark. Distribute **Activity 2-13 End Marks** and have students complete the page independently.

ACTIVITIES 2-14 and 2-15 teach rules about the **comma** and the use of the **colon and commas in a series.** Distribute **Activity 2-14 Colon and Commas in a Series.** Read the directions together. Complete items 1 and 2 with the class. Point out that the colon usually follows a phrase such as *the following* or *that includes*. It is not used after a verb. Have students work with partners to complete the page. Then distribute **Activity 2-15 More About Commas.** Tell students that when they write, commas will help to keep words and numbers from running together. Read the rules at the top of the page together. You may wish to complete the page with students.

ACTIVITY 2-16 teaches correct **punctuation of quotes**. Before distributing the page, tell students that quotes are the exact words someone says. Ask a student to give a sentence. Write on the board the sentence with the speaker's name: *Howard asked, "Who has finished?"* Point out the comma separating the speaker from the words, the open and closed quotation marks around the exact words spoken, the capital letter at the beginning of the quote, and the end punctuation mark inside the closed quotation mark. Distribute **Activity 2-16 Punctuating Quotations** and read the rules together. Have students complete the page.

ACTIVITY 2-17 teaches correct **punctuation of titles of books, movies, magazines, poems, and songs.** Write the following sentences on the board:

1. Have you read <u>The Adventures of Tom Sawyer</u>? (book)
2. My favorite movie is <u>Pinocchio</u>. (movie)

3. My brother's favorite magazine is <u>Cricket</u> magazine. (magazine)

4. I love the folktale "The Wind and the Sun." (folktale/story)

5. Shel Silverstein wrote the poem "Homework Machine." (poem/song)

Explain to students that titles of books, movies, and magazines should be underlined if they are writing by hand and either underlined or in italics if they are using a word processor. Titles of stories, poems, and songs should have quotation marks. Distribute **Activity 2-17 Punctuating Titles** and complete the page together. You may wish to follow up by having students play a game by writing the title of a favorite story, book, song, poem, or magazine on an index card and having a partner use the title correctly in a sentence.

ACTIVITY 2-18 reviews **punctuation problems**. Before distributing the page, review any punctuation skills students had trouble with. Then distribute **Activity 2-18 Punctuation Problems** and read the directions together.

ACTIVITIES 2-19 through 2-21 teach rules for **forming plurals**. Write on the board the words *leash/leashes, bus/buses, whiz/whizzes, loaf/loaves, memo/memos, potato/potatoes, key/keys, city/cities, mouse/mice, deer/deer*. Explain the rule for forming each plural. Point out that in some cases, students will need to memorize plural forms such as *roof/roofs* and *chief/chiefs*, or to go by the end sound when they say the word. Read the rules together and have students complete the page independently or with a partner. Make sure students have mastered the rules for the first activity before assigning the next page. Point out to students that correct formation of plurals will help them improve their writing.

ACTIVITIES 2-22 and 2-23 review **common rules for spelling**. Distribute **Activity 2-22 Spelling (Part One)** and read the rules together. Have students complete the page independently. Distribute **Activity 2-23 Spelling (Part Two)** and read the directions with the students. When they have completed the page, ask them to identify the rule for each correctly spelled word.

ANSWER KEY

2–1. CAPITAL LETTERS (PART ONE)

1. Sam, I, John F. Kennedy
2. Will, Harriet Tubman, Sojourner Truth
3. We, Chinese
4. P.J. Smith, New Year's Day
5. E. B. White, A. A. Milne
6. Our, Martin Luther King, Jr. Day
7. We're, Fourth, July, Yellowstone National Park
8. My, I, Laurel Music Camp, Alabama
9. Jill, Mother's Day
10. The, Smiths, Hudson Avenue, Toronto
11. Have, White House, Washington, D.C.
12. Many, Oregon Trail

2–2. CAPITAL LETTERS (PART TWO)

1. How, World War II
2. The, Wizard, Oz
3. Saturday, Sunday
4. The, Fox, Grapes
5. Principal Hall, Coach Wallace
6. June, July, August
7. Gold Rush, California
8. Civil War
9. The, Owl, Pussycat
10. Trumpet, Swan
11. Mount Rushmore, June
12. Will

2–3. ABBREVIATIONS

1. Mr.
2. NY
3. Dr.
4. Sept.
5. CA
6. Rd.
7. PA
8. Prof.
9. Fri.
10. Dr.
11. Jr.

2–4. COMPOUNDS WORDS
Part A

1. every thing
2. basket ball
3. back pack
4. stop light
5. every one
6. drug store
7. under pass
8. pocket book
9. high way
10. seat belts
11. thunder storm
12. grape fruits

Part B

Students lists and sentences will vary

2–5. SUBJECT, OBJECT, AND POSSESSIVE PRONOUNS

1. I (S)
2. him (O)
3. They (S)
4. my (P)
5. them (O)
6. his (P)
7. We (S)
8. it (O)
9. Your (P)
10. Their (P)
11. me (O)
12. our (P)

2–6. DEMONSTRATIVE AND INTERROGATIVE PRONOUNS

1. This
2. that
3. These
4. those
5. that
6. those
7. Which
8. Who
9. What
10. Who
11. Which
12. What

2–7. CHOOSING THE CORRECT PRONOUNS

1. their, P
2. He, S
3. These, D
4. Which, I
5. her, O
6. Yours, P
7. I, S
8. What, I
9. These, D
10. she, S
11. them, O
12. my, P
13. her, P
14. Which, I
15. her, O

2–8. PREFIXES

Answers will vary.

2–9. SUFFIXES

1. forgetful
2. mouthful
3. helpful
4. believable
5. willing
6. nicest
7. courageous
8. noticeable
9. arrangement
10. kindest
11. breakable
12. liveliest

2–10. APOSTROPHES AND CONTRACTIONS

1. he's
2. hasn't
3. won't
4. aren't
5. isn't
6. don't
7. she'll
8. can't
9. we're
10. shouldn't
11. they've
12. she'd

2–11. APOSTROPHES AND POSSESSIVE NOUNS

1. Karen's
2. boy's
3. ladies'
4. team's
5. children's
6. Archie's
7. hikers'
8. snow's
9. mouse's
10. girls'
11. animal's
12. book's

2–12. HYPHENS

Part A

1. all-around
2. part-time
3. thirty-five
4. twenty-two
5. seventy-five
6. twenty-five
7. Thirty-two
8. soft-spoken

Part B

Rachel and Erika had a lovely picnic in the park.

2–13. END MARKS

1. .
2. ?
3. ! (or .)
4. .
5. .
6. ?
7. .
8. !
9. ?
10. ?
11. .
12. .

2–14. COLON AND COMMAS IN A SERIES

1. Kentucky, Florida
2. nights: August
3. runs, and
4. following: be
5. giraffes, pandas
6. seats: Kenny
7. energetic, talented
8. *E.T.*, and
9. Fred, and
10. away: Herbie's
11. plates, napkins
12. Boston, and

2–15. MORE ABOUT COMMAS

1. The letter was addressed to Sally Smith at 796 East 116th Street, New York, NY.

2. I began my letter home with "Dear Mom and Dad," and then went on to describe my first week at camp.

3. The Pearson family picnic will be held on November 4, 2002, at Candlewood Lake.

4. My uncle's car has over 250,000 miles on it, and it's still running.

5. "Please, Jimmy, wipe your feet!" Mom shouted from the living room.

6. That performer's violin is worth $25,000!

7. Put your signature under *Sincerely*, at the end of a letter.

8. When I grow up, I will study animals that live in the ocean.

9. It is 2,700 miles from New York to Los Angeles, California.

10. Peter's new address is 4400 Sixth Street, Richmond, Virginia.

11. "Nadra, close the gate behind you," Kahlil said to his sister.

12. Wow, what a fantastic surprise!

2–16. PUNCTUATING AND CAPITALIZING QUOTATIONS

1. "I . . . partner."
2. "Iceland
3. concert?"
4. asked, "Who
5. life."
6. now?"
7. up!"
8. "Isn't
9. team!"
10. heavy,"
11. "Have . . . Canyon?"
12. league,"

2–17. PUNCTUATING TITLES

1. <u>Gone With the Wind</u>
2. "Aladdin and the Wonderful Lamp"
3. <u>A Thousand and One Nights</u>
4. <u>Sports Illustrated for Kids</u>
5. <u>Romeo and Juliet</u>
6. "Fifty Nifty United States"
7. <u>Zillions</u>
8. <u>Harry Potter and the Sorcerer's Stone</u>
9. <u>Seventeen</u>
10. <u>Tales of a Fourth Grade Nothing</u>
11. "Jabberwocky"
12. <u>Cobblestone</u>

2–18. PUNCTUATION PROBLEMS

1. C
2. . . . time?
3. . . . evening: Tom . . .
4. . . . "The Legend of Sleepy Hollow"?
5. C
6. . . . boys . . .
7. . . . they've . . .
8. C
9. C
10. . . . Francine.
11. mice's
12. C
13. <u>A League of Their Own</u>
14. C

2–19. PLURALS (PART ONE)

1. shelves
2. handkerchiefs
3. clocks
4. foxes
5. brushes
6. glasses
7. thieves
8. notebooks
9. watches
10. friends
11. roofs
12. answers

2–20. PLURALS (PART TWO)

1. turkeys
2. blueberries
3. copies
4. bays
5. dictionaries
6. keys
7. libraries
8. journeys
9. flies
10. sprays
11. highways
12. ladies
13. mysteries
14. days

2–21. IRREGULAR PLURALS

1. mice
2. children
3. teeth
4. oxen
5. deer
6. men
7. women
8. geese
9. feet
10. goldfish
11. news
12. trousers

2–22. SPELLING (PART ONE)

1. libraries
2. tripped
3. traced
4. swaying

5. sipping
6. swiped
7. keys
8. relying

9. swapping
10. stopped
11. spied (or spies)
12. tries

2–23. SPELLING (PART TWO)

Part A

1. clapped
2. lefties
3. tried
4. stopped

5. occurring
6. begging
7. passing
8. ruled

9. baking
10. liking
11. losing
12. hitting

Part B

Sentences will vary.

2–1. CAPITAL LETTERS (PART ONE)

Here are some rules for using capital letters.

> 1. Capitalize the first word in a sentence. (*Please mail this letter.*)
> 2. Capitalize the pronoun *I*. It always comes last. (*Do you think he and I can go?*)
> 3. Capitalize a person's name and initials. (*Her partner, Sheila Silverman, is better known as S.S.*)
> 4. Capitalize proper nouns. (*We will visit the Statue of Liberty.*)
> 5. Capitalize proper adjectives. (*This diner serves French toast.*)
> 6. Capitalize geographic features and place names. (*My aunt lives on Charles St. which is very near to the Mississippi River.*)
> 7. Capitalize the names of holidays. (*Our family enjoys Thanksgiving.*)

DIRECTIONS: Circle the letters that should be capitalized. There may be more than one in each sentence.

1. sam and i read about john f. kennedy.

2. will you write about harriet tubman or sojourner truth?

3. we ordered delicious chinese food last night.

4. p.j. smith will become our new mayor on new year's day.

5. Our librarian's favorite authors are e. b. white and a. a. milne.

6. our class will put on a play for martin luther king, jr. day.

7. we're spending the fourth of july in yellowstone national park.

8. my brother and i go to laurel music camp in alabama.

9. jill gave her mother flowers for mother's day.

10. the smiths live on hudson avenue in toronto.

11. have you been to the white house in washington, d.c.?

12. many people traveled west along the oregon trail.

2–2. Capital Letters (Part Two)

Here are some more rules for using capital letters.

1. Capitalize the names of historical periods and events. (*We're reading about the Great Depression. What are the dates of the Civil War?*)

2. Capitalize a person's title when it comes before the name. (*I have an appointment with Principal Hall.*)

3. Capitalize the days of the week and the months of the year. (*We will see them on the first Saturday in September.*)

4. Capitalize the first word in a direct quotation. (*"This is how to tie the knot," Bob told the class.*)

5. Capitalize the first word and important words in the titles of books, magazines, movies, stories, poems, and songs. (*We enjoyed listening to "Jack and the Beanstalk" when we were younger.*)

DIRECTIONS: Circle the letters that should be capitalized. There may be more than one in a sentence.

1. The teacher asked, "how many years did world war ii last?"

2. The woman said that many people came to see the movie <u>the wizard of oz</u>.

3. "Will you go to the carnival on saturday or on sunday?" Paul asked.

4. My favorite Aesop's fable is "the fox and the grapes."

5. The woman next to principal hall is coach wallace.

6. We have june, july, and august off from school.

7. Josh's report will be about the gold rush of 1848 in california.

8. Abraham Lincoln was president during the civil war.

9. Have you read the poem "the owl and the pussycat"?

10. Lena asked the librarian for the book <u>trumpet of the swan</u>.

11. The group's summer trip was to mount rushmore on june 14.

12. My sister asked, "will you help with this heavy package?"

2–3. ABBREVIATIONS

Here is the definition of abbreviations as well as rules and examples.

> An abbreviation is a shortened form of a word. Examples include: *Sr.* (senior), *Ave.* (Avenue), *SD* (South Dakota), and *Wed.* (Wednesday).
>
> 1. End abbreviations with a period. (*Wed., Apr., Prof,. St.*). State abbreviations do not end with a period (*PA* for Pennsylvania, *CA* for California, *TX* for Texas).
>
> 2. Capitalize abbreviations of streets (*Rd.* for Road) states (*NJ* for New Jersey), months (*Jan.* for January), days (*Mon.* for Monday), and titles of people (*Mr., Ms., Mrs., Miss, Dr., Prof.*).

© 2002 by The Center for Applied Research in Education

DIRECTIONS: On the line within each sentence, write the abbreviation for the word in parentheses.

1. My father's best friend is _____ Blassing. (**Mister**)

2. We wrote stories about Albany, _____. (**New York**)

3. Are you moving to 7635 Burlington _____? (**Drive**)

4. School will open during the second week of _____. (**September**)

5. Jaclyn vacationed in Los Angeles _____, CA. (**California**)

6. Sperling _____ is a beautiful street in our town. (**Road**)

7. The Amish live in the Lancaster, _____ area. (**Pennsylvania**)

8. The college students met with _____ Nidds yesterday. (**Professor**)

9. Where will we be going on _____ night? (**Friday**)

10. We read "I Have a Dream" by _____ Martin Luther King, Jr. (**Doctor**)

11. Ken Griffey, _____, is Mitch's favorite baseball player. (**Junior**)

2–4. COMPOUND WORDS

Here are the definition and the rule for compound words.

> A compound word is made up of two or more words joined together to form a new word. Examples of compound words include *baseball, starlight,* and *nobody.*

A. DIRECTIONS: Circle the compound word in each sentence. Then write the two words that make up the compound.

1. Yvonne had to bring everything with her.   _____

2. The basketball game will start in forty minutes.   _____

3. Is your backpack too heavy for you to carry?   _____

4. There were many cars waiting at the stoplight.   _____

5. Everyone takes the bus when it rains.   _____

6. Last night we met Davis in the drugstore.   _____

7. The trucks slowly went through the underpass.   _____

8. She found the receipt in her pocketbook.   _____

9. Which highway is the best route to take?   _____

10. The pilot told us to fasten our seatbelts.   _____

11. Where were you during that scary thunderstorm?   _____

12. Last night my mother bought six grapefruits.   _____

B. DIRECTIONS: On the back of this paper, brainstorm a list of compound words. See how many you can think of in five minutes. Then write a sentence using as many of the compound words as possible.

Name _____ **Date** _____

2–5. SUBJECT, OBJECT, AND POSSESSIVE PRONOUNS

Use the correct forms of pronouns when you write.

1. A subject pronoun can replace a noun as a sentence's subject. (*She* is a fine ballerina.) The subject pronouns are *I, he, she, it, you, we,* and *they.*

2. An object pronoun can replace a noun as an object in a sentence, following an action verb (They reminded *them* of the important date.) or after a preposition (We walked by *them*.). The object pronouns are *me, you, her, him, it, us,* and *them.*

3. A possessive pronoun shows ownership. (Brett needed *his* backpack.) The possessive pronouns are *her, hers, him, his, its, my, mine, our, ours, their, theirs, your,* and *yours.*

DIRECTIONS: Underline the pronouns in each sentence. Then write subject (S), object (O), or possessive (P) above each underlined pronoun. There is only one pronoun in each sentence.

1. I would like to congratulate Steve.

2. Tonight will be a happy occasion for him.

3. They brought several pictures from the event.

4. Here is my cousin now.

5. Barry sold them six tickets to the boat show.

6. Maybe Drew will ask the group over to his house.

7. We brought a flashlight to camp.

8. The volunteers may need to use it.

9. Your backpack is on the floor by the window.

10. The children carried their books.

11. The new zookeeper told me not to run.

12. Matt played our favorite game.

2–6. DEMONSTRATIVE AND INTERROGATIVE PRONOUNS

Here are the definitions of demonstrative and interrogative pronouns.

> 1. A demonstrative pronoun points out a specific person or thing. The demonstrative pronouns are *this, that, these,* and *those.*
>
> 2. An interrogative pronoun usually asks a question. The interrogative pronouns are *who, whom, what, which,* and *whose.*

DIRECTIONS: Circle the demonstrative pronouns in sentences 1–6. Then circle the correct interrogative pronouns in sentences 7–12.

1. This cartoon really makes my cousin laugh.

2. Can we take that bus to get to the arena, Michelle?

3. "These cakes are really fattening," Mom told her friends.

4. Could those musicians play at our town's festival?

5. "Is Trenton that state's capital city?" Mrs. Underwood asked her students.

6. Are you really going to use those facts in your report?

7. "(Which, Who) one should I select?" Izzy asked his brother.

8. "(What, Who) is your favorite cartoon character?" I asked my nephew.

9. (What, Who) is the best way to dock the boat?

10. (Who, What) were your best friends before you moved to Tulsa?

11. (Who, Which) people will we meet at Cindy's house?

12. (What, Whose) do you remember about your first train ride?

2–7. CHOOSING THE CORRECT PRONOUN

DIRECTIONS: Circle the correct pronoun in parentheses to complete each sentence. Then, on the line, write the letter that tells the type of pronoun that you circled: subject (S), interrogative (I), demonstrative (D), objective (O), or possessive (P).

1. ____ This dessert is (their, theirs) best recipe.

2. ____ (He, Him) and I will be at the park in an hour.

3. ____ (These, This) floats can be inflated very quickly with a pump.

4. ____ (Who, Which) boat did you choose for the trip?

5. ____ Did you know the pen was given to (her, she)?

6. ____ (Your, Yours) is the most interesting answer.

7. ____ Justine and (I, me) will be partners in this race.

8. ____ (What, Who) route will your dad take to get there?

9. ____ (That, These) cards could be traded in for good money.

10. ____ My guess is that (she, her) will be the next president of the club.

11. ____ When will the crowd see (them, they)?

12. ____ Please help me carry (mine, my) package.

13. ____ Wendy will tell (her, she) parents about the problem.

14. ____ (Which, Who) bookshelf will be better in their den?

15. ____ Let me tell (her, she) about it immediately.

2–8. PREFIXES

Here is the definition of prefixes and some examples.

A prefix is placed in front of a word to change its meaning. Here are some common prefixes and what they often (but not always) mean.

1. *re-* means *again* or *back*, as in *repay, revisit,* and *reopen.*
2. *pre-* means *before*, as in *preview, prerecord,* and *precooked.*
3. *im-* and *in-* mean *not,* as in *impossible* and *incomplete.*
4. *dis-* means *not,* as in *disagree* and *dishonest.*
5. *non-* means *not,* as in *nonfiction* and *nonsense.*
6. *anti-* means *against* or *opposite*, as in *antifreeze.*
7. *sub-* means *under*, as in *submarine* and *subway.*
8. *bi-* means *two*, as in *biweekly* and *bicycle.*

DIRECTIONS: Write some sentences on the lines below. Each sentence should contain at least one word that has a prefix. (You may select from the words on this page or choose others.)

1. _____

_____

2. _____

_____

3. _____

_____

4. _____

_____

5. _____

_____

6. _____

_____

Name _____   Date_____

2–9. SUFFIXES

Here are some rules to follow when adding suffixes.

A suffix is a word part added to the end of a base word. Examples of suffixes include: *-able* (agreeable), *-er* (stronger), *-ful* (powerful), *-ing* (willing), *-ion* (affection), *-less* (nameless), *-ly* (timely), and *-ness* (sharpness).

1. Do not drop the final *e* of the base word when adding a suffix that begins with a consonant (*excite + ment, care + less, arrange + ment*).

2. Drop the final *e* in a base word before adding a suffix that begins with a vowel (*believe + able = believable*) and (*rude + est = rudest*). Exception: Do not drop the final *e* in words that end with *ce* or *ge* (*changeable*).

3. When the root word ends in *y*, change the *y* to an *i* before you add the suffix (*lonely – y + i + ness = loneliness*) and (*lively – y + i + ness = liveliness*).

DIRECTIONS: Circle the correct spelling in parentheses to complete each sentence.

1. Mike does not always do his homework because he is so (forgetful, forgettful).

2. Carla could not answer because she had a (mouthful, mouthfull) of potatoes.

3. Maria tries to be (helpfull, helpful) by dusting and vacuuming.

4. The thief's excuse was not too (believeable, believable).

5. His favorite author is (willing, wiling) to appear at the bookstore.

6. My best friend, James, is the (nicest, niciest) boy in the class.

7. The (couragous, courageous) soldier was awarded a medal of bravery.

8. His change in attitude was very (noticable, noticeable).

9. The decorator made a beautiful (arrangement, arrangment) of flowers.

10. That is the (kindiest, kindest) thing he has ever done for his aunt.

11. Be careful handling that (breakable, breakeable) glass vase.

12. Todd's frisky kitten is the (livliest, liveliest) one in the litter.

2–10. APOSTROPHES AND CONTRACTIONS

Here are the rules for using an apostrophe in contractions.

> A contraction combines two words into one word leaving out one or more letters. An apostrophe (') replaces the missing letter or letters. Some common contractions involving the word *not* are as follows: *aren't* (are not), *can't* (cannot), *don't* (do not), *hadn't* (had not), *hasn't* (has not), *haven't* (have not), *isn't* (is not), *shouldn't* (should not), and *won't* (will not). Some common *pronoun–verb* contractions are *he's* (he is), *she'd* (she had or she would), *she'll* (she will), *they've* (they have), and *we're* (we are).

DIRECTIONS: Write the correct contraction on the line for the two words in parentheses.

1. They say _____ going to leave on the next train. (**he is**)

2. The doctor _____ called back yet. (**has not**)

3. Susan _____ believe what we have to tell her. (**will not**)

4. Luckily, our houses _____ in need of immediate repair after the hurricane. (**are not**)

5. This _____ the easiest trick to perform. (**is not**)

6. I _____ think she will be at the family's party. (**do not**)

7. Do you think that _____ be our next club president? (**she will**)

8. They _____ go to the movies tonight. (**cannot**)

9. Do they know that _____ moving in two months? (**we are**)

10. You _____ eat too much junk food. (**should not**)

11. I feel _____ earned the right to move on. (**they have**)

12. If _____ solved the puzzle, we would have won the match. (**she had**)

© 2002 by The Center for Applied Research in Education

2–11. APOSTROPHES AND POSSESSIVE NOUNS

Here are some rules for using the apostrophe in possessive nouns.

> The possessive form of a noun shows that someone or something possesses, or owns, something else.
>
> 1. To form the possessive of most *singular* nouns, add an apostrophe and *s* (*'s*), as in *dog's* bone. (Only one dog has ownership of the bone.)
>
> 2. To form the possessive of *plural nouns that end with s*, add an apostrophe (*'*) after the *s*, as in *girls'* room. (More than one girl has ownership of the room.)
>
> 3. To form the possessive of *plural nouns that do not end with s*, add an apostrophe and *s* (*'s*), as in *women's* club. (More than one woman has possession of the club.)

DIRECTIONS: On each line below, write the correct possessive form of the word in parentheses to complete the sentence.

1. Have you seen _____ new baseball glove? (**Karen**)

2. Here is the _____ brown coat. (**boy**)

3. The _____ coats are stored there. (**ladies**)

4. We spotted the _____ bus along the highway in Wisconsin. (**team**)

5. Several _____ stories were read by the teacher. (**children**)

6. Penny parked behind _____ pickup truck. (**Archie**)

7. Many _____ plans were changed due to the rainstorms. (**hikers**)

8. The _____ whiteness is attractive. (**snow**)

9. Did you find the _____ tracks near the stairs? (**mouse**)

10. Our _____ relay team easily won the county championship. (**girls**)

11. One _____ footprints caught our attention. (**animal**)

12. A _____ cover can make the book more appealing. (**book**)

© 2002 by The Center for Applied Research in Education

2–12. HYPHENS

Here are some rules for using hyphens and some examples.

> 1. Use hyphens to divide a word between syllables at the end of a line, as in:
>
>   *I like to play basketball after school, but my favorite spec-*
>   *tator sport is hockey.*
>
> 2. Use hyphens in compound words before nouns, as in:
>
>   I am going to get a *part-time* job this summer.
>   My neighbor is a *well-known* actor.
>
> 3. Use hyphens when writing the numbers from *twenty-one* to *ninety-nine*. Exception: numbers that end in zero (twenty, thirty).

A. DIRECTIONS: Insert a hyphen, where necessary, in the following sentences:

1. Soccer is my best sport, but my brother is a good all around athlete.

2. Alex's mom has a part time job at the local library in town.

3. J. J. plans to move to another state by the time he is thirty five.

4. Mark and Nicky inflated twenty two balloons before the party.

5. Have we traveled seventy five miles yet?

6. The alarm went off at twenty five minutes past six.

7. Thirty two fire engines were in the Fourth of July parade.

8. Many people easily see that Mom is a very soft spoken woman.

B. DIRECTIONS: Rewrite the following sentence on the lines below. End the first line after the first syllable in pic/nic. Remember to use a hyphen where the word breaks.

Rachel and Erika had a lovely picnic in the park.

_____

_____

_____

Name _____   Date _____

2–13. END MARKS

Use the correct punctuation mark to end a sentence.

> The end mark shows what type of sentence it is and appears at the end of a sentence. The end marks are the *period*, the *question mark*, and the *exclamation point*.
>
> 1. Use a period at the end of a sentence that makes a statement (*Kate is interested in the planets.*) or at the end of a sentence that gives a command or request that does not express strong feelings (*Please pass the carrots.*).
>
> 2. Use a question mark at the end of a sentence that asks a question. (*Are you awake?*)
>
> 3. Use an exclamation point at the end of a sentence that expresses strong feelings (*Watch out!*) or strong command (*Keep the noise down in there!*).

DIRECTIONS: Write the correct end mark for each sentence.

1. Steve is always nervous before he goes on stage

2. Do you think Grandpa would like to go skiing with us

3. Grab the rope now, Steve

4. You have read about the juggler's performance

5. Please help me make the bed, Hank

6. Whose coat is on the seat here, Jillian

7. He was laughing loudly during the comedy show

8. Wow, what a great party

9. May I help you, sir

10. Will this exercise help me develop stomach muscles

11. All the family members were there for the ceremony

12. My neighbor saw you at the television studio last week

2–14. COLON AND COMMAS IN A SERIES

Remember these rules for using a colon and commas in a series.

1. Use a comma to separate three or more items in a series such as *nouns, verbs,* or *adjectives.* Make sure to use a comma before the word *and* in the series.

    We studied about monkeys, sharks, and horses. (nouns)

    They wanted to read, discuss, and write more about the subject. (verbs)

    She is friendly, athletic, and interesting. (adjectives)

2. Use a colon when introducing a list of items, especially after the words *as follows* or *the following.* (*We will need the following supplies: tents, raincoats, and lanterns.*) Do not use a colon after a verb. (*Here are Bill, Saida, and Jon.*)

DIRECTIONS: Each sentence is missing either a colon or a comma. Insert the missing punctuation mark.

1. Uncle Dan's three favorite states are Kentucky Florida, and Alaska.

2. The orchestra will play on the following nights August 17, September 15, and October 21.

3. The coach walks, runs and swims to keep fit.

4. My list of rules for success includes all of the following be prompt, enjoy your work, and treat people fairly.

5. The following animals will be featured in the slide-show presentation: giraffes pandas, and monkeys.

6. Please help the following students find their seats Kenny, Michelle, and Melissa.

7. That famous entertainer is energetic talented, and terrific!

8. Our class will watch the following movies: *The Jungle Book, E.T.* and *Home Alone.*

9. Juan, Fred and Bridget will be playing at the music festival this month.

10. Please put these items away Herbie's hat, Mark's boots, and Georgia's socks.

11. Here are the plates napkins, and cups for the party.

12. This summer we will visit Atlanta, Boston and Chicago.

© 2002 by The Center for Applied Research in Education

2–15. MORE ABOUT COMMAS

Commas help keep words and numbers from running together.

1. Use a comma to separate appositives, or words that tell more about the noun or pronoun, from the rest of the sentence. (*Jack, our pet rabbit, has run away.*)

2. Use a comma after a noun of direct address. (*Peg, please turn off the lights.*)

3. Use a comma between items in addresses and dates, but not in ZIP Codes: (*I was born on July 14, 1993, in Youngstown, Ohio. We lived at 2550 First Ave., Chicago, IL 60473.*) There is no comma between the state and ZIP Code.

4. Place a comma after the greeting and after the closing when writing a friendly letter. (*Dear Aunt Sally, Your friend, Sincerely,*)

5. Use a comma to make numbers easy to read. Place commas after thousands, millions, billions, and so on. (*I think there are 500,000 pennies in the jar.*)

6. Use a comma after an introductory word or words at the beginning of a sentence. (*Last night, we made popcorn and watched a movie.*)

DIRECTIONS: Insert a comma in each sentence where it belongs. More than one comma may need to be added to each sentence.

1. The letter was addressed to Sally Smith at 796 East 116th Street New York NY.

2. I began my letter home with "Dear Mom and Dad" and then went on to describe my first week at camp.

3. The Pearson family picnic will be held on November 4 2002 at Candlewood Lake.

4. My uncle's car has over 250 000 miles on it, and it's still running.

5. "Please Jimmy wipe your feet!" Mom shouted from the living room.

6. That performer's violin is worth $25 000!

7. Put your signature under *Sincerely* at the end of a letter.

8. When I grow up I will study animals that live in the ocean.

9. It is 2 700 miles from New York to Los Angeles California.

10. Peter's new address is 4400 Sixth Street Richmond Virginia.

11. "Nadra close the gate behind you," Kahlil said to his sister.

12. Wow what a fantastic surprise!

2–16. PUNCTUATING AND CAPITALIZING QUOTATIONS

Here are some rules for punctuating and capitalizing quotations.

1. Place quotation marks *before* the *first* word and *after* the *last* word of a person's exact words. (*Ashley yelled to the fans, "We won the tournament!"*)

2. The first word of a person's exact words begins with a capital letter. (*Willie said, "This is the way to fix this problem."*)

3. A person's exact words are set apart from the rest of the sentence by a comma, a question mark, or an exclamation point.

   "This has to be the right way," the motorist responded. (comma)
   "Am I going to see you there?" Jill asked Nancy. (question mark)
   "This is tremendous!" the spectator screamed. (exclamation point)

DIRECTIONS: Correct each sentence below by adding missing punctuation marks or circling a letter that should be capitalized.

1. Monica responded, I am going to be your partner.

2. Iceland is a cold country," he added, as we walked down the hall.

3. "When did you leave the concert" my sister asked Kenny.

4. Our teacher asked "who is the current governor of our state?"

5. Dad always says, "These are the best days of your life.

6. I asked Randy, "Do you want to go to the video store now?

7. "Never give up! the coach shouted to her players.

8. isn't this your bracelet?" Jerry asked Janine.

9. "That's the winning run for the home team" the announcer shouted.

10. "Let's go home before the traffic gets heavy, Dad suggested.

11. Maureen asked Tim, have you been to the Grand Canyon?

12. "You are the best soccer player in this league" Mr. Glennon told Helen.

Name _____ Date _____

2–17. Punctuating Titles

Here are the rules for punctuating titles.

1. Underline the titles of books, magazines, and movies.

   Most of us liked the book <u>Cricket in Times Square</u>. (book)
   My little brother enjoys <u>Humpty Dumpty's Magazine</u>. (magazine)
   Did you see <u>1001 Dalmations</u> at this movie theater? (movie)

   (Note: When using a word processor for your writing, you can use either *underlines* or *italics* for the names of books, magazines, and movies.)

2. Use *quotation marks* for the titles of short stories, poems, and songs.

   "Once Down the Stairs" is a story that Carol wrote last year. (story)
   I like the poem "Things to Do If You Are a Subway." (poem)
   Our music teacher taught the class "You're a Grand Old Flag." (song)

DIRECTIONS: Insert underlines or quotation marks where they are needed in these sentences.

1. Grandma Shirley has seen Gone With the Wind ten times.

2. Aladdin and the Wonderful Lamp is my favorite bedtime story.

3. It's from the book called A Thousand and One Nights.

4. Mom gave me a subscription to Sports Illustrated for Kids for my birthday.

5. In tenth grade, we will probably see the movie Romeo and Juliet.

6. Our class is singing Fifty Nifty United States by Ray Charles.

7. Did you ever read Zillions magazine for children?

8. Harry Potter and the Sorcerer's Stone is a great book!

9. Seventeen is a very popular magazine for teenagers.

10. Wendy just read Judy Blume's book Tales of a Fourth Grade Nothing.

11. Jabberwocky is an hilarious poem by Lewis Carroll.

12. I read an article about the California missions in Cobblestone magazine.

2–18. PUNCTUATION PROBLEMS

DIRECTIONS: Only six of the following sentences are punctuated correctly. Write the letter C if the punctuation is correct. Correct the incorrectly punctuated sentences by either adding or deleting punctuation marks.

1. _____ Microphones, lights, and speakers were delivered to the arena.

2. _____ Were the cowboys hats dropped off in time.

3. _____ The following players will sign autographs this evening Tom Tresher, Mike Lyons, and Becky O'Brien.

4. _____ Who wrote the short story called The Legend of Sleepy Hollow?

5. _____ Penny will be twenty-four this September.

6. _____ Two of the boys' left their backpacks near the door.

7. _____ Do you think theyve had a terrific vacation?

8. _____ Here are some of this lady's thoughts on the subject.

9. _____ We've read books by these authors: Cleary, Blume, and Paterson.

10. _____ Please take your things to your room, Francine?

11. _____ They could see the mices' tail under the door.

12. _____ The speaker joked, laughed, and answered questions.

13. _____ A League of Their Own is my sister's favorite movie.

14. _____ Her legs, arms, and back hurt after she finished the marathon.

Name _____ Date_____

2–19. PLURALS (PART ONE)

Here are the rules for forming plurals and some examples.

1. A plural is usually formed by adding the letter *s*. Examples of plurals include: *rules, dates, names, animals, words, computers, tests,* and *friends.*

2. Nouns that end with *ch, sh, s, x,* or *z* form the plural by adding *es.* Examples of this rule include: *witch/witches, mess/messes, buzz/buzzes, brush/brushes,* and *fix/fixes.*

3. When a word ends with a single *f*, the plural is usually made by changing the *f* to a *v* and adding *es.* Examples of this rule include: *loaf/loaves, scarf/scarves, shelf/shelves, thief/thieves, elf/elves, leaf/leaves, hoof/hooves,* and *calf/calves.*

4. BUT . . . We form the plural of some words ending in *f* by just adding *s.* These words include: *roof* (*roofs*), reef (*reefs*), and *handkerchief* (*handkerchiefs*).

DIRECTIONS: Write the plural of the underlined word in the space after the sentence.

1. Put the books on the <u>shelf</u>.　　　　　　　　　　　_____

2. Use your <u>handkerchief</u> now.　　　　　　　　　_____

3. Look at the <u>clock</u> on the wall.　　　　　　　　　_____

4. The <u>fox</u> lives in the woods.　　　　　　　　　　_____

5. Place the <u>brush</u> on the table.　　　　　　　　　_____

6. Pour the milk into the <u>glass</u>.　　　　　　　　　_____

7. The <u>thief</u> broke into our neighbor's garage.　　_____

8. Did you have your <u>notebook</u> in school?　　　　_____

9. Leave your <u>watch</u> on the counter.　　　　　　　_____

10. Jason's <u>friend</u> came over to our house.　　　　_____

11. The worker went up to repair the <u>roof</u>.　　　　_____

12. Did you write down each <u>answer</u>?　　　　　　_____

2–20. Plurals (part two)

Here are some more rules for plurals.

1. Add *s* to most nouns that end in *o*. Examples of this rule include: *pianos, banjos, stereos,* and *shampoos.*

2. Some nouns ending in *o* form plurals by adding *es*. Examples include: *potato/potatoes, veto/vetoes, echo/echoes, tomato/tomatoes, buffalo/buffaloes,* and *cargo/cargoes.*

3. When a word ends with a vowel before the letter *y*, add *s*. Some examples include: *key/keys, way/ways, highway/highways, alley/alleys, birthday/birthdays, valley/valleys, monkey/monkeys,* and *boy/boys.*

4. When a word ends with a consonant before the letter *y*, change the *y* to *i* before adding the *es*. Examples include: *city/cities, story/stories, try/tries, fly/flies, fry/fries, country/countries, jury/juries,* and *baby/babies.*

DIRECTIONS: Write the plural of each word on the line that follows it.

1. turkey _____

2. blueberry _____

3. copy _____

4. bay _____

5. dictionary _____

6. key _____

7. library _____

8. journey _____

9. fly _____

10. spray _____

11. highway _____

12. lady _____

13. mystery _____

14. day _____

© 2002 by The Center for Applied Research in Education

2–21. IRREGULAR PLURALS

Here are some rules for forming irregular plurals.

Irregular plural nouns do not form plurals by adding *s* or *es*.

1. Some irregular nouns have the same form for singular and plural. Examples of these irregular nouns include: *elk, fish,* and *sheep.*

2. The plurals of some nouns are formed by a vowel change within the singular form or by a suffix added to the singular form. Examples of this rule are the following words: *man/men, ox/oxen, child/children, woman/women.*

3. A few nouns occur only in the plural form as in *news, scissors,* and *trousers.*

DIRECTIONS: On the line, write the correct form of the word in parentheses.

1. We found three _____ in our basement. (**mouse**)

2. Seventeen _____ entered yesterday's contest. (**child**)

3. Be true to your _____, or they will be false to you! (**tooth**)

4. Several _____ pulled the very heavy cart. (**ox**)

5. Those _____ were scared by the car's headlights. (**deer**)

6. How many _____ will it take to build that house? (**man**)

7. Talented _____ are the leaders of these important businesses. (**woman**)

8. Can you spot the three _____ on the side of the road? (**goose**)

9. Sometimes I feel like I have two left _____. (**foot**)

10. Three _____ swam happily in the bowl. (**goldfish**)

11. All this good _____ is exciting! (**news**)

12. Tom's and Huck's _____ were ripped. (**trousers**)

2–22. SPELLING (PART ONE)

Here are some rules and examples to help you with your spelling.

1. If a one-syllable word ends in a consonant, double the final consonant when adding -*ed* (trapped) or -*ing* (trapping).

2. If a word ends in a silent *e*, drop the *e* before adding -*ed* (raced) or -*ing* (racing).

3. If a word ends in *y* preceded by a consonant, change the *y* to *i* before you add the endings -*es* (countries) or -*ed* (pitied), but not -*ing* (frying).

4. If a word ends with a *y*, preceded by a vowel, just add -*ed* (swayed) or -*ing* (playing) or -*s* (donkeys).

DIRECTIONS: Write the correct spelling of each word in parentheses on the line to complete the sentence.

1. How many _____ carry this novel? (**library**)

2. The runner _____ over her own feet during the race. (**trip**)

3. You have really _____ this drawing so well, Lance. (**trace**)

4. The subway rider was _____ with the motion of the train. (**sway**)

5. We saw that the child was _____ from a bottle of milk. (**sip**)

6. The clerk _____ the credit card through the machine. (**swipe**)

7. Dad left all his _____ on the table inside the front door. (**key**)

8. We are _____ on you to complete your share of the work. (**rely**)

9. All the children were _____ their desserts with one another. (**swap**)

10. Every driver _____ so the children could exit the bus safely. (**stop**)

11. Les _____ on the spider busily weaving its web. (**spy**)

12. Mary _____ to do her best in all she does in and out of school. (**try**)

2–23. SPELLING (PART TWO)

A. DIRECTIONS: Circle the word that is spelled incorrectly in each group. Then spell the word correctly on the line after its number.

1. _____	flying	buying	claped
2. _____	leftys	parties	cities
3. _____	flapped	flapping	tryed
4. _____	bracing	crying	stoped
5. _____	controlled	occuring	tapping
6. _____	clapped	beging	prayed
7. _____	pasing	praising	pleasing
8. _____	faked	shaking	rulled
9. _____	making	bakeing	counties
10. _____	winning	likeing	buckling
11. _____	lossing	taking	shaded
12. _____	hiting	beginning	planned

B. DIRECTIONS: Write a sentence using one of the words spelled correctly in the list above.

_____

_____

_____

_____

FOURTH-GRADE LEVEL

MECHANICS AND USAGE
PRACTICE TEST

PRACTICE TEST: MECHANICS AND USAGE

DIRECTIONS: Four parts of each sentence are underlined. Each part has a letter under it. If the underlined part is incorrect, darken its circle above that letter on the Answer Sheet. If there is no error, darken the circle above the letter E.

1. <u>Bill and I</u> <u>are writing</u> short <u>stories</u> about the <u>pony express.</u> <u>No Error</u>
      A   B   C   D   E

2. The <u>dog's</u> leash <u>was hanging</u> on the <u>doorknob</u> when I found <u>it?</u> <u>No Error</u>
         A   B   C   D   E

3. Last <u>Monday,</u> <u>Taylor Lumber's</u> <u>finest</u> carpenter <u>rebuilt</u> our shed. <u>No Error</u>
        A   B   C   D   E

4. "<u>We</u> saw <u>gooses and deers</u> on <u>Bob's farm,"</u> Sharon said. <u>No Error</u>
     A   B   C   D   E

5. <u>Children,</u> please <u>wash</u> <u>dry,</u> and put away the <u>dishes.</u> <u>No Error</u>
       A   B C   D   E

6. <u>We</u> visited <u>these</u> <u>places</u> Niagara <u>Falls, Ellis Island,</u> and Gettysburg. <u>No Error</u>
     A   B C   D   E

7. Our <u>city's</u> <u>twenty-sixth</u> mayor is <u>Ms. Georgia</u> Owens from <u>Memphis.</u> <u>No Error</u>
       A   B   C   D   E

8. <u>Didnot</u> we read the story <u>"Rip Van Winkle"</u> in <u>Mrs.</u> <u>Branch's</u> class? <u>No Error</u>
     A   B   C   D   E

9. <u>Those</u> <u>girls'</u> parents spent <u>Thanksgiving</u> weekend in <u>Chicago, IL?</u> <u>No Error</u>
     A B   C   D   E

10. <u>Shel Silverstein</u> wrote <u>these</u> <u>poems:</u> "Tree House," "The <u>Fourth" and</u> "Boa Constrictor."
          A   B C   D
    <u>No Error</u>
      E

11. Bob Stone, Sandy Smith, and Charles Vargas will be runing in today's race. No Error
    A   B   C   D   E

12. The teacher asked, "Who can draw sheeps, oxen, and fish?" No Error
                A   B   C   D   E

13. Isn't Joe, Jr.'s favorite book *Winnie-the-Pooh* by a. a. milne? No Error
    A   B   C   D   E

14. This summer we'll visit Mesa Verde National Park in CO. No Error
    A   B   C   D   E

15. Juan watched two videoses: *Peter Pan* and *Wind in the Willows*. No Error
    A   B   C   D   E

Mechanics and Usage

PRACTICE TEST: ANSWER SHEET

Darken the circle above the letter that best answers the question.

1. ○ ○ ○ ○ ○
   A B C D E

2. ○ ○ ○ ○ ○
   A B C D E

3. ○ ○ ○ ○ ○
   A B C D E

4. ○ ○ ○ ○ ○
   A B C D E

5. ○ ○ ○ ○ ○
   A B C D E

6. ○ ○ ○ ○ ○
   A B C D E

7. ○ ○ ○ ○ ○
   A B C D E

8. ○ ○ ○ ○ ○
   A B C D E

9. ○ ○ ○ ○ ○
   A B C D E

10. ○ ○ ○ ○ ○
    A B C D E

11. ○ ○ ○ ○ ○
    A B C D E

12. ○ ○ ○ ○ ○
    A B C D E

13. ○ ○ ○ ○ ○
    A B C D E

14. ○ ○ ○ ○ ○
    A B C D E

15. ○ ○ ○ ○ ○
    A B C D E

Mechanics and Usage

KEY TO PRACTICE TEST

1. A ○ B ○ C ○ D ● E ○

2. A ○ B ○ C ○ D ● E ○

3. A ○ B ○ C ○ D ○ E ●

4. A ○ B ● C ○ D ○ E ○

5. A ○ B ● C ○ D ○ E ○

6. A ○ B ○ C ● D ○ E ○

7. A ○ B ○ C ○ D ○ E ●

8. A ● B ○ C ○ D ○ E ○

9. A ○ B ○ C ○ D ● E ○

10. A ○ B ○ C ○ D ● E ○

11. A ○ B ○ C ● D ○ E ○

12. A ○ B ● C ○ D ○ E ○

13. A ○ B ○ C ○ D ● E ○

14. A ○ B ○ C ○ D ○ E ●

15. A ○ B ● C ○ D ○ E ○

SECTION 3

WRITING SENTENCES

Teacher Preparation and Lessons

The ability to write and recognize a complete sentence is the basic building block of written expression. A common thread in the scoring of writing samples for the various state and national assessment tests is the student's ability to exhibit control over sentence boundaries. When guiding students through the activities in this section, it is important to keep in mind that this is the primary goal. You may wish to use the PRACTICE TEST at the end of the section as a pretest and/or posttest. Answer Keys for this section can be found on pages 80-86.

ACTIVITIES 3-1 through 3-4 help students recognize a sentence as a complete thought with a **subject** and **predicate.** Write on the board: *My best friend made these delicious cookies.* Point out that *my best friend* is the subject and *made these delicious cookies* is the predicate. Elicit additional examples of subjects and predicates. Distribute **Activity 3-1 Subjects and Predicates.** Read the introductory material and the directions together. Have students complete the page. To introduce **Activity 3-2 Simple and Complete Subjects,** refer to the sample sentence above. Point out that *My best friend* is the complete subject and *friend* is the simple subject. Have students substitute these subjects in the sentence: *The friendly baker; My grandmother in Georgia; Susie, May, and I.* Read the introductory material on the page with students. Make sure they understand the directions.

Repeat the procedure with **Activity 3-3 Simple and Complete Predicates.** Write on the board: *The friendly man helped us.* Point out that the simple subject is *man* and that the complete subject (all the words associated with the word *man*) is *The friendly man.* Also point out the complete predicate is *helped us* and the simple predicate is *helped.* Elicit additional examples of predicates to substitute for *helped us* in the sentence. Distribute the activity. Read and discuss the directions before students complete the activity. For further practice with subjects and predicates, distribute **Activity 3-4 Combining Subjects and Predicates** and have students complete the page independently.

ACTIVITIES 3-5 and 3-6 teach **compound subjects** and **compound predicates.** Explain to students that one way to improve their writing is to combine short, but related sentences into longer, more interesting sentences. Distribute **Activity 3-5 Compound Subjects and Predicates.** Read and discuss the introductory material. Then model for students how the two short sample sentences were combined into one longer sentence. Read the directions together. You may wish to complete the first item with students. Before distributing Activity 3-6, write this sentence on the board: *Regina and Marlene sang and danced in the school play.* Point out that *Regina and Marlene* is the compound (more than one) subject and *sang and danced* is the compound (more than one) predicate. Elicit additional examples of compound subjects and compound predicates. Distribute **Activity 3-6 More Compound Predicates.** Read and discuss the directions.

77

ACTIVITY 3-7 teaches **subject** and **verb agreement.** Point out that subject–verb agreement means that the subject must agree in number with the verb. Write these two sentences on the board: *The boy has a new coat.* and *These boys have new bicycles.* Explain to students that in the first sentence, the subject (*boy*) is singular (only one) and agrees with the singular verb or predicate (*has*). In the second sentence, the subject (*boys*) is plural and agrees with the plural verb (*have*). Answer the students' questions. Elicit additional examples of subject and verb agreement (e.g., *man walks, people walk, he has, they have*). Point out that the irregular verbs *are, were,* and *have* are plural, whereas *is, was,* and *has* are singular. Also, most regular verbs add an *s* for the third-person singular form (*he walks, they walk*). Distribute **Activity 3-7 Subject and Verb Agreement.** Read and discuss the directions and have students complete the page.

ACTIVITY 3-8 reviews **simple and compound sentences.** Distribute **Activity 3-8 Simple and Compound Sentences.** Read and discuss the preliminary teaching material. Point out the difference between the simple sentence (only one idea) and the compound sentence (two simple sentences joined by *and, but,* or *or*). Remind students that the conjunctions *and, but,* and *or* can join two words (tired *but* happy; milk *and* cookies; milk *or* juice). They can also join two simple sentences. (*I ate the small pie,* **and** *he ate the doughnut. I'll go to the library,* **and** *I'll read there. We ran quickly,* **but** *we missed the bus.*) Elicit other examples of simple sentences and compound sentences. Note the importance of a subject and predicate in each simple sentence. Read the directions and have students complete the page.

ACTIVITIES 3-9 and 3-10 introduce **complex sentences.** Write the following short, choppy sentences on the board: *Rosa wears boots. It rains.* Tell students that these two sentences can be combined into one meaningful sentence by using connecting words such as *before, whenever, while, as soon as,* and *because.* Tell students that sentences formed by combining two ideas with words such as these are called complex sentences. Write on the board: *Rosa wears boots whenever it rains. If it rains, Rosa wears boots.* Note that the part of a sentence that begins with a connecting word cannot stand alone because it does not express a complete thought. Have students underline the parts of the sentences on the board that cannot stand alone. Distribute **Activity 3-9 Complex Sentences.** Read the material in the box together and discuss the directions. You may wish to complete the page with students. Distribute **Activity 3-10 Writing Complex Sentences.** Write these two sentences on the board: *Whenever it rains, I go out. I go out whenever it rains.* Have students identify the connecting word *whenever* in each sentence. Point out that when an incomplete thought starting with the connecting word comes at the beginning of the sentence, it is followed by a comma. Read and discuss the items in the box. Review how the connecting words function in the sample sentences. Elicit other examples of complex sentences. Complete the activity with students.

ACTIVITY 3-11 introduces **sentence combining.** You may wish to complete Activities 3-12 and 3-13 on the coordinating conjunction before assigning Activity 3-11. Review briefly what students have learned about simple, compound, and complex sentences as well as compound subjects and predicates. Distribute **Activity 3-11 Combining Sentences.** Read the directions with students and use item 1 to model sentence combining.

ACTIVITIES 3-12 and 3-13 introduce **coordinating conjunctions.** Write the following sentences on the board: *Dad digs for clams, and Mom eats them. Dad likes seafood, but he does not like clams. Dad will grill tuna tonight, or he will bake snapper.* Point out that each longer sentence is made up of two shorter sentences joined by the connecting words *and, but,* or *or.* Tell students that these connecting words are called *conjunctions.* One way to avoid short choppy sentences when writing is to combine two short sentences into a longer sentence by using a conjunction. Elicit additional examples of sentences with coordinating conjunctions that combine two short sentences. Distribute **Activity 3-12 Coordinating Conjunctions.** Read and discuss the directions. During the next session, distribute **Activity 3-13 Coordinating Conjunctions and the Comma.** Begin by writing the sample sentences from the previous activity on the board. Point out the conjunctions *and, but,* and *or.* Explain that when one of these words is used to combine two simple sentences, it is preceded by a comma. Have students underline the conjunction in each sentence and circle the comma.

ACTIVITIES 3-14 **through** 3-16 introduce **sentence fragments.** Tell students that all sentences must express a complete thought. Emphasize that a sentence requires a subject and a predicate. If one of those is missing, the group of words is not a sentence and is called a sentence fragment. Write these fragments on the board: *Theo's birthday party last week; A boy who is in my reading class; makes lots of exciting trips.* Elicit from the class that these are not sentences because they do not state a complete thought. Have students suggest ways of making these fragments complete by adding either a subject or a predicate. Students may suggest: *I went to Theo's birthday party last week.* or *Theo's birthday party last week was a blast.* Repeat with the other fragments. Distribute **Activity 3-14 Sentence Fragments.** Discuss the preliminary material and read the directions. During the next two sessions, distribute **Activity 3-15 Finding Sentence Fragments** and **Activity 3-16 Correcting Fragments.** Read and discuss the directions together. You may want to have students complete Activity 3-15 independently and Activity 3-16 with a partner.

ACTIVITIES 3-17, 3-18, **and** 3-19 deal with **run-on sentences.** To begin, write the following on the board: *The teacher likes my work, I enjoy art class. Watch out for that car, it is speeding down the street. It's easy to find my house, it's the white one with the purple shutters.* Ask the class what is wrong with these sentences (each one contains two complete thoughts). Explain that these are called run-on sentences. Discuss and write on the board ways of correcting each of these. (For example, the first one could be divided into two sentences, or the connecting word *and* or *so* could be used.) Distribute **Activity 3-17 Run-on Sentences.** Read and discuss the directions. At the next session, distribute **Activity 3-18 Correcting Run-on Sentences.** After students have completed the page, have them share what they have written. Use **Activity 3-19 Revising Fragments and Run-ons** as a review. Have students share their revisions.

ACTIVITIES 3-20 **and** 3-21 provide two activities on forming sentences that are fun and easy to do. Distribute **Activity 3-20 Constructing Sentences by the Letters.** Make sure students understand the directions. Distribute **Activity 3-21 Unscrambling Sentences.** Read and discuss the directions. When students have completed these activities, have them share what they have written.

ACTIVITIES 3-22 **and** 3-23 review the **four types of sentences.** Distribute **Activity 3-22 Declarative, Interrogative, Exclamatory, and Imperative Sentences (Part One).** Read and discuss the items found within the box. Review the marks of punctuation used for each type of sentence. Read and discuss the directions. Distribute **Activity 3-23 Declarative, Interrogative, Exclamatory, and Imperative Sentences (Part Two).** Read the directions together and have students complete the page. When they have finished, have students share their answers.

ANSWER KEY

3–1. Subjects and Predicates

1. P	6. P	11. S
2. S	7. S	12. S
3. S	8. P	13. P
4. P	9. S	14. P
5. S	10. P	

3–2. Simple and Complete Subjects

(ss = simple subject; cs = complete subject)

1. movies (ss); Scary movies (cs)
2. gesture (ss); A thoughtful gesture (cs)
3. relatives (ss); My relatives in Germany (cs)
4. phone (ss); Someone's phone (cs)
5. man (ss); The man in the blue suit (cs)
6. residents (ss); The residents of that community (cs)
7. Jenny (ss); Six-year-old Jenny (cs)
8. location (ss); The new location of our former neighbor (cs)
9. friend (ss); Her friend in the boat (cs)
10. juggler (ss); The excellent juggler (cs)
11. family (ss); The whole family (cs)
12. leaders (ss); wise and caring leaders (cs)

3–3. Simple and Complete Predicates

(sp = simple predicate; cp = complete predicate)

1. took (sp); took pictures of people in the Dust Bowl during the 1930s (cp)
2. appeared (sp); appeared on the job yesterday (cp)
3. howled (sp); howled throughout the night (cp)
4. have opposed (sp); have opposed the new highway (cp)
5. wrote (sp); wrote a letter (cp)
6. signed (sp); signed the letter (cp)
7. lost (sp); lost his science journal while on the hike (cp)
8. had caused (sp); had caused damage last summer (cp)
9. dove (sp); dove for the penny at the bottom of the pool (cp)
10. walked (sp); walked into the room ten minutes late (cp)
11. are showing (sp); are showing in two theaters (cp)
12. are (sp); are biographies (cp)

3–4. COMBINING SUBJECTS AND PREDICATES

Part A

1. f
2. g
3. a
4. d
5. h
6. i
7. b
8. c
9. e
10. j

Part B
Sentences will vary.

3–5. COMPOUND SUBJECTS AND PREDICATES

Part A
(cs = compound subject; cp = compound predicate)

1. yelling and shouting (cp)
2. Mrs. Sanchez and her daughter (cs)
3. dances and plays (cp)
4. Jerry or his brother (cs)
5. Anita and her brother (cs)
6. pushed and shoved (cp)
7. hamburgers and fries (cs)
8. ladies and children (cs)
9. Josh and his father (cs)
10. dogs and cats (cs)

Part B
Sentences will vary.

3–6. MORE COMPOUND PREDICATES

Part A
1. read, discussed; read . . . friends
2. waved, ran; waved . . . track
3. talk, enjoy; talk . . . company
4. Try, do; Try . . . best
5. lived, moved; lived . . . later
6. listens, takes; listens . . . actions
7. sews, tells; sews . . time
8. writes, songs; writes . . . hobby
9. recycled, saved; recycled . . . cans
10. helps, notes; helps . . . accomplishments
11. told, made; told . . . happy
12. drank, ate; drank . . . day

Part B
Vera dried the seeds and sprouted them in water.

3–7. SUBJECT AND VERB AGREEMENT

1. has	5. barks	9. are
2. have	6. love	10. Have
3. write	7. wants	11. are
4. writes	8. is	12. Have

3–8. SIMPLE AND COMPOUND SENTENCES

1. S	5. C	9. C
2. S	6. C	10. C
3. S	7. S	11. S
4. S	8. C	12. S

3–9. COMPLEX SENTENCES
(The part that can stand by itself is listed first; the connecting word follows.)

1. the campers took shelter; When
2. I have not seen her; since
3. They smile; whenever
4. she ran toward it; As soon as
5. you must take the medicine every day; Until
6. let him go; If
7. make sure your facts are correct; Before
8. They went to the beach; because
9. we understood the problem better; After
10. These balloons popped; after
11. Keith says he's sorry; whenever
12. I hope he calls soon; Wherever

3–10. WRITING COMPLEX SENTENCES
(Sentences may vary. These are suggestions.)

1. After the pitcher threw the ball, the batter hit it into left field.
2. She smiled when she heard her name called for the award.
3. When the sun came out again, the swimmers went back into the water.
4. Talk with your parents while you wait for the bus to get here.
5. Because the dog ran out into the road, the driver swerved to avoid hitting the animal.
6. When the tide swept the ball away, the children were disappointed.
7. As soon as he feels tired, he takes a nap.
8. If you want to go with us to the football game, give us a call.

3–11. COMBINING SENTENCES

(These are possible answers.)

1. When the waiter brought out the food, the diners were talking to each other.
2. These children ran down the path, and their mother followed them.
3. The dentist examined Jim's teeth and then took an X-ray.
4. After Nadine Franklin made a great golf shot, the crowd cheered for her.
5. Gina smiled at her piano instructor and then completed her song.
6. I like to sunbathe and jog in the park.
7. Craig's family is moving to Detroit.
8. She combs her hair with her old brush.

3–12. COORDINATING CONJUNCTIONS

1. and (*or* but)	5. or	9. but
2. but	6. and	10. but
3. or	7. but (*or* and)	
4. and	8. and (*or* but)	

3–13. COORDINATING CONJUNCTIONS AND THE COMMA

1. and	5. Yes; wave, and	9. Yes; dessert, and
2. or	6. Yes; surfboard, or	10. Yes; cold, but
3. Yes; here, or	7. and	11. Yes; tall, but
4. Yes; video, but	8. Yes; game, and	12. and

3–14. SENTENCE FRAGMENTS

1. S	6. F	11. F
2. F	7. S	12. S
3. S	8. S	13. F
4. F	9. F	14. F
5. F	10. F	

3–15. FINDING SENTENCE FRAGMENTS

The five fragments are: Also, four packets of stamps. All over the world. Pictures in color of people and places. With many unusual names. Now, my favorite hobby.

Students may revise these fragments in different ways. Check to see that their revisions are correct.

3–16. CORRECTING FRAGMENTS

(Sentences will vary. These are possible answers. Check that the students have written complete sentences.)

1. The family was leaving on a jet plane this afternoon.
2. The package will be there in the morning.
3. Most of the bystanders were wondering what had happened.
4. Juan and his buddy were skipping stones across the lake.
5. The package was hidden by the lake behind our school.
6. The skater started to panic when the ice began to melt.
7. The roast beef and the potatoes were served by the students.
8. Since all of the sandwiches were delicious, we reordered from the same deli the following year.

3–17. RUN-ON SENTENCES

1. Mara always wanted to dance. She began taking lessons last week.
2. Alan rang the doorbell. There was no answer.
3. The kids are going out for pizza. Then they plan to see a movie.
4. I need a calendar for this year. My old one is lost.
5. Mrs. Sanders has a tiny dog. It is a Pomeranian.
6. My aunt has a vegetable garden. Tomatoes are her favorite plants.
7. I like August. My family goes to the beach almost every day that month.
8. The tornado swept through the city. It did not do much damage.
9. Our electricity went off during the storm. The repair crew fixed the problem this morning.
10. Ceil's pen exploded. The ink stained her hands.

3–18. CORRECTING RUN-ON SENTENCES

The five run-ons are: Jenna decided to run for class president, she thought she would be able to do the job. She made posters, she hung them up on the bulletin board in her classroom. Ethan was also running for president, he had many friends. Jenna thought that more students would vote for her, she was more qualified than Ethan. Jenna held her breath, she was relieved to see that she had won the election.

(A sample revision is given for each run-on sentence.)

Jenna decided to run for class president. She thought she would be able to do the job. She made posters and hung them up on the bulletin board in her classroom. Ethan was also running for president. He had many friends. Jenna thought that more students would vote for her because she was more qualified than Ethan. Finally, it was time for the class to vote. Jenna held her breath. She was relieved to see that she had won the election.

3–19. REVISING FRAGMENTS AND RUN-ONS

Paragraph One: The eight fragments are: Going to the store. Who is twenty years old. And likes to buy me gifts. Although he does not really like it. To buy some new CDs. My brother soft rock. Jazz and soft rock. Each okay.

(This is a sample revision. Other revisions are possible.)

I enjoy going to the store. I always like shopping with my older sister, Eileen, who is twenty years old. She likes to buy me gifts. Although he does not really like it, sometimes my brother Bob will come along with us. Yesterday the three of us went to the music store to buy some new CDs. Each of us bought CDs that we like. My brother likes soft rock. My sister likes jazz bands. I enjoy both jazz and soft rock. Each is okay.

Paragraph Two: The entire paragraph consists of six run-ons.

(This is a possible revision. Others are possible.)

The five workers are digging a long and wide trench next to the house across the street from me. They are working very hard. They started at eight o'clock, and they have taken only one break for water. The water is cold and refreshing. Their boss seems to be proud of their efforts. He has stood over the trench and has laughed along with them. I think they will be digging for the rest of the afternoon. My friend thinks the same. What a tiring job it must be! They are very fit men. I hope they rest well after their work is done. I know I would!

3–20. CONSTRUCTING SENTENCES BY THE LETTERS

(Sentences will vary. These are possible answers.)

1. My brother is tall.
2. He will be there tomorrow.
3. Water spilled on the floor.
4. They will choose the captain.
5. Tom was tracking the satellite yesterday.
6. We talk to the family often.
7. You can go with us.
8. These ten shirts look very interesting.
9. Take these to my sister.
10. We are the champions.

3–21. UNSCRAMBLING SENTENCES

(These are possible answers. There may be others.)

1. She yelled loudly.
2. Michael drew the picture.
3. We often see him.
4. He scored the first run.
5. The family bought a new car.

6. Did she smile at him?

7. He was wearing his new slacks.

8. Will you help me with my homework?

9. They will see you now.

10. We have to read two books this summer.

3–22. DECLARATIVE, INTERROGATIVE, EXCLAMATORY, AND IMPERATIVE SENTENCES (PART ONE)

1. period
2. period (*or* exclamation point)
3. question mark
4. period
5. question mark
6. exclamation point
7. period
8. period (*or* exclamation point)
9. question mark
10. period

3–23. DECLARATIVE, INTERROGATIVE, EXCLAMATORY, AND IMPERATIVE SENTENCES (PART TWO)

1. INT
2. DEC
3. IMP
4. EXC
5. IMP
6. EXC
7. INT
8. DEC
9. DEC
10. EXC
11. INT
12. IMP

3–1. SUBJECTS AND PREDICATES

Be sure your sentences are complete thoughts.

A sentence expresses a complete thought. It always has a **subject** and a predicate. The subject tells who or what is doing the action. The predicate tells what the subject is doing or gives more information about the subject. In the sentence *My friend, Mitch, recited the speech,* the subject is *My friend, Mitch* and the predicate is *recited the speech.*

DIRECTIONS: If the underlined part of the sentence is the subject, write S on the line. If the underlined word or words is the predicate, write P on that line.

1. _____ The band <u>played in the parade</u>.

2. _____ <u>My mother</u> works in the library.

3. _____ <u>Sophia</u> dropped a book on her way to school.

4. _____ Jason <u>pointed to the caribou</u>.

5. _____ <u>The watchmen</u> heard an odd sound.

6. _____ Maria <u>borrowed two books from the library</u>.

7. _____ <u>These children</u> greeted the circus clown.

8. _____ The vice-president <u>shook many hands at the event</u>.

9. _____ <u>They</u> will certainly believe your version of the story.

10. _____ We <u>have many more miles ahead of us</u>.

11. _____ <u>Many of the newspaper deliverers</u> work very hard.

12. _____ <u>She</u> never disappoints the coach.

13. _____ The umpire <u>called the runner out at third base</u>.

14. _____ Thunder <u>rumbled</u> under the darkened sky.

Name _____ Date _____

3–2. SIMPLE AND COMPLETE SUBJECTS

Know the difference between a simple subject and a complete subject.

> 1. The simple subject is the noun or pronoun that tells who or what the sentence is about.
>
> 2. The complete subject includes the simple subject and all the words that tell more about it. In the sentence *The tall, handsome man often took long walks after supper*, the simple subject is *man* and the complete subject is *The tall, handsome man*.

DIRECTIONS: Underline the complete subject in each sentence. Then circle the simple subject.

1. Scary movies attract large audiences.

2. A thoughtful gesture can make another person very happy.

3. My relatives in Germany send packages to my sister and me.

4. Someone's phone rang in the middle of the rehearsal.

5. The man in the blue suit is talking with Mr. Holden.

6. The residents of that community requested the help of the Red Cross.

7. Six-year-old Jenny developed a passion for riding ponies.

8. The new location of our former neighbor is Boise, Idaho.

9. Her friend in the boat waved to us as she passed by.

10. The excellent juggler entertained the crowd.

11. The whole family attended the ceremony.

12. In Otto's opinion, wise and caring leaders are hard to find.

3–3. SIMPLE AND COMPLETE PREDICATES

Know the difference between a simple predicate and a complete predicate.

1. A simple predicate is the main verb of the sentence. It can be an action verb or a linking verb. Any helping verb is included. In the sentence *Mom's flowers have bloomed all summer*, the simple predicate is *have bloomed*.

2. A complete predicate includes the simple predicate and all the words that go with it. In the sentence *The Conners family vacations on Cape Cod each summer*, the simple predicate is *vacations* and the complete predicate is *vacations on Cape Cod each summer*.

DIRECTIONS: Underline the complete predicate in each sentence. Then circle the simple predicate.

1. Dorothea Lange took pictures of people in the Dust Bowl during the 1930s.

2. All the workers appeared on the job yesterday.

3. The wind howled throughout the night.

4. Pennsylvania residents have opposed the new highway.

5. The students in Miss Smith's class wrote a letter.

6. All of my classmates signed the letter.

7. He lost his science journal while on the hike.

8. Many floods had caused damage last summer.

9. The children dove for the penny at the bottom of the pool.

10. James walked into the room ten minutes late.

11. Two of the movies are showing in two theaters.

12. All of the books on that shelf are biographies.

3-4. COMBINING SUBJECTS AND PREDICATES

A. DIRECTIONS: Combine each complete subject in Column A with the correct predicate in Column B. Each is used only once. Write the letter of the correct predicate on the line in front of its subject.

A	B
_____ 1. Little Miss Muffet	a. usually dress alike.
_____ 2. My social studies teacher	b. writes best-selling novels.
_____ 3. The Bailey twins	c. are champion terriers.
_____ 4. My television set	d. has a large screen.
_____ 5. Thanksgiving and July Fourth	e. goes into extra innings.
_____ 6. The robin	f. sat on a tuffet.
_____ 7. The famous author	g. gives a quiz every Friday.
_____ 8. My uncle's two dogs	h. are fun holidays.
_____ 9. Sometimes, a baseball game	i. built a nest in the tree.
_____10. My mother and my father	j. were married twenty years ago.

B. DIRECTIONS: Combine subjects from Column A with predicates from Column B to create silly sentences. For example, *My television set built a nest in the tree.* Write your sentences on the lines below. Have fun!

_____

_____

_____

_____

_____

_____

_____

© 2002 by The Center for Applied Research in Education

© 2002 by The Center for Applied Research in Education

Name _____ Date _____

3–5. COMPOUND SUBJECTS AND PREDICATES

Keep these rules in mind.

1. There can be more than one subject in a sentence. When there are *two* or *more* subjects in a sentence joined by *and* or *or*, the sentence has a compound subject. In the sentence *Jon and Lisa walked to school together*, the compound subject is *Jon and Lisa*.

2. There can be more than one predicate in a sentence. When there are *two* or *more* predicates in a sentence joined by *and* or *or*, the sentence has a compound predicate. In the sentence *Bernie worked out and jogged at the gym*, the two verbs that form the compound predicate are *worked out* and *jogged*.

A. DIRECTIONS: Underline the compound subject or the compound predicate in each sentence.

1. The fans were yelling and shouting in the ballpark.

2. Mrs. Sanchez and her daughter came to visit today.

3. Julia's sister dances and plays the violin.

4. Jerry or his brother watched the video last night.

5. Anita and her brother were joking at the table.

6. The man pushed and shoved the door.

7. The hamburgers and fries were delicious.

8. Two ladies and three children came into the store.

9. Josh and his father painted the room.

10. The dogs and cats in the kennel are making loud noises.

B. DIRECTIONS: On the back of this sheet, write a sentence about a place you went to with a friend. In your sentence, use a compound subject and a compound predicate.

3–6. MORE COMPOUND PREDICATES

Remember these ideas about compound predicates.

> **When there are two verbs in a sentence joined by *and* or *or*, the sentence has a compound predicate.**
>
> 1. Here are two short sentences: *The performers sang joyfully on stage. The performers danced joyfully on stage.* These sentences express complete thoughts, but nearly all of the words are repeated.
>
> 2. The two sentences can be combined into one sentence: *The performers sang and danced joyfully on stage.* This sentence has a compound predicate, *sang and danced joyfully on stage*, that includes the two verbs *sang* and *danced*.

A. DIRECTIONS: Circle the two verbs that make up the compound predicate in each sentence. Then underline the complete predicate.

1. Dale read a book and discussed it with friends.

2. The champion waved to the crowd and ran around the track.

3. Many people talk to pets and enjoy their company.

4. Try your hardest and do your best.

5. He lived in Nebraska and moved to Georgia thirty years later.

6. Our employer listens to our concerns and takes necessary actions.

7. Her aunt sews dresses and tells stories at the same time.

8. Mrs. Gavin writes stories and sings songs as a hobby.

9. We recycled newspapers and saved bottles and cans.

10. Your principal helps her students and notes their accomplishments.

11. One man told jokes and made the crowd happy.

12. The mall builders drank water and ate lunch on that very hot day.

B. DIRECTIONS: On the back of this sheet, combine these two sentences into one longer sentence with a compound predicate: *Vera dried the seeds. Vera sprouted the seeds in water.*

© 2002 by The Center for Applied Research in Education

© 2002 by The Center for Applied Research in Education

Name _____ Date _____

3–7. SUBJECT AND VERB AGREEMENT

Be sure your subject and verb are in agreement.

1. The verb or predicate in a sentence must agree in number with the *subject (noun or pronoun).*

2. Singular means only one. *Basket* is a singular noun. *She* is a singular pronoun. Plural means more than one. *Baskets* is a plural noun. *They* is a plural pronoun.

3. A singular subject takes a singular verb. *Russell has a ticket to the concert.* In this sentence, *Russell* is the *subject* and *has* is the *verb.* Both are singular.

4. A plural subject takes a plural verb. *My parents have two minivans.* In this sentence, *parents* is the *plural subject* and *have* is the *plural verb.*

DIRECTIONS: Complete these sentences by filling in the correct verb.

1. Shauna _____ a bike. (**has, have**)

2. Her neighbors _____ three bikes. (**has, have**)

3. My favorite authors _____ exciting books. (**write, writes**)

4. His favorite author _____ exciting mystery stories. (**write, writes**)

5. The dog in the next yard _____ throughout the day. (**bark, barks**)

6. My three cats _____ to be fed three times a day. (**love, loves**)

7. Mark _____ to go to camp next summer. (**want, wants**)

8. The show _____ about to start. (**is, are**)

9. These pictures of the lighthouse _____ great! (**is, are**)

10. _____ they finished the mural yet? (**Has, Have**)

11. Where _____ my keys, Frankie? (**is, are**)

12. _____ you seen them, Leslie? (**Has, Have**)

3–8. SIMPLE AND COMPOUND SENTENCES

Remember the difference between a simple sentence and a compound sentence.

1. A simple sentence has only one idea. It has *one complete subject* and *one complete predicate*. An example of a simple sentence is: *The jogger headed for the finish line.*

2. A compound sentence has *two simple sentences* that are joined by *and*, *but*, or *or*. An example of a compound sentence is: *The jogger headed for the finish line, and her friends cheered her on.* The word *and* joins the two simple sentences.

3. NOTE: The words *and*, *but*, and *or* are also used to form compound subjects and compound predicates. *The jogger pumped her arms and headed for the finish line* is an example of a simple sentence. In this sentence, the word *and* joins two verbs, *pumped* and *headed*, not two simple sentences.

DIRECTIONS: Write the letter S if the sentence is a simple sentence. Write the letter C if the sentence is a compound sentence.

1. _____   The jar was left on the counter.

2. _____   He washed the car and cleaned the pool today.

3. _____   Jill and her sister were there before.

4. _____   They sat by the ocean and told funny stories to each other.

5. _____   I walked the dog, and Tom fed the cats.

6. _____   She went to the wrong room, but her teacher did not punish her.

7. _____   These men cheered for their sons.

8. _____   The man cheered for his son, and the boy waved back to him.

9. _____   Many people want to go to the concert, but there are not that many tickets.

10. _____   I wanted to sleep late, but the fire siren woke me up.

11. _____   My relatives can see the mountains and the lake from their backyard.

12. _____   Many authors and their readers enjoy discussing books and characters.

© 2002 by The The Center for Applied Research in Education

Name _____ Date _____

3–9. COMPLEX SENTENCES

Use complex sentences correctly to make your writing clear.

1. A complex sentence has two closely related ideas. The main idea is a *simple sentence* that makes sense by itself and can stand alone. The other idea cannot stand alone. It depends on the main idea to make sense.

2. The two ideas are often connected with one of the following words or phrases: *until, after, as soon as, because, before, if, since, when, while, whenever,* or *wherever.*

3. Here are four complex sentences with a connecting word or words shown underlined. These words introduce the idea that cannot stand alone: <u>Until</u> *you do better in school, you cannot play soccer.* <u>As soon as</u> *you are finished, put your paper on my desk. John walked home* <u>after</u> *eating dinner at Marty's house. They will be moving* <u>because</u> *Mr. Rollins has taken a new job.*

4. NOTE: When the idea with the connecting word begins the sentence, a comma is needed to separate it from the main idea.

DIRECTIONS: Underline the part of the sentence that can stand alone. Circle the word that connects the two ideas.

1. When the sky darkened, the campers took shelter.

2. I have not seen her since we were in the second grade.

3. They smile whenever they think about summer camp.

4. As soon as Smokey saw her food dish, she ran toward it.

5. Until you feel better, you must take the medicine every day.

6. If he hollers, let him go.

7. Before you write the e-mail, make sure your facts are correct.

8. They went to the beach because it was so hot at home.

9. After we spoke with the teacher, we understood the problem better.

10. These balloons popped after the party was already over.

11. Keith says he's sorry whenever he makes a mistake.

12. Wherever he is, I hope he calls soon.

3–10. WRITING COMPLEX SENTENCES

Keep these rules in mind when using complex sentences.

---

1. The following words are used to join or connect the two ideas in a complex sentence: *after, as soon as, because, before, if, since, until, when, while, whenever,* and *wherever.*

2. Here are some examples of complex sentences: <u>*Whenever*</u> *she is cold, she puts on a sweater.* <u>*Since*</u> *I am older than you, I can give you permission. You can do it* <u>*if*</u> *you try.*

3. If the word that joins the two ideas *starts* the sentence, insert a comma after the end of the first idea.

4. If the word that joins the ideas comes *after* the first idea, no comma is needed.

DIRECTIONS: Combine each pair of sentences using any of the connecting words listed in the beginning of the box above. Write your complex sentences on another sheet of paper.

1. The pitcher threw the ball. The batter hit it into left field.

2. She smiled. She heard her name called for the award.

3. The sun came out again. The swimmers went back into the water.

4. Talk with your parents. You wait for the bus to get here.

5. The dog ran out into the road. The driver swerved to avoid hitting the animal.

6. The tide swept the ball away. The children were disappointed.

7. He feels tired. He takes a nap.

8. You want to go with us to the football game. Give us a call.

© 2002 by The Center for Applied Research in Education

3–11. COMBINING SENTENCES

DIRECTIONS: Combine each pair of sentences. A combined sentence might have a compound subject and/or a compound predicate. It might be a simple sentence, a compound sentence, or a complex sentence. Check that you use correct punctuation. You might need to change some words.

1. The waiter brought out the food. The diners were talking to each other.

   _____

   _____

2. These children ran down the path. The children's mother followed them down the path.

   _____

   _____

3. The dentist examined Jim's teeth. Then the dentist took an X-ray of Jim's teeth.

   _____

   _____

4. Nadine Franklin made a great golf shot. The crowd cheered for her.

   _____

   _____

5. Gina smiled at her piano instructor. Gina completed her song.

   _____

   _____

6. I like to sunbathe in the park. I like to jog in the park.

   _____

   _____

7. Craig is moving. His family will be living in Detroit.

   _____

   _____

8. She combs her hair. She combs her hair with her old brush.

   _____

   _____

3–12. COORDINATING CONJUNCTIONS

Use coordinating conjunctions to make your writing easier to read.

The coordinating conjunctions *and, but,* and *or* can be used to join two simple sentences.

1. The conjunction *and* joins two related sentences that are equal. (*I like basketball, and he likes soccer.*)

2. The conjunction *but* joins two sentences that have related but opposing *information.* (*I went to the store, but it was closed.*)

3. The conjunction *or* suggests one possibility or the other. (*Tonight I will listen to music, or I will read a book.*)

4. Conjunctions also can be used to join words (*peanut butter and grape jelly; he and I*).

DIRECTIONS: Complete each sentence. Write *and, but,* or *or* depending upon the meaning of the sentence.

1. Billy wanted to sell lemonade, _____ I wanted to sell cookies.

2. Dad wanted to sleep late, _____ the dog's loud barking woke him up.

3. You can do your homework in my room _____ in the library.

4. Stewart washed the car, _____ Marilyn waxed it.

5. You can repair the window now, _____ you can repair it later.

6. My brother _____ my sister will be there during the night.

7. Sharon wanted to leave, _____ her ride had not arrived.

8. Yesterday, the Dolphins won, _____ the Raiders tied.

9. The children wanted to go to the beach, _____ their parents had other plans for them.

10. Many are called, _____ few are chosen.

© 2002 by The Center for Applied Research in Education

Name _____   Date _____

3–13. COORDINATING CONJUNCTIONS AND THE COMMA

Remember the comma with conjunctions.

1. A comma is used before the conjunctions *and, but,* or *or* whenever they are used to join two simple sentences. Here are some examples: *Joey loves to read, and Kate loves to act. You can have a peanut butter and jelly sandwich, or you can have a tuna fish sandwich. I wanted to buy a pair of sneakers, but the store didn't have my size.*

2. Do not use a comma when the conjunction joins two nouns in a compound subject. (*He and I joined the club. Biscuits or French bread will be fine.*)

3. Do not use a comma when the conjunction joins the verbs in a compound predicate. (*Boxer jumped and skipped down the street.*)

DIRECTIONS: Circle the conjunction in each sentence. Write YES when the conjunction joins two simple sentences. Then insert the comma where it belongs in the sentence.

1. _____ I want to buy a new bicycle and use it this weekend.

2. _____ You may have peaches or ice cream for dessert, Sue.

3. _____ The seagulls will land here or they will land down the beach.

4. _____ My sister wants to rent a video but I would like to go to the movies.

5. _____ Shelly didn't see the wave and she didn't realize it would knock her down.

6. _____ Your uncle can use this surfboard or he can use Dan's kayak.

7. _____ What are they serving for dinner and dessert tonight, Lydia?

8. _____ Henry will go to the football game and watch the soccer match on TV.

9. _____ You can bring the dessert and I will bring the kites.

10. _____ The lake's water was cold but I went in anyway.

11. _____ Louis is tall but he does not play on our basketball team.

12. _____ Nancy opened and closed the window.

Name _____ Date _____

3–14. SENTENCE FRAGMENTS

Avoid sentence fragments in your writing.

> 1. A sentence is a group of words that has a subject and a verb, and expresses a complete thought. Look at the following example: *The mirror fell from the wall last night.* In this sentence, *mirror* is the subject, *fell* is the verb, and all the words express a complete thought.
>
> 2. A group of words that looks like a sentence but is incomplete and does not express a complete thought is called a sentence fragment. *After every game.* is a fragment. It does not have a subject, a verb, or express a complete thought.

DIRECTIONS: On the line next to each group of words, write F if it is a fragment or S if it is a sentence.

1. _____ Here is a message for your mother.

2. _____ My mother, father, brother, and uncles.

3. _____ Mike was standing outside.

4. _____ Sitting on the stoop with her friends next to her.

5. _____ Anna, my very best friend in the world.

6. _____ Even though I do not know how to bowl.

7. _____ The dogs were barking.

8. _____ Tests usually make me nervous.

9. _____ Although Sarah was happy to have her own room.

10. _____ Joe and his trumpet in the marching band.

11. _____ Thursdays at three o'clock.

12. _____ I was finally called to read.

13. _____ My Spanish teacher, Mrs. Lambert.

14. _____ Much to my surprise.

3–15. FINDING SENTENCE FRAGMENTS

DIRECTIONS: The following paragraph contains five fragments. Underline the fragments. Then rewrite the paragraph, changing the five fragments into five sentences.

> My grandfather thought that I should have a hobby. He gave me a book for collecting stamps. Also, four packets of stamps. At first, I thought it would be boring. Then I began to examine the stamps. They were from many countries. All over the world. Many of them were beautiful. Pictures in color of people and places. I did not know there were so many countries. With many unusual names. I soon became interested in stamp collecting. Now, my favorite hobby.

_____

_____

_____

_____

_____

_____

_____

_____

_____

_____

_____

_____

Use another sheet of paper if you need more space to write.

Name _____ Date _____

3-16. CORRECTING FRAGMENTS

DIRECTIONS: Each group of words below is a fragment. Add words to each fragment to make it a complete sentence. You do not have to start your new sentences with the words that start these fragments. Write your sentence on the lines below each group of words.

1. Leaving on a jet plane.

_____

_____

2. There in the morning.

_____

_____

3. Wondering what had happened.

_____

_____

4. Juan and his buddy.

_____

_____

5. By the lake behind our school.

_____

_____

6. When the ice started to melt.

_____

_____

7. The roast beef and the potatoes.

_____

_____

8. Since all of the sandwiches.

_____

_____

© 2002 by The Center for Applied Research in Education

Name _____ Date _____

3–17. RUN-ON SENTENCES

Know when to rewrite to avoid run-on sentences.

> 1. When a sentence continues past the point where it should stop, it is called a run-on sentence. The following group of words is a run-on: *My mother went to the store, she bought me a new T-shirt.* This group of words would be better written as two separate sentences: *My mother went to the store. She bought me a new T-shirt.*
>
> 2. Make sure to begin each sentence with a capital letter and end it with a period, an exclamation point, or a question mark.

DIRECTIONS: On another sheet of paper, rewrite each run-on sentence as two separate sentences.

1. Mara always wanted to dance, she began taking lessons last week.

2. Alan rang the doorbell, there was no answer.

3. The kids are going out for pizza, then they plan to see a movie.

4. I need a calendar for this year, my old one is lost.

5. Mrs. Sanders has a tiny dog, it is a Pomeranian.

6. My aunt has a vegetable garden, tomatoes are her favorite plants.

7. I like August, my family goes to the beach almost every day that month.

8. The tornado swept through the city, it did not do much damage.

9. Our electricity went off during the storm, the repair crew fixed the problem this morning.

10. Ceil's pen exploded, the ink stained her hands.

3–18. CORRECTING RUN-ON SENTENCES

DIRECTIONS: Underline the five run-on sentences in this paragraph. Then correct them by rewriting the paragraph on the lines below.

> Jenna decided to run for class president, she thought she would be able to do the job. She made posters, she hung them up on the bulletin board in her classroom. Ethan was also running for president, he had many friends. Jenna thought that more students would vote for her, she was more qualified than Ethan. Finally, it was time for the class to vote. Jenna held her breath, she was relieved to see that she had won the election.

_____

_____

_____

_____

_____

_____

_____

_____

_____

_____

_____

_____

Use another sheet of paper if you need more space to write.

3–19. REVISING FRAGMENTS AND RUN-ONS

DIRECTIONS: Paragraph One has eight fragments, and Paragraph Two has six run-ons. On a separate sheet of paper, correct these problems by writing complete and clear sentences. You can add or delete words from the original paragraphs.

PARAGRAPH ONE

Going to the store. I always like shopping with my older sister, Eileen. Who is twenty years old. And likes to buy me gifts. Sometimes my brother, Bob, will come along with us. Although he does not really like it. Yesterday, the three of us went to the music store. To buy some new CDs. Each of us bought CDs that we like. My sister likes jazz bands. My brother soft rock. I enjoy both of these. Jazz and soft rock. Each okay.

PARAGRAPH TWO

The five workers are digging a long and wide trench next to the house across the street from me, they are working very hard. Starting at eight o'clock, they have taken only one break for water, the water is cold and refreshing. Their boss seems to be proud of their efforts, he has stood over the trench and has laughed along with them. I think they will be digging for the rest of the afternoon, my friend thinks the same. What a tiring job it must be, they are very fit men. I hope they rest well after their work is done, I know I would!

3–20. CONSTRUCTING SENTENCES BY THE LETTERS

DIRECTIONS: Here is a challenging activity for you! The letters after each number are the first letters of the words in the sentence that you will make up. So if the letters are J-j-o-t-f, the sentence could be *Joe jumped over the fence.* Of course, many sentences can be made up for each group of letters. Write your sentence on the lines. You may change end punctuation if you wish.

1. M b i t. _____

_____

2. H w b t t. _____

_____

3. W s o t f. _____

_____

4. T w c t c. _____

_____

5. T w t t s y. _____

_____

6. W t t t f o. _____

_____

7. Y c g w u. _____

_____

8. T t s l v i. _____

_____

9. T t t m s. _____

_____

10. W a t c. _____

_____

© 2002 by The Center for Applied Research in Education

Name _____   **Date** _____

3–21. UNSCRAMBLING SENTENCES

DIRECTIONS: Unscramble the following sentences. The word with the capital letter begins the sentence. Use correct end punctuation. Write your answers on the lines.

1. loudly She yelled _____

_____

2. drew picture the Michael _____

_____

3. see him often We _____

_____

4. first scored run the He _____

_____

5. The a new car bought family _____

_____

6. she smile Did him at _____

_____

7. wearing his was He new slacks _____

_____

8. me with Will you my homework help _____

_____

9. now will They see you _____

_____

10. We two books to read have this summer _____

_____

3–22. DECLARATIVE, INTERROGATIVE, EXCLAMATORY, AND IMPERATIVE SENTENCES (PART ONE)

Use the four types of sentences correctly.

1. A declarative sentence makes a statement. It is followed by a period. (*This is a declarative sentence. You are a good writer.*)

2. An interrogative sentence asks a question. It is followed by a question mark. (*Is this an interrogative sentence? Is this sentence asking a question?*)

3. An exclamatory sentence expresses strong feelings. It is followed by an exclamation point. (*What a great day this is! How beautiful you look!*)

4. An imperative sentence gives a command or makes a request. It is usually followed by a period, unless it expresses strong feeling. (*Please take this to the cleaners. Turn the computer off, please. Stop talking right now!*)

DIRECTIONS: Insert the correct punctuation mark (period, question mark, or exclamation point) at the end of each sentence below.

1. Sheila is going to camp

2. Wait a minute

3. May I go to the park tomorrow

4. I cannot see the sunset from here

5. What is the answer to this question

6. Wow, what a terrific performance

7. The dog is wagging his tail

8. Please leave now

9. Do you understand this math problem

10. Three monkeys escaped from their cages yesterday

Name _____   Date _____

3–23. DECLARATIVE, INTERROGATIVE, EXCLAMATORY, AND IMPERATIVE SENTENCES (PART TWO)

DIRECTIONS: Tell whether each sentence is a declarative sentence (DEC), interrogative sentence (INT), an exclamatory sentence (EXC), or an imperative sentence (IMP). Write the appropriate abbreviation in the space before each sentence.

1. _____   How are you feeling these days, Mike?

2. _____   These flowers are very pretty.

3. _____   Take these to your uncle.

4. _____   What a terrific day for the beach!

5. _____   Turn off the television set.

6. _____   How beautiful you look!

7. _____   Are you going to Carlo's party tomorrow night, Kendra?

8. _____   There are many ways to fix the problem.

9. _____   This song makes me think about you.

10. _____   Wow, you are terrific, Steve!

11. _____   Can you give us a better reason for your decision?

12. _____   Let me see it now.

FOURTH-GRADE LEVEL

WRITING SENTENCES
PRACTICE TEST

PRACTICE TEST: WRITING SENTENCES

DIRECTIONS: Read each question carefully. Think about what it is asking. Decide if A, B, C, or D answers each question. Then on the Answer Sheet, darken the circle above the letter that best answers the question. Make sure you read all the answers before making your decision.

1. Which sentence(s) below is (are) an example of a *declarative sentence*?
   - (A) Heather helped her dad.
   - (B) What did you do today?
   - (C) Watch out!
   - (D) A and C

2. Which sentence(s) below is (are) *interrogative*?
   - (A) Everyone enjoyed the picnic.
   - (B) Can you find your brother in this old picture?
   - (C) I've lost my house keys.
   - (D) A and B

3. In which sentence is the *complete subject* underlined?
   - (A) My brothers and sisters <u>will sing at dinner</u>.
   - (B) My <u>brothers and sisters</u> will sing at dinner.
   - (C) <u>My brothers and sisters</u> will sing at dinner.
   - (D) My brothers and sisters will sing <u>at dinner</u>.

4. Which sentence has a *compound subject and a compound predicate*?
   - (A) I read the story.
   - (B) Jan and I read and discussed the story.
   - (C) Bill and I discussed the story.
   - (D) None of the above

5. In which sentence is the *subject–verb agreement* correct?
   - (A) The children writes letters home every day.
   - (B) John write letters home every day.
   - (C) John writes letters home every day.
   - (D) None of the above

6. Which sentence(s) is (are) an example of a *simple sentence*?
   - (A) I washed windows.
   - (B) I washed windows and waxed the car.
   - (C) I washed windows, and I waxed the car.
   - (D) A and B

PRACTICE TEST: WRITING SENTENCES *(Continued)*

7. Which sentence(s) is (are) an example of a *compound sentence*?
   - (A) The weather was sunny and hot.
   - (B) The weather was sunny, and it was hot.
   - (C) The weather was hot.
   - (D) A and C

8. In which sentence is the *conjunction* in italics?
   - (A) <u>Mary and Ted</u> are friends.
   - (B) Mary and <u>Ted</u> are friends.
   - (C) Mary and Ted <u>are</u> friends.
   - (D) Mary <u>and</u> Ted are friends.

9. In which sentence does the *conjunction join two simple sentences*?
   - (A) Juan jogged to the store and to the park.
   - (B) Danny jogged to the store, and Juan jogged to the park.
   - (C) Juan and Danny jogged to the store and to the park.
   - (D) None of the above

10. In which sentence is the *incorrect conjunction* used?
    - (A) Ed wants an apple, or he wants a peach.
    - (B) Sue wants to paint, but Alice wants to draw.
    - (C) Alice is doing her homework, or it's almost finished.
    - (D) Maxine went to school, or she went to the library.

11. In which sentence is the *comma in the correct place?*
    - (A) Bob, and I are in the same class.
    - (B) Pia, Anna, and Tina, work in the principal's office.
    - (C) Joe is home from work, but Jon isn't home yet.
    - (D) None of the above

12. Which is *not* an example of a *complex sentence?*
    - (A) Before the storm, it became very still.
    - (B) We stayed inside until the storm let up.
    - (C) As a result of the story, many trees fell.
    - (D) My sister and I were worried.

© 2002 by The Center for Applied Research in Education

13. In which sentence can the underlined part *stand alone?*

   (A) <u>Before you sit down</u>, hang up your coat.
   (B) Hang up <u>your coat before</u> you sit down.
   (C) Before you sit down, <u>hang up your coat</u>.
   (D) None of the above

14. Which group of words is a *sentence fragment?*

   (A) Don't forget your lunch money.
   (B) He was in a hurry.
   (C) He'll be hungry today!
   (D) None of the above

15. Which group of words is a *run-on sentence?*

   (A) The boy left his coat in class. The school is closed.
   (B) The boy left his coat, the school is closed.
   (C) The boy left his coat in class, but the school is closed.
   (D) None of the above

Name _____   Date _____

Writing Sentences
PRACTICE TEST: ANSWER SHEET

Darken the circle above the letter that best answers the question.

1. ○ ○ ○ ○
   A B C D

2. ○ ○ ○ ○
   A B C D

3. ○ ○ ○ ○
   A B C D

4. ○ ○ ○ ○
   A B C D

5. ○ ○ ○ ○
   A B C D

6. ○ ○ ○ ○
   A B C D

7. ○ ○ ○ ○
   A B C D

8. ○ ○ ○ ○
   A B C D

9. ○ ○ ○ ○
   A B C D

10. ○ ○ ○ ○
    A B C D

11. ○ ○ ○ ○
    A B C D

12. ○ ○ ○ ○
    A B C D

13. ○ ○ ○ ○
    A B C D

14. ○ ○ ○ ○
    A B C D

15. ○ ○ ○ ○
    A B C D

Writing Sentences

KEY TO PRACTICE TEST

© 2002 by The Center for Applied Research in Education

1. **A** B C D

2. A **B** C D

3. A B **C** D

4. A **B** C D

5. A B **C** D

6. A B C **D**

7. A **B** C D

8. A B C **D**

9. A **B** C D

10. A B **C** D

11. A B **C** D

12. A B C **D**

13. A B **C** D

14. A B C **D**

15. A **B** C D

WRITING PARAGRAPHS

Teacher Preparation and Lessons

Recognizing and writing paragraphs is a necessary prerequisite for essay writing. The activities in Section 4 help students to organize their thinking as well as their writing and to communicate thoughts and ideas clearly to the reader. These skills are an important component of the scoring process in both state and national standardized assessment tests for writing. Selected answers are given on page 120. The PRACTICE TEST on pages 142-146 assesses students' ability to apply their knowledge of language and writing skills in a sample writing passage. The rubric and student samples can be used to assist in assessing students' writing.

ACTIVITIES 4-1 through 4-4 are designed to help students **organize paragraphs.** The first two activities deal with writing topic sentences. Write the following on the board:

> *It is no fun to be in a car that breaks down on the road.*
> *I never thought that moving to a new house would be so hard!*
> *How would you feel if your family was really weird?*

For each sentence, elicit (1) what a paragraph that might follow is about; (2) what type of sentence it is (declarative, interrogative, exclamatory); and (3) how this topic sentence grabs the reader's interest. Distribute **Activity 4-1 Writing a Topic Sentence (Part One)** and read the directions together. When the exercise has been completed, read aloud each topic sentence. Distribute **Activity 4-2 Writing a Topic Sentence (Part Two)** . Read the directions together and instruct students to write a topic sentence for each paragraph. Share and discuss the results.

The next two activities deal with writing **concluding sentences**. Distribute **Activity 4-3 Writing a Concluding Sentence (Part One)** . Read the introductory sentence and the paragraph at the top together. Discuss how the last sentence sums up the topic. Then read the directions aloud. When the exercise has been completed, have students share their concluding sentences. Follow the same procedure for **Activity 4-4 Writing a Concluding Sentence (Part Two)**.

ACTIVITIES 4-5, 4-6, and 4-7 help students **develop a topic.** Distribute **Activity 4-5 Developing the Topic (Part One)** and read part A together. Elicit: (1) the topic sentence, (2) which sentences develop the topic, and (3) how the concluding sentence brings the subject to a conclusion. Read the directions for part B. When the exercise has been completed, collect the papers and read several paragraphs aloud for discussion of how successfully each is organized. Distribute **Activities 4-6 Developing the Topic (Part Two)** and **4-7 Developing the Topic (Part Three)** . Read the directions aloud and have students share their completed paragraphs.

ACTIVITIES 4-8 and 4-9 are designed to help students use tense consistently. Distribute **Activity 4-8 Using Tense Consistently (Part One)** . Read part A with students and have them identify where the tense changes in the example. Make sure students understand how to complete part B. Distribute **Activity 4-9 Using Tense Consistently (Part Two)** . Read the directions and discuss why it is appropriate to change tense in the example. Read the directions for parts B and C. When completed, have students share and discuss their answers.

ACTIVITIES 4-10 and 4-11 teach students to use the **transitional words and phrases.** Write the following words and phrases on the board: *Next, In fact, Besides, Soon, However, Next time, At last, Therefore,* and *Of course.* Tell the class that these are examples of transitional words and phrases that help our ideas flow together smoothly when we speak and write. Write and say these sentences: *He was late for class. In fact, because of the storm, almost everyone was late.* Point out how the phrase *In fact* helps the reader make a smooth transition, or shift, from one idea to the next. Elicit additional pairs of sentences using the transitional words on the board. Distribute **Activity 4-10 Using Transitional Words and Phrases (Part One).** Have one student read the paragraph aloud while omitting the underlined transitional words and phrases. Then ask another student to read the same paragraph with the underlined words. Discuss how these words make the paragraph flow smoothly. Then have students prepare and share their lists of transitional words and phrases. Read and discuss directions for part B. When students have completed their paragraphs, have several read aloud to compare transitional phrases. Distribute **Activity 4-11 Using Transitional Words and Phrases (Part Two).** You may wish to complete part A together. Write students' sentences on the board and discuss the transitional words. Then have students complete part B. Have students compare their completed paragraphs.

ACTIVITIES 4-12 and 4-13 deal with **staying on the subject.** Distribute **Activity 4- 12 Staying on the Subject (Part One)** . Read the paragraph together. Discuss where the subject begins to change and why this is confusing. Make sure students understand the directions and have them complete the page. Distribute **Activity 4-13 Staying on the Subject (Part Two).** Read directions together. Have students identify the point at which the subject suddenly changes in the first paragraph. Then have students share their completed paragraphs for part B. Follow with a class discussion as to whether or not the writer stayed on the subject.

ACTIVITIES 4-14 and 4-15 help students **avoid unrelated detail** and **put sentences in order.** Distribute **Activity 4-14 Avoiding Details Unrelated to the Topic.** Ask students to identify the topic sentence in the sample paragraph and point out details that are unrelated to the topic. Discuss why the corrected paragraph is stronger. For part B, have students read their completed paragraphs aloud while class members listen for any irrelevant details. Distribute **Activity 4-15 Putting Sentences in Order.** Read the directions for parts A and B and have students complete the page.

ACTIVITIES 4-16 through 4-21 involve students in **using the writing process.** These activities guide students through prewriting, writing the first draft, revising, and writing the final copy of two paragraphs. Discuss the value of prewriting and producing a first draft. The directions for revising should be discussed. It is important that students understand exactly what to look for during the revision process. You may wish to teach students proofreading marks for indenting, inserting, adding, deleting, and correcting spelling mistakes. A reproducible chart with proofreading marks can be found on page 343. Encourage students to refer to it as they make revisions. Before writing a final copy, have students exchange papers and offer additional suggestions for revision. It is always easier to see the flaws in someone else's work, and this practice helps students to be more critical of their own writing. Teacher assistance, as described above, is useful, but the directions contained in these activities are clear enough for students to work independently.

Practice Test: Writing Paragraphs

The sample student paragraphs A and B on page 146 are rated a 6 and a 1.

Paragraph A contains a strong topic sentence that creates interest and a good concluding sentence that sums up the information. Many transitional words and phrases help the ideas flow smoothly. The paragraph is well-developed with relevant details. Sentences are well-constructed and punctuated correctly. Tenses are consistent. Sensory words add interest and variety. The usage problem (*me* instead of *my just sitting there*) and an unclear pronoun (*I became better at it.*) do not interfere with understanding. This paragraph was rated a 6.

Paragraph B makes an attempt at a topic sentence and a closing sentence, but neither one clearly states the topic. There are many usage and mechanics errors, and the content is unfocused. Sentences are short and choppy and they are not punctuated correctly. There is one fragment. This very weak paragraph received a score of 1.

ANSWER KEY

4–8. USING TENSE CONSISTENTLY (PART ONE)

Part A

Suddenly, they see . . .

Part B

1. <u>My dad and I each take a big cloth</u> . . .
2. <u>He lifted the heaviest weights</u> . . .
3. <u>Our dog sits in a corner</u> . . .

4–9. USING TENSE (PART TWO)

Part B

1. <u>Yesterday, Jeb got</u> . . .
2. <u>Then she gets home</u> . . .

Paragraph #1 should be checked.

Part C

Paragraphs will vary.

4–12. STAYING ON THE SUBJECT (PART ONE)

1. <u>I have never gone horseback riding</u> . . .
2. <u>A few years ago</u> . . .
3. <u>My main interest</u> . . .

4–15. PUTTING SENTENCES IN ORDER

Part A

Once, I got my friend, Jonathan, into trouble at school. I saw him put a snake into Anita Cardoza's pocket. I asked him in a loud voice what he was doing. Anita put her hand into her pocket and screamed. Everyone heard and turned to look at Jonathan. It was really my fault that Jonathan got punished.

Part B

Summer is my favorite season of the year. First of all, we get a break from school. In July, I go to a wonderful camp that I love. In August, I have lots of time to fool around. I like to read, swim, and go biking in my free time. I feel sad when summer finally comes to an end.

4–1. WRITING A TOPIC SENTENCE (PART ONE)

DIRECTIONS: A *topic sentence* tells what the paragraph is about. It is usually the first sentence of a paragraph. In the following paragraphs, however, the topic sentence is in the middle of the paragraph. Find the topic sentence and circle it.

1.   Last year, I made three New Year's resolutions. I didn't manage to stick to any of them. New Year's resolutions are hard to keep. I resolve never to make another New Year's resolution. That should take care of the resolution problem once and for all.

2.   Everyone was happy when we won the opening game of the season. The second game was a heart-breaker that we lost by just one run. The season that just ended was the worst in our team's history. When our best pitcher broke his arm, we did not win any more games.

3.   Mrs. Colvino next door gives me fresh-baked cookies every day. The Robinsons on the other side let me play with their kittens. The greatest people live on my street. Best of all, my best friend, Greg, lives just down the block. What kid wouldn't be happy on a street like this?

4–2. WRITING A TOPIC SENTENCE (PART TWO)

DIRECTIONS: Each of these paragraphs is missing a topic sentence. On the lines, write a different type of topic sentence for each paragraph. Write one *declarative sentence*, one *interrogative sentence*, and one *exclamatory sentence*.

1.   First, we made a list of what I would need. Then we spent days gathering everything together. Finally, the day came to pack and meet the bus. The best part about camp is seeing your friends again.

_____

_____

_____

2.   When I woke up in the morning, I saw a box in the corner of my room. I looked inside, and there was a little puppy, wagging its tail. It was what I wanted more than anything else. I named the puppy Max, and I know we'll be great friends. That was one birthday I'll never forget.

_____

_____

_____

3.   The trip there would be uncomfortable if our car was not air-conditioned. When we arrive, we spread our blanket on a spot near the ocean. I spend most of the day in the water riding the waves. We go home at the end of the day tired and covered with sand, but happy.

_____

_____

_____

4–3. WRITING A CONCLUDING SENTENCE (PART ONE)

The concluding (last) sentence in a paragraph is often used to sum up the topic, as in the following example:

> Every kid ought to get an allowance. The amount depends on several things. One is age. Naturally, older kids need more money and should get bigger allowances. A family's income is also important. Even a small amount, however, is better than nothing. All kids need to discuss allowances with their families.

DIRECTIONS: Add a concluding sentence to each of the following paragraphs:

1.   Yesterday was the worst day of Brian's life. In the morning, he overslept and was late to school. His teacher was angry when he told her he had left his homework on his desk at home. He failed a test in math. On the way home in the afternoon, he scratched his arm on a thorn.

_____

_____

_____

2.   Maria was afraid to go into her house. Something looked wrong. The front door was standing wide open. There was no sign of their dog, Woofer, who always ran to greet Maria when she returned home.

_____

_____

_____

3.   I saw something weird yesterday afternoon. There were two cats on Mrs. Malcolm's lawn. One was black, and the other was gray. They were staring at each other. The gray one hissed. Then the black one hissed. Then they each turned around and ran in opposite directions.

_____

_____

_____

4–4. WRITING A CONCLUDING SENTENCE (PART TWO)

DIRECTIONS: Write a concluding sentence for each paragraph below.

1.   March 16 was the windiest day of the year. When I walked out of school, a gust of wind caught my hat and whipped it right off my head. I had to run a long way before I could catch my hat, as it kept dancing away from me. Sharp blasts kept lashing me from behind all the way home. _____

_____

_____

_____

_____

2.   Thanksgiving is just one week away. I love this holiday because my whole family is together. Uncle Jack lives in Texas. Aunt Sofia lives in Idaho, and Grandma is in Florida. They all come to our house for dinner. _____

_____

_____

_____

_____

3.   Yesterday, I was home with a cold. Here is what happened. I watched TV. I played games on my computer. My mom brought me lunch on a tray. Even my little brother was nice to me. _____

_____

_____

_____

_____

© 2002 by The Center for Applied Research in Education

Name _____ Date _____

4–5. DEVELOPING THE TOPIC (PART ONE)

A. DIRECTIONS: A paragraph is like a story, with a beginning, middle, and end. The first sentence states what the story is about. The sentences that follow tell the details of the story. The last sentence provides an ending to the story. In the paragraph below, draw a single line under the topic sentence. Then draw a double line under the middle sentences that develop the story. Finally, circle the ending sentence (conclusion).

> If I could change one thing about myself, it would be my size. I am the shortest person in my class. I've always been short. This does not affect my social life. I have lots of friends. It would be nice, however, not having to look up to all the other people in the world. Maybe some day I'll suddenly shoot up in size and no longer be a "shorty."

B. DIRECTIONS: You are going to write a paragraph on a similar topic. What is one thing you would like to change about yourself? Write a *topic sentence* first. Then develop the topic with at least four *middle sentences*. Write a *concluding sentence* to sum up your ideas. Write your paragraph on the lines below.

_____

_____

_____

_____

_____

_____

_____

_____

_____

_____

_____

_____

(Use the back of this sheet if you need more space to write.)

4–6. DEVELOPING THE TOPIC (PART TWO)

DIRECTIONS: Each of the following sentences is the topic sentence of a paragraph. Complete each paragraph by developing the topic and then adding a concluding sentence.

1.   Patrick likes to cook._____

_____

_____

_____

_____

_____

2.   My new pet is great._____

_____

_____

_____

_____

_____

3.   Yesterday, I went shopping with my mom._____

_____

_____

_____

_____

_____

© 2002 by The Center for Applied Research in Education

4–7. DEVELOPING THE TOPIC (PART THREE)

DIRECTIONS: The five sentences below can be combined into one paragraph, but they are not in the right order. On another sheet of paper, unscramble them and copy them in the correct order to form a paragraph. The *topic sentence* should come first, the *concluding sentence* last, and the three sentences that *develop the topic* should be placed in a logical order in between. Remember to indent your paragraph.

1. We arrive home at night, happily tracking sand all over the house.
2. It is fun to spend a summer day at the beach.
3. The first thing we do is spread out our blanket, and then we run to the water.
4. I spend most of the time swimming with my dad.
5. We take time out to get some lunch on the boardwalk.

DIRECTIONS: Here are five more scrambled sentences. Put them into a paragraph, following the directions as above. Remember to indent your paragraph.

1. He is the art teacher at my school.
2. Mr. Wilson is my favorite teacher.
3. His classroom is messy but fun.
4. Thanks to Mr. Wilson, art is the best period of the day for me.
5. It is filled with crayons, paints, clay, and easels.

4–8. USING TENSE CONSISTENTLY (PART ONE)

A. DIRECTIONS: It is confusing when a writer switches tense in the middle of a paragraph for no good reason, as in this example:

> *Bobby and Max went for a bike ride. They rode across town to the bike path along Green Park. They pedaled side by side in the direction of the ice cream shop. Suddenly, they see Bobby's brother. They rode right past him without a word.*

This paragraph is written in past tense. Where does it suddenly change tenses?

_____

_____

_____

B. DIRECTIONS: Each paragraph below switches tense in the middle. Underline the sentences where this incorrect change begins.

1.   Last Sunday, I helped my dad wash the car. First, we took out the garden hose and hosed it down completely. Then I filled up a bucket of water. My dad and I each take a big cloth and scrub down the really dirty spots. Then we polished it with clean cloths until it shone.

2.   Andy Colville is the strongest kid I know. He has muscles that are as hard as steel. He lifted the heaviest weights and somehow made it look easy. When he walks into a gym, everyone stops to stare.

3.   We had a big storm here last Tuesday. The rain came pelting down in heavy sheets. The wind blew so hard that two trees in our front yard were uprooted. Our dog sits in a corner, trembling. I didn't blame him. It was really scary.

4–9. USING TENSE CONSISTENTLY (PART TWO)

A. DIRECTIONS: Sometimes, there is a good reason to switch tenses in the middle of a paragraph, as in this example:

> *Our reading teacher this year is really cool. His name is Mr. Bonato. He is a young guy with long hair and merry blue eyes. We do fun things in his class. Last year, we had Mr. Malcolm. He was okay, but not as much fun as Mr. Bonato.*

The first four sentences are in the present tense. Then the paragraph changes to the past tense. This is correct. Do you know why?

B. DIRECTIONS: Both paragraphs below switch tense in the middle. Underline the sentence that switches tense. Then put a check next to the paragraph that switches tenses correctly.

_____ 1. Jeb loves to get mail. Usually, everything in the mailbox is addressed to Jeb's parents. Once in a while, there is an envelope with Jeb's name on it. Yesterday, Jeb got three things in the mail. They were all birthday cards.

_____ 2. Alison had a good day in school yesterday. She wore her new jeans and cherry-colored sweater. She got A's on two tests. She had her favorite lunch of cheeseburger and cole slaw. Then she gets home and finds that her mom expects her to clean her room. That's enough to spoil the day.

C. DIRECTIONS: Finish the paragraph below. Add at least three more detail sentences and a concluding sentence to the topic sentence. Be sure you do not change tense in the middle of your paragraph unless there is a good reason to do so.

There is one day of the week that is my favorite._____

_____

_____

_____

_____

(Use the back of this sheet if you need more space to write.)

4–10. USING TRANSITIONAL WORDS
AND PHRASES (PART ONE)

A. DIRECTIONS: Here are some transitional words and phrases:

nevertheless	also	therefore	soon
at that time	then	first	however
next	now	in fact	naturally
for example	of course	besides	all in all

Write five sentences on the back of this sheet. Use one of these transitional words in each sentence.

B. DIRECTIONS: Fill in the following blank spaces with transitional words or phrases.

1. Tony is Adam's best friend. _____, they sometimes fight. _____, when this happens, they make up right away. Last week, _____, they had the biggest fight of their lives. _____, they haven't spoken to each other since then.

2. _____, Rina likes the way she looks. _____, there are some things about her appearance that bother her. _____, she wishes she had a shorter nose. _____, she doesn't like the shape of her eyebrows. _____, she could be better-looking than she is.

Name _____ **Date** _____

4–11. USING TRANSITIONAL WORDS
AND PHRASES (PART TWO)

A. DIRECTIONS: Note the underlined words and phrases in the following paragraph. Note how choppy the paragraph would be if these were omitted. Copy these transitional words and phrases on the lines below. Then add at least five additional transitional words or phrases to the list.

> *I used to like to play basketball, but I don't any longer. First of all, my two best friends are on a different team this year. Also, we have a different coach who doesn't like me. Besides, the other kids have all grown, so now I'm the shortest one on the team. All in all, I can see that basketball will not be great this year.*

_____ _____ _____

_____ _____ _____

_____ _____ _____

_____ _____ _____

B. DIRECTIONS: The following paragraph needs some transitional words to make it smoother and clearer. Rewrite it on the lines below, adding transitional words or phrases.

Matt and Frankie were shooting baskets on the court. Three older guys came over. Matt thought they were being friendly. They did not look friendly. They seemed tough. The bigger one told Matt and Frankie to get out. Matt wanted to stand up to them. Matt and Frankie decided to leave.

_____

_____

_____

_____

_____

_____

(Use the back of this sheet if you need more space to write.)

4–12. STAYING ON THE SUBJECT (PART ONE)

The following paragraph is confusing because it suddenly changes subjects:

> *My sister and I had a fight last night. I found her reading my diary. I couldn't believe my eyes! She waved it in my face and asked why I had written such mean things about her. I told her she had no right to be reading my personal stuff. She screamed at me, and I screamed at her. Once I wrote a story in my diary about an imaginary planet named Gof. It was a neat story.*

This paragraph wanders away from the topic beginning with the sentence *Once I wrote a story* . . . . A paragraph should stick to the topic stated in the opening sentence.

DIRECTIONS: The following paragraphs change subject in the middle. Underline the sentences that do not relate to the topic.

1. My Uncle Hank's house is very unusual. It is miles out into the country. There are no other homes nearby. Uncle Hank's house is very old. It was built in 1805 and used to be a stable for horses. I have never gone horseback riding, but my friend, Jeni, went once and said it was fun.

2. My favorite sport is swimming. There is a pool in my school, and I practice there almost every day. I am also lucky enough to have a pool near my house where I can swim all summer. A few years ago, someone painted that pool light green. The painter was visiting our neighbor.

3. Here is my idea of a perfect teacher. The most important thing is that he or she should truly like kids. A perfect teacher is kind and patient and makes the subject interesting. My main interest is animals because I want to become a veterinarian one day.

4–13. STAYING ON THE SUBJECT (PART TWO)

A. DIRECTIONS: The following paragraph changes subject. This is confusing to the reader. Underline the sentence where the subject suddenly changes from the one stated in the topic sentence.

> *Yesterday, I went shopping at the new market on Main Street. It was the biggest market I had ever seen. The fruit department alone was as large as most complete stores. I bought two bananas and a pound of grapes. I once visited a vineyard in California where they grow grapes.*

A sudden change of subject, as in this example, is confusing to the reader because it is off the topic.

B. DIRECTIONS: The following paragraph changes subject. Cross out the sentences that do not relate to the topic. Then rewrite and complete the paragraph on the lines below. Be sure it sticks to the topic.

> *My little brother, Denny, is a real pest. He bothers me all the time. He comes into my room and stares at me while I am doing my homework. I hate that! Denny always wants me to play games with him. Our cousin, Sandy, is the same age as Denny. She has big, brown eyes.*

Rewrite and complete the paragraph below, staying on the subject.

_____

_____

_____

_____

_____

_____

_____

(Use the back of this sheet if you need more space to write.)

4–14. AVOIDING DETAILS UNRELATED TO THE TOPIC

A. DIRECTIONS: The following paragraph contains unnecessary and unrelated details that take the reader's attention away from the topic. Locate and cross out these unrelated details that have nothing to do with the topic.

> *It is easy to make a chocolate banana frosted. First, cut a soft banana into the blender. We used to have an old blender, but last year my mom bought a new blender. Add two tablespoons of milk, and blend for one minute. Add one cup of milk and two tablespoons of chocolate syrup. Blend for one minute. I like to use a timer. It has a loud ring. The last thing to add is one big scoop of ice cream. Blend for just 30 seconds, and then pour into a glass. Enjoy your delicious chocolate banana frosted.*

Here is the same paragraph without the unrelated details:

> *It is easy to make a chocolate banana frosted. First, cut a soft banana into the blender. Add two tablespoons of milk, and blend for one minute. Add one cup of milk and two tablespoons of chocolate syrup. Blend for one minute. The last thing to add is one big scoop of ice cream. Blend for just 30 seconds, and then pour into a glass. Enjoy your delicious chocolate banana frosted.*

B. DIRECTIONS: Cross out the sentences with unrelated details in the following paragraph. Then write the paragraph correctly on the lines below.

> *One person from American history whom I admire a lot is Abraham Lincoln. I believe he was our greatest president. He did not let our Union be split up into two separate countries. He freed the slaves. He was also a kind and thoughtful person. My mom is a kind person. She always forgives me when I do something wrong.*

_____

_____

_____

_____

(Use the back of this sheet if you need more space to write.)

4–15. PUTTING SENTENCES IN ORDER

A. DIRECTIONS: The six sentences below can be combined into one paragraph. But they are not in the right order. Can you unscramble them and copy them in the right order into a paragraph? The *topic sentence* should come first. The *concluding sentence* should be last. The other four sentences should be arranged in a logical order in between.

1. Everyone heard and turned to look at Jonathan.
2. Anita put her hand into her pocket and screamed.
3. It was really my fault that Jonathan got punished.
4. Once, I got my friend, Jonathan, into trouble at school.
5. I asked him in a loud voice what he was doing.
6. I saw him put a snake into Anita Cardoza's pocket.

_____

_____

_____

_____

_____

B. DIRECTIONS: Here are some more scrambled sentences. Put them in the correct order and combine them into a paragraph on the lines below.

1. First of all, we get a break from school.
2. In July, I go to a wonderful camp that I love.
3. Summer is my favorite season of the year.
4. In August, I have lots of time to fool around.
5. I feel sad when summer finally comes to an end.
6. I like to read, swim, and go biking in my free time.

_____

_____

_____

_____

4–16. USING THE WRITING PROCESS: PREWRITING

A. DIRECTIONS: Are there some things about your school or your home you wish could be different? Choose *one* thing you would like to change.

 1. Check the box below that shows *where* this change will take place. (If you check "Other," describe where it is.)

❑ School

❑ Home

❑ Other (_____)

 2. Describe the change briefly. (You don't need a sentence here—just words and phrases, such as *the amount of my allowance, class size,* etc.) _____

_____

B. DIRECTIONS: You are going to write a paragraph about your wish to make a change. It will be easy to do if you first complete this **brainstorming list.**

 1. Write a **topic sentence** to introduce the subject, such as: *My allowance is so small that the whole thing usually disappears in just one day.*

_____

_____

 2. List **three reasons** why the present situation is not good. (You don't need sentences here—just words and phrases.)

_____

_____

_____

 3. List ways in which things will be improved if this change is made. (Remember, just use words and phrases.)

_____

_____

_____

 4. Write a **concluding sentence**, such as: *Life would be much better with a larger allowance.*

_____

_____

Name _____ **Date** _____

4–17. USING THE WRITING PROCESS: WRITING THE FIRST DRAFT

DIRECTIONS: Write the first draft of a paragraph about something you wish could be changed in your home, school, or other place.

> A. Copy the topic sentence from your brainstorming list.
>
> B. Develop the topic. Write a sentence for each reason listed on your brainstorming list.
>
> C. Write a sentence for each item in #3 of your brainstorming list.
>
> D. Copy the concluding sentence from your brainstorming list.

Write your paragraph below. This is just a **first draft**, so don't be concerned about spelling or grammar. Concentrate on getting your thoughts on paper.

_____

_____

_____

_____

_____

_____

_____

_____

_____

_____

_____

_____

_____

(Use the back of this sheet if you need more space to write.)

4–18. USING THE WRITING PROCESS: REVISING AND WRITING A FINAL COPY

A. DIRECTIONS: Correct and revise the first draft of your paragraph.

1. Does your topic sentence state the subject? Can you make it more interesting?
2. Do you develop the topic in a logical order in the sentences that follow?
3. Do you stay on the subject?
4. Does your concluding sentence sum up the topic?
5. Are your sentences complete? Do subjects and verbs agree?
6. Check your spelling with a dictionary.

B. DIRECTIONS: When your paragraph is as good as you can make it, write the final copy below. Indent at the beginning of the paragraph.

_____

_____

_____

_____

_____

_____

_____

_____

_____

_____

_____

(Use the back of this sheet if you need more space to write.)

© 2002 by The Center for Applied Research in Education

Name _____   Date _____

4–19. MORE ON USING THE WRITING PROCESS: PREWRITING

A. DIRECTIONS: You are going to write a paragraph describing a place you know well. Here are some suggestions:

❏ Your room at home
❏ One of your classrooms
❏ The street on which you live
❏ A place where you felt happy
❏ A place that made you sad
❏ A theme park
❏ Other (_____)

Check one of the above choices. If you checked "Other," write what it is.

B. DIRECTIONS: It will be easy to write this paragraph if you first complete this **brainstorming list.**

1. In the left-hand column, list all the words and phrases you can think of that describe this place. Include *sensory words, colorful adjectives,* and at least one *simile.*

2. In the right-hand column, list all the words and phrases you can think of that describe your feelings about this place.

BRAINSTORMING LIST	
Description of Place	**Your Feelings**

C. DIRECTIONS: Write a topic sentence for the beginning of your paragraph.

_____

_____

_____

4–20. MORE ON USING THE WRITING PROCESS: WRITING THE FIRST DRAFT

DIRECTIONS: Write the first draft of a paragraph about a place you know well.

1. Copy the topic sentence from your brainstorming list.

2. Develop the topic by describing what this place looks like. Use the descriptive words and phrases on your brainstorming list.

3. Develop the topic further by describing your feelings about this place. Use the words and phrases from your brainstorming list.

4. Write a concluding sentence.

Write your paragraph below. This is just a **first draft**, so don't be concerned about spelling or grammar. Concentrate on getting your thoughts on paper.

_____

_____

_____

_____

_____

_____

_____

_____

_____

_____

_____

_____

_____

4–21. More on Using the Writing Process: Revising and Writing a Final Copy

A. DIRECTIONS: Correct and revise the first draft of your paragraph.

---

1. Does your topic sentence state the subject? Can you make it more interesting?

2. Do you develop the topic in a logical order in the sentences that follow?

3. Can you add *colorful adjectives* and *sensory words* to make the description more vivid?

4. Does your description contain at least one *simile?* If not, add one.

5. Does your concluding sentence sum up the topic?

6. Are your sentences complete? Do subjects and verbs agree?

7. Check your spelling with a dictionary.

B. DIRECTIONS: When your paragraph is as good as you can make it, write the final copy below. Indent at the beginning of the paragraph.

_____

_____

_____

_____

_____

_____

_____

_____

_____

_____

_____

(Use the back of this sheet if you need more space to write.)

FOURTH-GRADE LEVEL

WRITING PARAGRAPHS

PRACTICE TEST

PRACTICE TEST: WRITING PARAGRAPHS

DIRECTIONS: Write a paragraph of at least six sentences describing someone you admire. Explain how this person has influenced you in a positive way.

© 2002 by The Center for Applied Research in Education

CHECKLIST

Make sure to:

_____ 1. Write a topic sentence that creates interest.

_____ 2. Use only the details that stay on the subject.

_____ 3. Write a concluding sentence that sums up the topic.

_____ 4. Avoid run-on sentences and sentence fragments.

_____ 5. Check for correct subject–verb agreement.

_____ 6. Use punctuation marks and capital letters correctly.

_____ 7. Look for misspelled words.

_____ 8. Indent your paragraph.

Follow these four steps to write your paragraph:

- FIRST: On the page labeled PREWRITING, brainstorm ideas for your paragraph. Write words and phrases that show what makes this person special.

- SECOND: On a separate sheet of paper, write the first draft of your paragraph. Use the items in the checklist as a guide.

- THIRD: Revise and edit your first draft. Make sure that you have written complete sentences and that they are organized logically.

- FOURTH: On a separate sheet of paper, write the final draft of your paragraph.

PRACTICE TEST: WRITING PARAGRAPHS *(Continued)*

Prewriting

Use the lines below to brainstorm ideas for your paragraph. Then, in the space, organize your ideas in a way that is workable for you.

_____

_____

_____

_____

_____

_____

_____

_____

Scoring Guide

SCORE	1	2
Content and Organization	– lacks topic sentence and/or concluding sentence – details do not stay on the subject	– may lack topic and/or concluding sentence – details do not stay on the subject
Usage	– tense is inconsistent – no subject–verb agreement	– tense is inconsistent – little subject–verb agreement
Sentence Construction	– too many fragments and/or run-ons	– much greater sentence variety needed
Mechanics	– numerous punctuation and capitalization errors	– numerous punctuation and capitalization errors

SCORE	3	4
Content and Organization	– may lack topic and/or concluding sentence – some details stay on the subject	– may lack topic and/or concluding sentence – details stay mostly on the subject
Usage	– several errors in tense and in agreement	– some errors in tense and agreement but they don't affect meaning
Sentence Construction	– some fragments and run-on sentences	– few fragments and run-on sentences
Mechanics	– some punctuation and capitalization errors	– some punctuation and capitalization errors

SCORE	5	6
Content and Organization	– has a topic and/or concluding sentence – most details stay on the subject	– has interesting topic sentence and good concluding sentence(s) – all details stay on the subject
Usage	– few errors	– very few errors (if any)
Sentence Construction	– few errors	– very few errors (if any)
Mechanics	– few errors	– very few errors (if any)

PRACTICE TEST: WRITING PARAGRAPHS *(Continued)*

Student Samples

DIRECTIONS: Rate the paragraphs with a score from 1 (lowest) to 6 (highest). Use the information on the scoring guide to help you.

PARAGRAPH A

My father always loved basketball. His athletic abilities earned him a full scholarship to college. From there, he played in the Spanish Professional Basketball League. I spent much time in stuffy, smelly gyms watching my father practice either alone or with his team. Instead of me just sitting there, I would dribble and shoot the basketball. After some time, I became better at it and really started to enjoy the game. Thanks to my father, now I want to become a professional basketball player too!

Score _____

PARAGRAPH B

I likes go sking on the water, it was so fun. The sky blue. good for my health too My broter teached me to do this last year when we was vaction. my friends goes with me now. My broter too some times. I guess my broter who is my admire the mostest.

Score _____

ESSAY-WRITING TECHNIQUES

Standardized Testing Information

Essay writing is the heart and basic structure of standardized writing tests. In almost all cases, students are evaluated on their abilities to state a theme and develop it in a clear and logical fashion, leading toward a satisfactory conclusion. Three types of essays are required: **expository/informational, narrative/imaginative,** and **persuasive.** Some tests require students to write samples of each of these; other tests ask for only one.

Most standardized tests encourage students to use the following steps in the writing process to create a final writing test passage: **prewriting** (brainstorming, clustering, outline), writing a **first draft**, making **revisions**, and writing a **final copy.** Pennsylvania, for example, assigns two 40-minute sessions over two days for the writing test. During Session 1, the student is instructed to "think about what you want to say, make notes, and write a draft of your paper." During Session 2, the student is directed to "read the prompt, read your draft, make any changes in your draft you feel are necessary, and when you are satisfied with what you have written, copy it onto the FINAL COPY pages of the assessment folder."

Other state and national standardized tests follow a similar procedure. Students are given one or more topics on which to write (sometimes called "prompts" or "strands") and are expected to produce a final copy, which meets grade standards for achievement. Scorers are given a rubric that lists the traits upon which the samples are evaluated. Among the traits usually listed are:

- clearness of beginning, middle, and end
- logical progression of writing
- a response that stays on topic
- use of details to support that topic
- use of a variety of words and sentence patterns with correct spelling and usage of most high-frequency, grade-appropriate language
- correct capitalization and punctuation at grade level

It is encouraging to note that many school districts are now mandating regularly scheduled writing assignments, sometimes on a daily basis, in their classrooms. One learns to write by writing. That is not enough, however. An aspiring violinist may practice assiduously and often, but will never become an accomplished musician without guidance and instruction in the techniques and methods of playing the violin. In the same way, the student-writer needs instruction and guidance in order to communicate clearly and effectively. The sections on writing essays, and the ones on writing letters and stories (which are sometimes also included on standardized writing tests), offer a wealth of suggestions and activities to augment the teacher's own writing instruction. Most of the activities in these sections will have multiple parts in order to include practice in all the steps of the writing process.

Teacher Preparation and Lessons

The activities in Section 5 provide students with practice in developing the simple essay by using the writing process. The activities cover: (1) organizing thoughts logically, (2) writing the introductory paragraph, (3) developing the topic, (4) staying on the subject, and (5) writing a concluding paragraph. Provide students with an overview of the strategies in this section. You may wish to define the essay as a short piece of writing that tells about something that happened to them or someone else (narrative), describes a process or place (informational), or tries to persuade someone to do something or to think a certain way (persuasive). Selected answers are given on page 152. The PRACTICE TEST on pages 173-177 assesses students' ability to apply their knowledge of language and writing skills in a sample essay.

ACTIVITIES 5-1 through 5-6 focus on organizing thoughts logically through **brainstorming** and **clustering.** Discuss the advantage of making lists before going shopping or having a party. Elicit that the advantages of shopping lists and party lists include not forgetting something you need, saving time, and being more efficient and organized. Discuss why this sort of preparation can also be helpful when writing an essay and what kinds of prewriting activities can be helpful (for example, lists, research, outlines, discussions, interviews). Distribute **Activity 5-1 Brainstorming (Part One).** Read and discuss the description of brainstorming. Then read and, if necessary, clarify the directions. When students have finished brainstorming, have them read their lists aloud or exchange them with a partner. Distribute **Activity 5-2 Brainstorming (Part Two).** Read the directions aloud for parts A and B. When students have completed their lists, have them shared aloud or exchanged and passed around.

Distribute **Activity 5-3 Clustering (Part One).** Read and discuss the description of clustering and the example. Then read and, if necessary, clarify the directions. When students have completed the clustering activity, have them share their clusters aloud or exchange and pass them around. Distribute **Activity 5-4 Clustering (Part Two).** Review the definition of clustering, and discuss the suggestions set forth. Read the directions aloud. When students have completed the activity, have them share their clusters with a partner.

Explain that an **outline** is a simple plan for a piece of writing. To create an outline, the first step is to write the title. The main ideas are listed next to Roman numerals I, II, III, and so on. Details or examples are listed next to capital letters A, B, C, and so on. Create a simple essay outline on the board such as the one on page 149 with the input of the class.

Point out that to develop the essay, sentences are written for each item in the outline.

Distribute **Activity 5-5 Outlining (Part One).** Read aloud the directions and the entries in the outline. Help students complete their outlines. When several have been completed, make transparencies and display them on an overhead projector. Have them read aloud and discussed. Distribute **Activity 5-6 Outlining (Part Two).** Read directions aloud. Have students share their completed outlines with a partner.

COOKING AND SERVING A MEAL

I.   Getting ready
    A. Number of diners
    B. Set the table

II. Cooking the meal
    A. Choose recipes
    B. Choose cooking utensils
    C. Set out all ingredients
    D. Follow directions on recipe

III. Serving the meal
    A. Choose serving platters and bowls
    B. Decide the order in which to serve

ACTIVITIES 5-7 through 5-12 deal with **writing the introductory paragraph.** Read the following paragraph to the class:

> *For many people, holidays are a time for giving gifts. It is great to get presents. Giving them can also be a lot of fun. I look forward to making special gifts for the people I like best.*

Identify this as the **introductory paragraph** of an essay. Elicit that the subject of the essay is "gift giving," and that the purpose of this paragraph is to state the topic. Distribute **Activity 5-7 Stating the Topic (Part One).** Read the directions for parts A and B aloud and clarify if necessary. When the students have completed their introductory paragraphs, have them share them with the class. Repeat the procedure for **Activity 5-8 Stating the Topic (Part Two).**

Tell students that they might want to write one or more sentences in the introductory paragraph in the form of a question in order to get the reader's attention. Read the following paragraph to the class:

> *Have you ever thought about what life on Earth will be like in the future? What about the year 5310? It's difficult to imagine what a typical day will be like for an average kid thousands or even hundreds of years from now.*

Elicit from students that the use of **questions** in this introductory paragraph makes it exciting and provokes the reader's interest. Distribute **Activity 5-9 Introductory Paragraph with a Question (Part One).** Read and discuss the directions. When students have completed parts A and B, have them share their paragraphs with the class. Repeat the procedure with **Activity 5-10 Introductory Paragraph with a Question (Part Two).**

Another way to attract readers' attention is to write an exclamatory statement at the beginning of an introductory paragraph. Read the following paragraph to the class:

> *Turn off that TV! Studies have shown that people who*
> *watch less TV get a better education, make more money, and*
> *have more friends than those who watch TV a lot.*

Elicit from the class how this introductory paragraph gets the reader's interest by making a **surprising statement.** Distribute **Activity 5-11 Introductory Paragraph with a Surprising Statement**. Read the directions aloud. When students have completed parts A and B, have them read their paragraphs aloud. Tell the class to listen for the surprising statement at the beginning of each introductory paragraph as it is read aloud.

A third way to attract attention is to include an anecdote or story in the introductory paragraph of an essay. Read the following paragraph to the class:

> *When I first began to get an allowance, I spent it as fast*
> *as I received it. Then I noticed that my older sister had a lot of*
> *money, whereas I was usually broke. I realized that she always*
> *saved some of her allowance. Now, I have figured out a way to*
> *accumulate money, too.*

Elicit that the author has used an **interesting anecdote**, or story, to begin an essay. Distribute **Activity 5-12 Introductory Paragraph with an Anecdote**. Read the directions aloud for parts A and B. When students have completed their paragraphs, have them read aloud and discuss each one after listening for the anecdote.

ACTIVITIES 5-13 and 5-14 focus on **developing essay topics**. One way to develop the topic introduced in the introductory paragraph is to **use examples** in the next one or two paragraphs. Distribute **Activity 5-13 Developing the Topic Using Examples (Part One).** Read aloud and discuss the explanation and the sample. Elicit that the first paragraph in this essay states the topic. Discuss how the topic is developed in the second paragraph by using examples. Read aloud and, if necessary, clarify directions. When students have completed their paragraphs, have them read aloud and discuss each one after listening for examples. Distribute **Activity 5-14 Developing the Topic Using Examples (Part Two)**. Read the directions aloud. Have students read aloud their completed paragraphs or share them with a partner.

ACTIVITIES 5-15 and 5-16 help students avoid **writing details that are not related** to the topics of their essays. Distribute **Activity 5-15 Avoiding Details Unrelated to the Topic (Part One).** Read both paragraphs in Part A aloud and discuss which paragraph is better and why. Then have students cross out unrelated details in each paragraph in part B. Distribute **Activity 5-16 Avoiding Details Unrelated to the Topic (Part Two).** You may wish to have students underline the unrelated details in each paragraph. Have each corrected paragraph read aloud.

ACTIVITIES 5-17 and 5-18 deal with **staying on the subject**. Distribute **Activity 5-17 Staying on the Subject (Part One).** Read the introduction and the sample essay aloud. Discuss how and where the writer gets lost (goes off the subject), and students' answers to the questions. When students have finished part B, have them share their paragraphs. Ask listeners if the writers stayed with the subject. Distribute **Activity 5-18 Staying on the Subject (Part Two).** Read the directions and have students underline the unrelated details in the list. Have students share their paragraphs with a partner. Tell students to listen for instances of the writer failing to stay on the subject.

ACTIVITIES 5-19 and 5-20 teach how to write a **concluding paragraph** in an essay. To begin, review the purposes of an introductory paragraph and paragraphs that develop the topic. Then write each of the following purposes of a concluding paragraph: (1) to restate the topic in the introductory paragraph; (2) to summarize the points in the body of the essay; and (3) to bring the essay to an end. Distribute **Activity 5-19 Concluding Paragraph (Part One).** Read the introductory material together and have students read aloud and discuss what they have written for part B. Distribute **Activity 5-20 Concluding Paragraph (Part Two).** Read the directions aloud. When students have completed their paragraphs, have them read aloud and discussed.

Practice Test: Essay-Writing Techniques

The sample student essays A and B on page 177 are given a rating of 5 and 3, respectively.

Essay A has good organization, specific detail, and logical reasoning. Though there is a run-on at the end of the second paragraph, the other well-written sentences include the simple, compound, and complex types. Usage and mechanics also have merit. Additionally, there is a pleasant tone to the author's essay. This essay scored a 5.

Essay B is filled with mechanical mistakes (misspellings and the incorrect capitalization of certain pronouns in certain places). Run-ons and fragments are also present. Incorrect compounds and the inconsistency of subject pronouns (*we, I, You*) is distracting. Yet, there is a topic sentence, three paragraphs, supportive details and examples, and an ambitious attempt to show why the writer enjoys playing sports. This essay scored a 3.

ANSWER KEY

5–15. AVOIDING DETAILS UNRELATED TO THE TOPIC (PART ONE)

<u>Part A.</u> Paragraph #2 should be marked as the better paragraph. The sentences with unrelated details that should be underlined in Paragraph #1 are:

<u>My family visited Boston once because our cousin lives there.</u>
<u>We had a lot of fun.</u>

<u>Part B.</u> The following sentences with unrelated details should be crossed out:

Paragraph 1:   <u>Once I went with my father when he voted, . . .</u>
<u>Two years ago, my family went on a trip to Mexico, . . .</u>

Paragraph 2:   <u>Once, I was real sick with the flu. It was awful. I hated . . .</u>

5–16. AVOIDING DETAILS UNRELATED TO THE TOPIC (PART TWO)

Students should rewrite each paragraph without the following sentences:

Paragraph 1:   My family doctor's . . .
There's a YMCA . . .

Paragraph 2:   There are many great beaches . . .
Once I saw a movie . . .

5–17. STAYING ON THE SUBJECT (PART ONE)

<u>Part A.</u> 1. My Favorite Month *or* The month of May

2. Actually, my house

5–18. STAYING ON THE SUBJECT (PART TWO)

1. cactus plant,

2. *Paragraphs will vary.*

5–1. BRAINSTORMING (PART ONE)

Brainstorming is a way of setting down and organizing your thoughts and ideas before you begin to write an essay or other piece of writing. If you develop a detailed brainstorming list before you begin a writing project, you will be ready to turn out a clear and well-organized piece of work.

DIRECTIONS: Prepare a brainstorming list for an essay on the subject "My Family," as follows: In the first column, list the names of your family members. In the second column, next to each name, write as many words and phrases as you can think of to describe that person's appearance, personality, and character. In the third column, jot down words and phrases that describe actions that show what he or she is like.

© 2002 by The Center for Applied Research in Education

Name	Description	Actions

Use the back of this sheet if you need more space for your brainstorming list.

5–2. Brainstorming (part two)

A. DIRECTIONS: Prepare a brainstorming list for an essay on the subject "Times That I've Been Happy." In the first column, list the dates. In the second column, name the event that occurred on that date. In the third column, list as many words and phrases you can think of that could be used to describe the event and your feelings about it.

Date	Event	Description

B. DIRECTIONS: Prepare a brainstorming list for an essay on the subject "My Favorite Games." In the first column, write the names of three games. In the second column, write a list of words and phrases describing each game. In the third column, write a list of words and phrases describing what you like about the game.

Name of Game	Description	Why You Like It

© 2002 by The Center for Applied Research in Education

5–3. CLUSTERING (PART ONE)

Clustering is a type of brainstorming before writing an essay or other piece of writing. It is an effective way to jot down and organize ideas. It is also fun. Here is the way clustering is done:

1. Draw a large circle on a piece of paper. Write the subject in the middle of the circle in BIG letters.

2. Using somewhat smaller print, write the main points about this subject in different parts of the circle around the subject.

3. Near the main point, write descriptive words and phrases for each in even smaller letters.

Here is an example of clustering for an essay called "An Unusual Family."

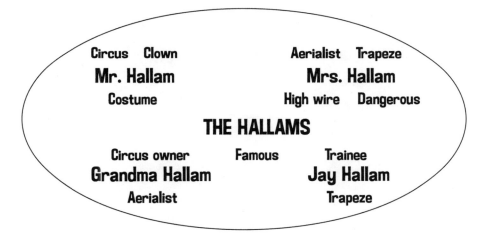

DIRECTIONS: On another sheet of paper, prepare a cluster for an essay called "Favorite Baseball Teams."

© 2002 by The Center for Applied Research in Education

5–4. CLUSTERING (PART TWO)

Clustering is a type of brainstorming before writing an essay or other piece of writing. It helps the writer to organize his or her thoughts. When preparing a cluster, set the subject in the center of the circle. Write the main points around the subject. Then surround the main points with words and phrases that describe and add details for each point.

Use big lettering for the subject, small letters for the main points, and even smaller writing for the descriptive details.

Write more details than you think you will need in your essay. The bigger your cluster, the more choice you will have.

DIRECTIONS: In the circle below, prepare a cluster for an essay called "Favorite Holidays." It has been started for you with the subject name in the center.

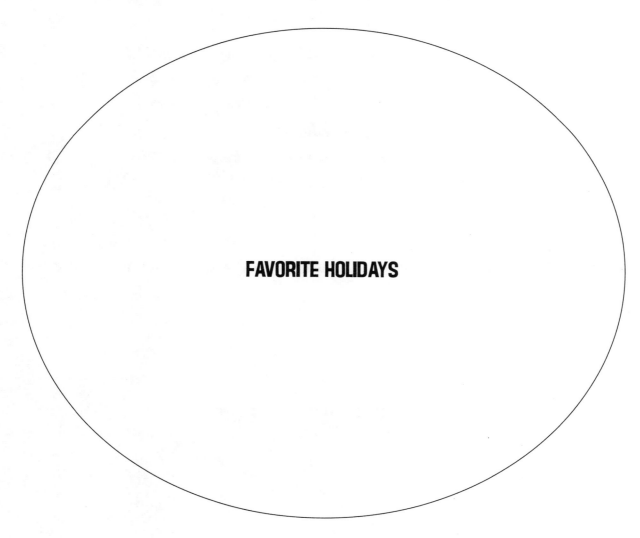

FAVORITE HOLIDAYS

5–5. Outlining (part one)

DIRECTIONS: An outline is like a skeleton. It is the "bare bones" of an essay. Using the form below, complete this outline for an essay called "Giving a Surprise Party."

Giving a Surprise Party

I.   Topic Paragraph

    A. _____

    B. _____

II. Invitations

    A. _____

    B. _____

III. Other Planning

    A. _____

    B. _____

IV. Running the Party

    A. Activities

       1. _____

       2. _____

       3. _____

    B. Food

       1. _____

       2. _____

       3. _____

V.   Conclusion

    A. _____

    B. _____

Name _____ Date_____

5–6. Outlining (Part Two)

DIRECTIONS: Write an outline for the following essay.

The House I Live In

On another sheet of paper, write an outline for an essay on "My Neighborhood."

Name _____ **Date** _____

5–7. STATING THE TOPIC (PART ONE)

DIRECTIONS: The purpose of the introductory paragraph of an essay or other piece of writing is to tell the reader what it is about—to state the topic. Write an introductory paragraph that clearly states the topic for each essay below.

How to Be a Friend

_____

_____

_____

_____

_____

_____

_____

_____

My Favorite Place to Be

_____

_____

_____

_____

_____

_____

_____

_____

5–8. STATING THE TOPIC (PART TWO)

DIRECTIONS: The purpose of the introductory paragraph of an essay is to tell the reader what the essay is about. Write an introductory paragraph that clearly states the topic for each essay below.

An Exciting Journey

_____

_____

_____

_____

_____

_____

_____

The Nicest People I Know

_____

_____

_____

_____

_____

_____

_____

_____

© 2002 by The Center for Applied Research in Education

5–9. INTRODUCTORY PARAGRAPH WITH A QUESTION (PART ONE)

DIRECTIONS: One way to get the reader's attention in an introductory paragraph is to ask a question or questions. Write an introductory paragraph that includes a question for each essay below.

My Best Friend

_____

_____

_____

_____

_____

_____

_____

_____

_____

Computer Games

_____

_____

_____

_____

_____

_____

_____

_____

5–10. INTRODUCTORY PARAGRAPH WITH A QUESTION (PART TWO)

DIRECTIONS: One way to get the reader's attention in an introductory paragraph is to ask a question. Write an introductory paragraph that includes a question for each essay below.

Being a Good Sport

_____

_____

_____

_____

_____

_____

_____

_____

My Favorite Room at Home

_____

_____

_____

_____

_____

_____

_____

_____

© 2002 by The Center for Applied Research in Education

5–11. INTRODUCTORY PARAGRAPH WITH A SURPRISING STATEMENT

DIRECTIONS: A surprising or shocking statement in your introductory paragraph can really catch the reader's attention. Write an introductory paragraph that includes a surprising statement for each essay below. (Remember that your paragraph must state the topic of the essay whether in your surprising statement or in another sentence.)

Things I Would Never Do

_____

_____

_____

_____

_____

_____

_____

_____

How to Change the School Cafeteria

_____

_____

_____

_____

_____

_____

_____

_____

5–12. INTRODUCTORY PARAGRAPH WITH AN ANECDOTE

DIRECTIONS: Telling an anecdote (little story) in your introductory paragraph can arouse the reader's interest. Write an introductory paragraph that includes an anecdote for each essay below. (Remember that your paragraph must also state the topic of the essay!)

Embarrassing Moments

_____

_____

_____

_____

_____

_____

_____

Shopping Trips I Do Not Enjoy

_____

_____

_____

_____

_____

_____

_____

5–13. Developing the Topic Using Examples
(Part One)

Here are two paragraphs of a three-paragraph essay called "If I Were Principal." Notice how the topic is introduced in the first paragraph and developed in the second paragraph by using examples.

> Would you like to be principal of our school? I would! It would be neat! Of course, it would also be a big challenge. Even so, there are some things I would change if I had that power.
>
> The first thing I would do is lengthen the school day. Then there would be more time for clubs and sports. Second, I would send out an order to discontinue all homework. All necessary work would be completed during the school day. Another change would come in the cafeteria food. There would be lots more pizza, hot dogs, burgers, and fries.

DIRECTIONS: Here is the introductory paragraph of a three-paragraph essay called "Save Our Earth." Write a second paragraph for this essay that develops the topic using three examples.

> Will our children and grandchildren be able to breathe fresh air? Will they have food to eat that is not polluted? It is up to us to take steps now to preserve Earth for them.

_____

_____

_____

_____

_____

_____

_____

_____

Use the back of this sheet if you need more space to write.

5–14. DEVELOPING THE TOPIC USING EXAMPLES
(PART TWO)

DIRECTIONS: Below are two introductory paragraphs. Write a second paragraph for each essay that develops the topic by using examples.

Winter Fun

Some people don't like winter because it is too cold. Not I! I love this season because there are so many wonderful things to see and do.

_____

_____

_____

_____

_____

_____

Great Americans

There have been many great people in the history of America who have used their ability to make it a better country. There are a few, however, who stand out above the rest.

_____

_____

_____

_____

_____

_____

© 2002 by The Center for Applied Research in Education

Name _____ Date _____

5–15. AVOIDING DETAILS UNRELATED TO THE TOPIC
(PART ONE)

A. DIRECTIONS: Read the two paragraphs below. One of them is better because it sticks to the point of the topic. Can you identify which one does this? In one of the paragraphs, there are details that have nothing to do with the topic. Check the paragraph with these details and underline the sentence(s).

❑ On December 16, 1773, an amazing event took place in Boston Harbor. Workmen and merchants, dressed in Native American clothing, boarded a ship bringing tea into Boston Harbor. My family visited Boston once because our cousin lives there. We had a lot of fun. Anyway, these colonists protested unfair taxes by dumping the tea overboard. This became known as the "Boston Tea Party."

❑ On December 16, 1773, an amazing event took place in Boston Harbor. Workmen and merchants, dressed in Native American clothing, boarded a ship bringing tea into Boston Harbor. These colonists protested unfair taxes by dumping the tea overboard. This became known as the "Boston Tea Party."

B. DIRECTIONS: In the following paragraphs, cross out any sentences not related to the topic.

Election Day in the United States always falls on the first Tuesday after the first Monday in November. In this country, the government is elected by the people. Once I went with my father when he voted and watched him pull down the levers in the booth. In some parts of the world, the people have no power. They must obey a government and laws they did not choose. Two years ago, my family went on a trip to Mexico, but I don't know what kind of government they have there.

Michael E. DeBakey was born in Louisiana on September 7, 1908. Dr. DeBakey was a pioneer in heart surgery. He developed new methods and procedures that gave patients many extra years of life. Once, I was real sick with the flu. It was awful. I hated being in bed all day. The work of Dr. DeBakey and other heart surgeons gave new hope to people with heart disease.

5–16. AVOIDING DETAILS UNRELATED TO THE TOPIC
(PART TWO)

DIRECTIONS: Each of the following paragraphs contains details that have nothing to do with the topic. Rewrite each paragraph correctly on the lines below.

> Basketball is a popular game in the U.S. and in many other countries, too. Did you know that basketball has only been in existence a little more than a hundred years? It was invented by Dr. James Naismith. My family doctor's name is Dr. Naismith, which is a funny coincidence. This game was played for the first time by students at the YMCA Training School in Springfield, Massachusetts. There's a YMCA two blocks from my house. The date of this first game was January 20, 1892.

_____

_____

_____

_____

Use the back of this sheet if you need more space to write.

> In 1492, it was commonly believed that Earth was flat. Christopher Columbus said it was round. Lots of people thought he was crazy. Columbus set out to prove he was right by sailing westward across the Atlantic Ocean. There are many great beaches on the Atlantic Coast where you can swim and surf. People warned Columbus that he would topple off Earth's edge. The journey was dangerous, but he kept on going. Once I saw a movie about a ship that sank in the Atlantic Ocean. On October 12, Columbus and his crew landed in the New World.

_____

_____

_____

_____

Use the back of this sheet if you need more space to write.

© 2002 by The Center for Applied Research in Education

5–17. STAYING ON THE SUBJECT (PART ONE)

A. DIRECTIONS: Here is part of an essay called "My Favorite Month." It begins nicely, but at one point the writer gets lost and fails to stay on the subject.

> Every year, my heart seems to swell on the first day of May. That's because May is my favorite month, and I look forward to it all year. There are lots of reasons why I feel this way.
>
> I enjoy May temperatures. Sometimes, it is cool but not too cold. Many days are warm but not hot. Every week, new flowers bloom in the garden such as lilies, tulips, and daffodils. After school, my friends and I can play outdoors, which is better than being stuck in the house. Actually, my house was recently remodeled and there is lots more room to play inside. My room was enlarged, and I now have two huge closets. Dad built a recreation room in the basement with shelves for games and a ping-pong table.

1. State the subject of this essay. _____

2. Write the first three words of the sentence where the writer gets lost and fails to stay on the subject. _____

B. DIRECTIONS: Write the first two paragraphs of an original essay on the same subject, "My Favorite Month." Write an introductory paragraph that states the subject. Then develop the subject in the next paragraph, being sure to stay on the subject.

_____

_____

_____

_____

_____

_____

_____

_____

Use the back of this sheet to continue your writing.

© 2002 by The Center for Applied Research in Education

5–18. Staying on the Subject (Part Two)

DIRECTIONS: It is important, when writing, to stay on the subject. Read the following brainstorming list for an essay called "Taking Care of Your Pet." Then answer the questions below.

BRAINSTORMING LIST FOR "TAKING CARE OF YOUR PET"		
Kind of Pet	**Duties**	**Supplies Needed**
Puppy	walking, feeding, bathing, playing, training	leash, tag, flea collar, dog toys, food and water bowls
Cat	feeding, cleaning litter box, playing	litter box, food and water bowls, scratching post, toys
Cactus plant	watering	watering can

1. Which item does not belong on this list? _____

2. Write the first two paragraphs of this essay. Introduce the topic in the first paragraph. Then develop the topic in the second paragraph. Be sure you stay on the subject.

_____

_____

_____

_____

_____

_____

_____

_____

_____

_____

Use the back of this sheet to continue your writing.

© 2002 by The Center for Applied Research in Education

5–19. Concluding Paragraph (part one)

Every piece of writing needs to have an ending. Otherwise, the reader is left hanging, waiting for what comes next. In an essay, this is done with the concluding paragraph. The concluding paragraph:

- Restates the topic that is in the introductory paragraph
- Summarizes the points in the body of the essay
- Brings the essay to an end

Here is a concluding paragraph for an essay called "Buying Holiday Gifts":

> I'm always exhausted after my shopping trip in December, but it is a good sort of tiredness. It is fun and exciting to stroll through the gaily-decorated stores purchasing gifts for all the family and friends I love.

Notice how the concluding paragraph sums up the essay, restates the topic, and brings it to a satisfactory end.

DIRECTIONS: Write a concluding paragraph for the following essay.

> Can you imagine a world without telephones? We might be living in such a world today if it had not been for the inventor of the telephone, Alexander Graham Bell.
>
> Bell was born on March 3, 1847. In 1876, he spoke these famous words to his assistant: "Mr. Watson, come here." These were the first words ever spoken on the telephone. It changed the lives of everyone on Earth. Bell was proudest of the work he did throughout his life teaching and helping the deaf, but the world will always know him best as the inventor of the telephone.

_____

_____

_____

_____

_____

Use the back of this sheet if you need more space to write.

5–20. CONCLUDING PARAGRAPH (PART TWO)

A. DIRECTIONS: Write a concluding paragraph for the following essay called "My Neighborhood." Be sure to restate the topic, summarize the essay, and bring it to an end.

> I would hate to live anywhere else but in my neighborhood. I have lived there all my life, and I love everything about it.
>
> Our neighbors are great. The Olsons live in the brown house to our right. They are an older couple whose children are grown, and they are very friendly. Sometimes, in fact, they seem like grandparents because they are always giving me little gifts. On the other side of us live the Santoros. They have three teenage girls who are a lot of fun and sometimes baby-sit for my little sister. Best of all, my best friend, Luis, lives just down the street. We enjoy going on the bike trail that begins a block away. There is a shopping mall around the corner, and my school is only three blocks away.

_____

_____

_____

Use the back of this sheet if you need more space to write.

B. DIRECTIONS: Write a concluding paragraph for the following essay called "A Scary Moment."

> Have you ever been so frightened that you couldn't talk or move? That's what happened to me last Tuesday. It was the scariest moment of my life.
>
> I had just arrived home after school. I was surprised to see the front door wide open. I rushed inside and called, "Mom!" Mom is always there when I get home, but there was no answer this time. I ran through every room, upstairs and down, calling to her. I couldn't find her anywhere. That's when I began to get scared. What had happened to my mother? Imagine my relief when she walked into the house. She had gone next door to help our neighbor.

_____

_____

_____

Use the back of this sheet if you need more space to write.

© 2002 by The Center for Applied Research in Education

FOURTH-GRADE LEVEL

ESSAY-WRITING TECHNIQUES
PRACTICE TEST

PRACTICE TEST: ESSAY-WRITING TECHNIQUES

DIRECTIONS: Write an essay of three or more paragraphs about something you enjoy doing. Explain why this activity is important to you.

CHECKLIST

Make sure to:

_____ 1. Write an introductory paragraph that states the topic.

_____ 2. Begin with a surprising statement, a story, or a question.

_____ 3. Write one or two paragraphs that develop the topic.

_____ 4. Use only those details and examples that are related to the topic.

_____ 5. Write a concluding paragraph to sum up.

_____ 6. Check that pronouns agree with antecedents.

_____ 7. Indent each paragraph's first line.

_____ 8. Write the essay's title above the first sentence.

Follow these four steps to write your essay:

- FIRST, on the page labeled PREWRITING, brainstorm some ideas for an essay topic. Then list words and phrases that support the topic you've chosen.

- SECOND, write the first draft of your essay. Use the items in the checklist as a guide. Write a title for the essay at the top.

- THIRD, revise and edit your first draft. Your sentences should be organized in a logical order. Check that your sentences each have a subject and a predicate.

- FOURTH, on a separate sheet of paper, write the final draft of your essay.

PRACTICE TEST: ESSAY-WRITING TECHNIQUES *(Continued)*

Prewriting

Use the lines below to brainstorm some ideas for a topic. Then, in the space, organize your ideas for the topic you have selected in a list, a cluster, or an outline.

_____

_____

_____

_____

_____

_____

_____

Scoring Guide

SCORE	1	2
Content and Organization	– lacks introductory and concluding paragraphs – topic not developed – details and examples missing	– may lack an introductory and/or concluding paragraph – topic not developed – some details and examples
Usage	– numerous incorrect pronouns, compound words, and comparison adjectives	– many incorrect pronouns, compound words, and comparison adjectives
Sentence Construction	– far too many fragments and/or run-on sentences	– sentence variety is needed – many run-ons and/or fragments
Mechanics	– numerous serious errors prevent understanding	– numerous serious errors prevent understanding

SCORE	3	4
Content and Organization	– may lack introductory and/or concluding paragraph – topic is somewhat developed – some details add meaning	– attempt made at an introductory and/or concluding paragraph – attempt made at topic development – details help meaning somewhat
Usage	– several incorrect pronouns, compounds, and comparison adjectives	– some incorrect pronouns, compounds, and comparison adjectives
Sentence	– frequent run-ons and/or	– a few run-ons and/or fragments
Mechanics	– spelling and punctuation errors are obvious	– some errors but they don't take away from meaning

SCORE	5	6
Content and Organization	– usually has introductory and concluding paragraphs – topic is well developed – good details add meaning	– has effective introductory and concluding paragraphs – topic is fully developed – excellent details focus meaning
Usage	– few errors	– very few errors (if any)
Sentence Construction	– some variety of simple, compound, and complex sentences	– excellent variety of simple, compound, and complex sentences
Mechanics	– few errors	– very few errors (if any)

PRACTICE TEST: ESSAY-WRITING TECHNIQUES *(Continued)*

Student Samples

DIRECTIONS: Read the sample student essays below. Rate each paragraph with a score from 1 (lowest) to 6 (highest). Use the information in the scoring guide to help you.

ESSAY A
Playing Sports

Have you given up on playing sports? Some people keep away from sports because they think that they are not athletic. This is a big mistake because everyone gets something out of being in some kind of sports.

Getting into sports will make your body stronger, and you will feel healthier. Running, walking, and jumping will help you to be fitter too. You will be able to live longer if you are helther, sports can do that for you.

Sports can help you to make friends. If you are on the same team and practice together, you will share some good and bad times. As a result, you will be better friends, I think. They can make a friendship stronger, and that friendship can last a very long time.

As you can see, taking part in sports can be good for you. Sports will make your body stronger, and through sports you can make many good friends, too.

Score _____

ESSAY B
Playing Sports

I like to play sports because its so very much fun. Me and my frends play soccer and base ball in the feilds near my house, then we went home to have a cold drink. May be lemonade or water. Other times we played baskit ball on the court near my house. That is also much fun too. If You win, You are happy, if You do not win, You are not to happy. So it is beter to win because You will be hapy too—just like I am happy when I win.

My best day in sports was when my team won the town trofey in baskit ball.

We worked hard to do our best. It worked because we won out of the fourty teams last winter. Six games and we were the winners. May be We will win it again next winter.

Those reasons tell you why I like playing sports.

Score _____

WRITING INFORMATIVE ESSAYS

Standardized Testing Information

Students in grade 4 may be required to write informative essays on their state or national writing tests. According to the National Assessment of Educational Progress (NAEP), **informative (expository)** writing "communicates information to the reader to share knowledge or to convey messages, instructions, and ideas." The topics that students are given in the NAEP tests require them to "write on specified subjects in a variety of formats, such as reports, reviews, and letters." NOTE: Information on the NAEP can be found at www.NAGB.org. or at www.nces.ed.gov/nationsreportcard.

The NAEP offers guidelines, or rubrics, for scoring its writing test as does each state. Below is an example of the official scoring guide for the Oregon writing assessment for grade 4. Guidelines for the Oregon writing assessment focus on four areas to rate students' samples:

- Ideas/Content
- Organization
- Voice
- Word Choice

Scores in each area range from 1 to 6, with 6 being the highest. Some excerpts from the guidelines for the highest and lowest scores follow:

Ideas/Content

- A high score of 6 calls for the writing to be "exceptionally clear, focused, and interesting. It holds the reader's interest throughout. Main ideas stand out and are developed by strong support and rich details suitable to audience and purpose."

- The lowest score in this area is awarded if "the writing lacks a central idea or purpose" and is characterized by "ideas that are extremely limited or simply unclear."

Organization

- The highest rating calls for organization that "enhances the central idea and its development."

- The minimal score in this area is for writing that "lacks coherence; organization seems haphazard and disjointed."

Voice

- The highest score is given when the writing is "appropriate for the topic, purpose, and audience," and is "expressive, engaging, or sincere."

- The low score in this area goes to writing that "lacks a sense of involvement or commitment."

Word Choice

- A high score of 6 goes to writing where "words convey the intended message in an exceptionally interesting, precise, and natural way appropriate to audience and purpose."

- The lowest score is for writing that "shows an extremely limited vocabulary or is so filled with misuses of words that the meaning is obscured."

Scores of 2 through 5 in each category are suggested for writing samples that fall between these two extremes, with specific guidelines laid out for each score.

This is just one example, but it is typical of scoring nationwide and should provide some idea of how to set writing goals for students, how to evaluate writing assignments, and what areas need to be marked for improvement.

Teacher Preparation and Lessons

In an effort to give students maximum writing experience, this section offers eight three-part activities. The eight activities are designed to provide a variety of interesting experiences in **informative/expository** writing with guidelines and supportive instructions that student-writers can use to hone their writing skills. Students are encouraged to use the **steps of the writing process** as described below.

Each activity has three parts.

- **Part One** consists of **prewriting activities** such as **brainstorming, outlining,** or **clustering.** These can be done individually, with class participation, or by some combination of these two procedures.

- **Part Two** is the **writing of a first draft.** Students should be encouraged to write freely at this point without worrying about grammar, spelling, or punctuation. The aim is to overcome the blocks that so many student-writers face by making this part of the process less threatening.

- **Part Three** offers directions for **revising and writing a final copy.** You may wish to teach students the proofreading marks found on page 343, and encourage them to use the marks to make their revisions. The revision/editing process can be performed by the individual student-writer alone, in association with the teacher, or with class participation by having students exchange papers and make suggestions for revision. Peer editing can be valuable for both the writer and the "editor," since it is easier for anyone (child or adult) to recognize the flaws in someone else's writing and then transfer this knowledge to one's own work. Teachers are urged to use this occasionally in their lessons on revision.

Most of these activities require writing simple, three-paragraph **informative** essays, but several more complex essay-writing activities are also included.

Practice Test: Writing Informative Essays

The sample student essays A and B on page 210 are given a rating of 6 and 5, respectively.

Essay A is well-developed and gives details in a logical sequence. The introductory paragraph gives the reader incentives to make the pie. The essay's sentence construction, sentence variety, tone, and content are excellent. Contractions are used correctly; transition words, vivid verbs, and sensory words create interest. Although *get* is not a specific or vivid verb, the remainder of the essay is clear and understandable. The essay scored a 6.

Essay B is well-developed and logical with fine directions and reminders (*Make sure you've tied the knot snugly, but not too tight.*). There are good transitional words and phrases (*now, at this point, here, finally*) and colorful adjectives and verbs (*separate, slip, snug, tight*). Except for two fragments, the sentences are appropriate and clear. Usage and mechanics are fine. Additionally, the second paragraph sums up the topic and has an appealing tone to it. This essay was scored a 5 and not a 6 mostly because of the two incomplete sentences.

Name _____   Date _____

6–1. WRITING ABOUT A HOBBY OR INTEREST (PREWRITING)

A. DIRECTIONS: What do you know a lot about? Is there some subject you know more about than most other kids your age? Perhaps you have a hobby, or have read a lot about a particular topic, such as pets, movies, sports, fixing things, camping, and so on. Do you know the rules of some game, or how to cook a meal? In the box below, list several subjects or activities you know fairly well.

B. DIRECTIONS: Choose one of the subjects above and circle it. Prepare a **brainstorming list** below. In the first column, list as many words and phrases you can think of that describe this activity. In the second column, write words and phrases that describe why you like this activity and how you first became interested in it.

BRAINSTORMING LIST	
Description of Activity	**Why I Like It**

Use the back of this sheet if you need more space for your brainstorming list.

6–2. WRITING ABOUT A HOBBY OR INTEREST (FIRST DRAFT)

DIRECTIONS: Write the first draft of a three-paragraph essay on the subject you have chosen. It will be easy to do if you follow this guide. This is just a first draft so don't be concerned about spelling and grammar. Concentrate on getting your thoughts on paper.

First Paragraph: Your introductory paragraph introduces the topic in an interesting way. Sometimes, using a question or surprising statement can be used, such as "Would it surprise you to learn that a kid my age is a gourmet chef?" Write your first paragraph (*at least three sentences*) below or on another sheet of paper.

_____

_____

_____

Second Paragraph: The second paragraph is the main part of your essay. Select the best words and phrases from both columns of your brainstorming list, and develop your topic (*at least four sentences*) below or on the other sheet of paper.

_____

_____

_____

_____

_____

_____

Concluding Paragraph: The third and last paragraph restates and sums up your topic. It is satisfying to the reader if you refer to something in the introductory paragraph, such as "Perhaps I'm not really a gourmet chef yet, but I'm on my way." Write your concluding paragraph (*at least two sentences*) below or on the other sheet of paper.

_____

_____

_____

6–3. WRITING ABOUT A HOBBY OR INTEREST (FINAL COPY)

A. DIRECTIONS: Correct and revise your first draft.

> 1. Are your sentences complete? Do subjects and verbs agree?
> 2. Does your first paragraph introduce the topic in an interesting way?
> 3. Does the second paragraph develop the topic? Have you chosen the most interesting words and phrases from your brainstorming list?
> 4. Does the final paragraph restate and sum up the topic?
> 5. Use a dictionary to check spelling.

B. DIRECTIONS: Begin the final copy of your essay below and continue on the back of this sheet. Put a title on the first line, and indent at the beginning of each paragraph.

_____

_____

_____

_____

_____

_____

_____

_____

_____

_____

_____

_____

_____

_____

_____

_____

6–4. DESCRIBING YOUR DEAREST POSSESSION (PREWRITING)

If you had to give up all your possessions except for one, what would that one thing be? Surely, it would be something you care a lot about. Perhaps it is a pet, a special toy or game, or a book you love to read over and over.

A. DIRECTIONS: You are going to write about your dearest possession. It will be easy to do if you first complete a **brainstorming list.**

Write the name of your favorite thing on the top line. In the first column, list words and phrases that can be used to describe your favorite thing. In the second column, list your feelings about this thing. In the third column, list words and phrases that describe why it is so important to you.

BRAINSTORMING LIST

My favorite thing is _____

Description	My Feelings	Why It Is Important

B. DIRECTIONS: On the back of this sheet, write a **first sentence** for your introductory paragraph. Write something that will catch the reader's interest, such as, *I was only five years old when we got Caesar, but he changed my life forever.*

6–5. DESCRIBING YOUR DEAREST POSSESSION
(FIRST DRAFT)

DIRECTIONS: Write the first draft of a three-paragraph essay on the topic "My Dearest Possession." It will be easy to do if you follow this guide. This is just a first draft so don't be concerned about spelling and grammar. Concentrate on getting your thoughts on paper.

    First Paragraph: Write your introductory paragraph (*at least two sentences*) below on another sheet of paper. It introduces the topic in an interesting way. Begin with the sentence you wrote on your brainstorming page.

_____

_____

_____

    Second Paragraph: The second paragraph is the main part of your essay. Select the best words and phrases from your brainstorming list to develop the topic (*at least four sentences*) by describing: (1) the thing you are writing about, (2) your feelings about it, and (3) why it is so important to you. Write your second paragraph below or on the other sheet of paper.

_____

_____

_____

_____

_____

    Concluding Paragraph: The third and last paragraph restates and sums up your topic, as in this example: "Caesar has brought me so much joy! I could not imagine life without him. He is the only thing I own that I would never give up." Write your concluding paragraph (*at least two sentences*) here or on the other sheet of paper.

_____

_____

_____

© 2002 by The Center for Applied Research in Education

6–6. DESCRIBING YOUR DEAREST POSSESSION
(FINAL COPY)

A. DIRECTIONS: Correct and revise your first draft.

> 1. Are your sentences complete? Do subjects and verbs agree?
>
> 2. Does the introductory paragraph begin in an interesting way?
>
> 3. Does the second paragraph develop the topic? Have you chosen the best words and phrases from your brainstorming list to describe your dearest possession, to explain how you feel about it, and why it is so important to you? Did you leave anything out that would make this thing more vivid to the reader?
>
> 4. Does the concluding paragraph restate and sum up the topic?
>
> 5. Use a dictionary to check your spelling.

B. DIRECTIONS: Begin the final copy of your essay below and continue on the back of this sheet. Write the title on the first line, and indent at the beginning of each paragraph.

Name _____ **Date**_____

6–7. DESCRIBING YOUR CLASSROOM
(PREWRITING)

A. DIRECTIONS: You are going to describe *your classroom* to someone who has never seen it! Can you describe it in such a way that the reader will be able to *see* it? Here is a **brainstorming list** for you to complete that will help you write this essay. In the first column, write words and phrases to describe all the objects in the classroom, such as desks, posters, and so on. In the second column, list words and phrases to describe the people in the classroom. In the third column, list words and phrases that describe the activities that take place in your classroom.

BRAINSTORMING LIST FOR "MY CLASSROOM"		
Objects	People	Activities

B. DIRECTIONS: On the back of this sheet, write a **first sentence** for your introductory paragraph. Write something that will spark the reader's interest, such as *You would not believe some of the things that can be seen in my classroom!*

6–8. DESCRIBING YOUR CLASSROOM (FIRST DRAFT)

DIRECTIONS: Begin the first draft of an essay called "My Classroom" below, and continue on the back of this sheet. It will be easy if you keep your brainstorming list in front of you as you write.

- State the topic in your introductory paragraph (*at least two sentences*) in an interesting way. Use the first sentence you wrote in your brainstorming list.

- Develop the topic in the second paragraph (*at least four sentences*). Use the words and phrases in your brainstorming list to describe the objects, people, and activities.

- Restate and sum up the topic in your concluding paragraph (*at least two sentences*).

This is just a first draft, so don't worry about spelling and grammar. Concentrate on getting your thoughts on paper. Write the title on the first line, and indent at the beginning of each paragraph. Use the back of this paper if you need more room.

© 2002 by The Center for Applied Research in Education

6–9. Describing Your Classroom (final copy)

A. DIRECTIONS: Correct and revise your first draft.

> 1. Look around your classroom. Do you see anything interesting or unusual that you could add to your essay?
>
> 2. Are your sentences complete? Do subjects and verbs agree?
>
> 3. Does the introductory paragraph begin in an interesting way? Can you add or change anything to make it more exciting?
>
> 4. Is the topic developed in your second paragraph? Can you think of any words or phrases that would describe your classroom better? Have you used active verbs to describe what goes on there?
>
> 5. Does the concluding paragraph restate and sum up the topic?
>
> 6. Use a dictionary to check your spelling.

B. DIRECTIONS: When your essay is as interesting and well-written as you can make it, write your final copy below and continue on the back of this sheet. Put the title on the first line and indent at the beginning of each paragraph.

_____

_____

_____

_____

_____

_____

_____

_____

_____

_____

6–10. Writing About a Day to Remember
(Prewriting)

DIRECTIONS: You are going to write an essay called "A Day to Remember" about a day in your life that stands out in your memory. It might have been a special birthday, or a trip with your family, or your worst day ever at school. Choose a day to write about. Begin by preparing a **cluster,** using the circle at the bottom of the page.

1. Write the special date in the middle of the circle using large letters.

2. In smaller print (or a different pencil color), write the events that make this day memorable around the date.

3. In even smaller print (or another color), write descriptive words and phrases around each event.

Here is an example of a cluster. ⟶

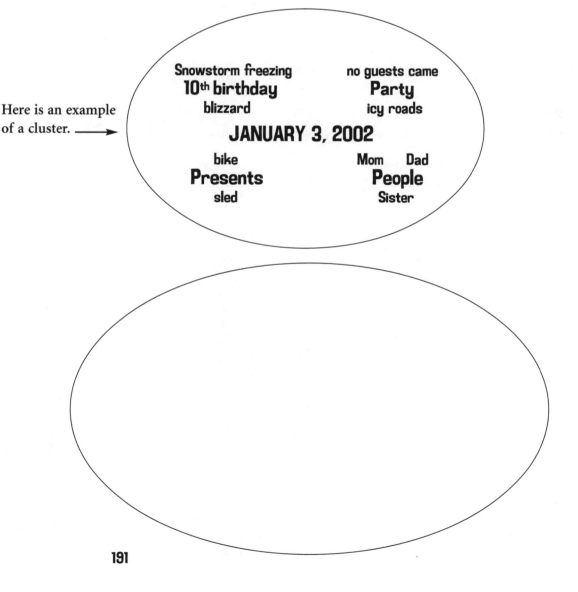

6–11. WRITING ABOUT A DAY TO REMEMBER
(FIRST DRAFT)

DIRECTIONS: Write the first draft of an essay called "A Day to Remember." It will be easy if you keep your cluster handy and follow this guide. This is just a draft, so don't worry about spelling and grammar. Concentrate on getting your thoughts on paper.

First Paragraph: Write your introductory paragraph (*at least two sentences*) below or on another sheet of paper. It introduces the topic in an interesting way. Sometimes, telling a little story can be exciting, as, "I was late to school, failed two tests, and made a fool of myself in gym. Would you believe that these were not even the worst things that happened that day? It sure was a day to remember."

_____

_____

_____

Second Paragraph: Develop the topic in the second paragraph. Use your cluster to help organize your ideas. Write the second paragraph (*at least four sentences*) here or on the other sheet of paper.

_____

_____

_____

_____

Concluding Paragraph: Write your concluding paragraph (at least two sentences) here or on the other sheet of paper. The third and last paragraph restates and sums up your topic, as in this example—"I wish I could forget that awful day and the terrible things that happened. I just can't get it out of my mind! I hope I never have such a day again."

_____

_____

_____

© 2002 by The Center for Applied Research in Education

6–12. WRITING ABOUT A DAY TO REMEMBER
(FINAL COPY)

A. DIRECTIONS: Correct and revise your first draft.

1. Are your sentences complete? Do subjects and verbs agree?
2. Does your first paragraph introduce the topic in an interesting way?
3. Does the second paragraph develop the topic? Is it organized clearly? Do you stay on the topic?
4. Does the concluding paragraph restate and sum up the topic?
5. Use a dictionary to check your spelling.

B. DIRECTIONS: Begin the final copy of your essay below and continue on the back of this sheet. Indent at the beginning of each paragraph.

A Day to Remember

_____

_____

_____

_____

_____

_____

_____

_____

_____

_____

_____

_____

_____

6–13. WRITING ABOUT WHAT YOU WANT TO BE
(PREWRITING)

All young people have hopes and dreams about what they want to be when they are grown. Maybe your dreams aren't realistic. Many people, however, have realized dreams that seemed impossible. In this essay, called "What I Want to Be," you are going to write about one career that appeals to you the most, no matter how impossible it may seem now.

A. DIRECTIONS: It will be easier to write this essay if you first complete this **brainstorming list.** In the first column, state the career that interests you, and the names of anyone you know or have heard of in that career. In the second column, list the reasons why you want that career. (You don't need complete sentences here—just words and phrases.) In the third column, list what you will need to succeed in that career, such as education, personality, character, and so on.

BRAINSTORMING LIST		
Career and Names	**Reasons**	**Requirements**

B. DIRECTIONS: On the back of this sheet, write a catchy **first sentence,** such as *Even people who think they know me well will never, never suspect what I want to do most when I am grown.*

6–14. WRITING ABOUT WHAT YOU WANT TO BE
(FIRST DRAFT)

DIRECTIONS: Begin the first draft of an essay called "What I Want to Be" below and continue on the back of this sheet. It will be easy if you use your brainstorming list.

- State the topic in the introductory paragraph (*at least two sentences*) in an interesting way. Use the first sentence you wrote on the brainstorming page unless you think of something even better.

- Develop the topic in the second paragraph (*at least four sentences*). Organize the information in your brainstorming list and present it clearly.

- Restate and sum up the topic in your concluding paragraph (*at least two sentences*).

This is just a first draft, so concentrate on getting your thoughts on paper without being concerned about spelling and grammar. Indent at the beginning of each paragraph. (Use the back of this page if you need more room.)

What I Want to Be

_____

_____

_____

_____

_____

_____

_____

_____

_____

_____

_____

_____

_____

_____

_____

6–15. WRITING ABOUT WHAT YOU WANT TO BE
(FINAL COPY)

A. DIRECTIONS: Correct and revise the first draft of your essay, "What I Want to Be."

1. Are your sentences complete? Do subjects and verbs agree?
2. Does your first paragraph introduce the topic in an interesting way?
3. Does the second paragraph develop the topic? Did you leave out anything important about your career goal? Did you describe the career clearly?
4. Does the concluding paragraph restate and sum up the topic?
5. Do you have unnecessary words that clutter your writing? If so, cut them out.
6. Can you add anything else that will make your career dream as exciting to the reader as it is to you?
7. Use a dictionary to check your spelling.

B. DIRECTIONS: When your draft is as perfect as you can make it, begin the final copy below and continue on the back of this sheet. Indent at the beginning of each paragraph.

What I Want to Be

_____

_____

_____

_____

_____

_____

_____

_____

_____

Name _____ Date _____

6–16. Describing an American Holiday (prewriting)

If you were to meet someone from another country, would you be able to explain our **national holidays** to that person? In this activity, you are going to write a five-paragraph essay describing an American holiday.

A. DIRECTIONS: Choose the holiday you are going to write about by checking the box next to one of the following:

❑ Independence Day (Fourth of July)   ❑ Memorial Day
❑ Thanksgiving Day   ❑ Labor Day

B. DIRECTIONS: Prepare a **cluster** for your essay in the circle below. Using large letters, write the name of the holiday you have chosen in the middle of the circle. Use smaller letters (or another pencil color) to write the main points around the name of the holiday, such as **event celebrated, celebrations, meaning,** and so on. Use even smaller letters (or another color) to write descriptive words around each point, such as **Revolution, Declaration of Independence, founding fathers, parades, fireworks,** and so on.

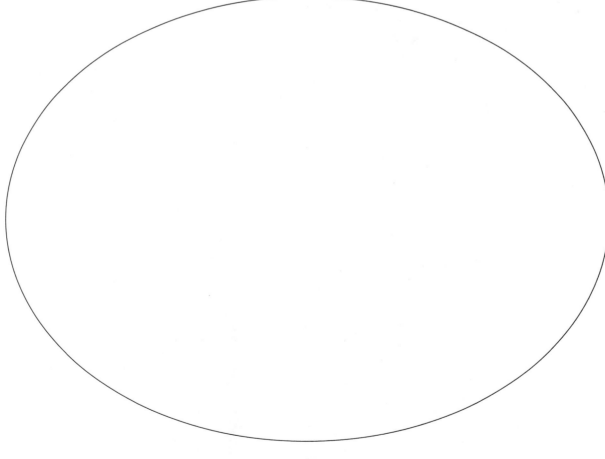

6–17. DESCRIBING AN AMERICAN HOLIDAY (FIRST DRAFT)

DIRECTIONS: Write the first draft of a five-paragraph essay called "An American Holiday: _____." Use your cluster as a guide.

- The first paragraph (*at least two sentences*) introduces the topic in an interesting way. Be sure to include the name of the holiday you have chosen.

- The next three paragraphs develop the topic. The second paragraph (*at least two sentences*) tells what this holiday celebrates and how it began.

- The third paragraph (*at least three sentences*) describes how the holiday is celebrated.

- The fourth paragraph (*at least two sentences*) discusses the meaning of this holiday.

- The concluding paragraph (*at least two sentences*) restates and sums up the topic.

Begin your essay below and continue on the back of this sheet. Write the name of the holiday on the title line, and indent at the beginning of each paragraph.

An American Holiday: _____

_____

_____

_____

_____

_____

_____

_____

_____

_____

_____

Name _____   **Date** _____

6–18. DESCRIBING AN AMERICAN HOLIDAY
(FINAL COPY)

A. DIRECTIONS: Correct and revise the first draft of your essay about an American holiday.

1. Are your sentences complete? Do subjects and verbs agree?
2. Does the first paragraph introduce the topic in an interesting way?
3. Do the next three paragraphs develop the topic? Does each paragraph discuss one of your main points listed in the cluster?
4. Does the concluding paragraph restate and sum up the topic?
5. Use a dictionary to check your spelling.

B. DIRECTIONS: Is your draft as perfect as you can make it? Now, begin the final copy below and continue on the back of this sheet. Write the name of the holiday on the title line, and indent at the beginning of each paragraph.

An American Holiday: _____

_____

_____

_____

_____

_____

_____

_____

_____

_____

_____

_____

_____

Name _____   Date _____

6–19. EXPLAINING A GAME (PREWRITING)

Can you explain a game to someone who doesn't know how to play it? It could be a board game like Monopoly® or Scrabble®, or a ball game such as soccer or hockey, or any other kind of game. You might even choose a TV game show such as "Wheel of Fortune."

A. DIRECTIONS: Write the name of the game. _____

B. DIRECTIONS: Prepare a **brainstorming list.** In the first column, write words and phrases that describe the goals and purpose of this game, and how the winner is determined. In the second column, write words and phrases that describe the tools used in the game. (Example: For Monopoly® you might list *board, dice, houses, hotels, tokens, money, deed cards, chance cards,* etc.) In the third column, write words and phrases that describe how the game is played. (Example: For Monopoly® you might list *throw dice, move token, pass Go, buy property, build houses and hotels,* etc.)

BRAINSTORMING LIST		
Goals and Purposes	**Tools**	**How Game Is Played**

C. DIRECTIONS: A writer's confidence increases when he or she decides exactly how to begin. Can you think up a good **opening sentence** for your essay that will grab the reader's interest? (Example: *If you want to know how it feels to be incredibly rich, try playing Monopoly®.*) Write your opening sentence on the back of this sheet.

6–20. EXPLAINING A GAME (FIRST DRAFT)

DIRECTIONS: Write the first draft of a five-paragraph essay about the game you have chosen. Use your brainstorming list as a guide.

- The first paragraph (*at least two sentences*) introduces the topic in an interesting way. Be sure to include the name of the holiday you have chosen.

- The next three paragraphs develop the topic. The second paragraph (*at least two sentences*) tells what this holiday celebrates and how it began.

- The third paragraph (*at least three sentences*) describes how the holiday is celebrated.

- The fourth paragraph (*at least two sentences*) discusses the meaning of this holiday.

- The concluding paragraph (*at least two sentences*) restates and sums up the topic.

Begin your essay below and continue on the back of this sheet. Write the name of the game on the title line, and indent at the beginning of each paragraph.

_____

_____

_____

_____

_____

_____

_____

_____

_____

_____

_____

_____

_____

_____

_____

6–21. Explaining a Game (final copy)

A. DIRECTIONS: Correct and revise the first draft of your essay describing a game.

---

1. Are your sentences complete? Do subjects and verbs agree?

2. Does the first paragraph introduce the topic in an interesting way?

3. Do the next three paragraphs develop the topic? Does each paragraph discuss one main point (goals and purposes, tools, how the game is played)?

4. Is there anything that should be explained more clearly so the reader will be able to understand this game?

5. Does the concluding paragraph restate and sum up the topic?

6. Use a dictionary to check your spelling.

B. DIRECTIONS: When your draft is as perfect as you can make it, begin the final copy below and continue on the back of this sheet. Write the name of the game on the title line, and indent at the beginning of each paragraph.

_____

_____

_____

_____

_____

_____

_____

_____

_____

_____

_____

Name _____   Date _____

6–22. CHOOSING A SUBJECT TO WRITE ABOUT
(PREWRITING)

A. DIRECTIONS: Choose one of the following subjects to write about and check the box. (Pick one that you know and can describe.)

❑ Growing Flowers in a Garden   ❑ Our Sun and Solar System

❑ What You Can See in a Zoo   ❑ Prehistoric Life

❑ Cooking a Meal   ❑ A Team Sport

B. DIRECTIONS: Prepare a **brainstorming list** for the topic you have chosen. In the first column, write words and phrases to introduce your topic. In the second column, write words and phrases you can use in your description of the topic. In the third column, write words and phrases that describe the importance of this topic and why you have chosen it.

BRAINSTORMING LIST		
Introduction	**Description**	**Importance**

C. DIRECTIONS: Take some time to decide on an **opening sentence** that will grab the reader's interest. You could try a question or a surprising statement. Write your opening sentence on the back of this sheet.

Name _____ **Date** _____

6–23. CHOOSING A SUBJECT TO WRITE ABOUT
(FIRST DRAFT)

DIRECTIONS: Write a draft for a three-paragraph essay about the topic you chose in your prewriting activity.

First Paragraph: The first paragraph introduces the topic in an interesting way. Use the opening sentence you wrote under your brainstorming list and write the first paragraph *(at least two sentences)* here or on another sheet of paper.

_____

_____

_____

Second Paragraph: The second paragraph is the main part of your essay and develops the topic. Select words and phrases from your brainstorming list that describe this topic and its importance, and write the second paragraph *(at least four sentences)* here or on the other sheet of paper.

_____

_____

_____

_____

_____

_____

_____

Concluding Paragraph: The concluding paragraph restates and sums up the topic. It can be more satisfying to the reader if you refer to something you mentioned in the introductory paragraph. Write your concluding paragraph *(at least two sentences)* here or on the other sheet of paper.

_____

_____

_____

6–24. CHOOSING A SUBJECT TO WRITE ABOUT
(FINAL COPY)

A. DIRECTIONS: Correct and revise the first draft of your essay.

---

1. Does the first paragraph introduce the topic? Can you think of a way to introduce it in a more interesting manner?

2. Does the second paragraph develop the topic? Change anything that is not explained clearly. Have you left out anything important?

3. Does the concluding paragraph restate and sum up the topic?

4. Are your sentences complete? Do subjects and verbs agree?

5. Are the words you have chosen the best ones? Can you make your writing more vivid by using some sensory language?

6. Use a dictionary to check your spelling.

B. DIRECTIONS: Is your draft as perfect as you can make it? Begin the final copy below and continue on the back of this sheet. Write the name of the topic on the title line, and indent at the beginning of each paragraph.

_____

_____

_____

_____

_____

_____

_____

_____

_____

_____

FOURTH-GRADE LEVEL

WRITING INFORMATIVE ESSAYS
PRACTICE TEST

PRACTICE TEST: WRITING INFORMATIVE ESSAYS

DIRECTIONS: Write an essay explaining how to do or make something. You should describe something that you can do well. It might be how to paint a picture, how to do a magic trick, how to plant a garden, how to memorize a list of numbers, or how to make a favorite dessert.

CHECKLIST

Make sure to:

_____ 1. Choose a topic on something you do well.

_____ 2. Introduce your topic by using a question, surprising statement, or anecdote.

_____ 3. Develop the topic logically and use only details related to the topic.

_____ 4. Stay on the subject.

_____ 5. Use contractions correctly; use vivid verbs and sensory words.

_____ 6. Sum up the topic near the end of your essay.

_____ 7. Indent each paragraph before the first line.

_____ 8. Write the essay's title at the top of the page.

Follow these four steps to write your essay:

- FIRST, on the page labeled PREWRITING, brainstorm some ideas for your essay. After selecting a topic, write down words and phrases to develop the topic.

- SECOND, on a separate sheet of paper, write the first draft of your essay. Try to use transition words to connect the steps for carrying out the process.

- THIRD, revise and edit your first draft. Make sure your sentences are organized logically.

- FOURTH, on a separate sheet of paper, write the final draft of your essay.

PRACTICE TEST: WRITING INFORMATIVE ESSAYS *(Continued)*

Prewriting

Use the lines below to brainstorm some ideas for a topic. Write down any ideas that come to mind about your topic. Then, in the space, organize your ideas in a list, a cluster, or an outline.

_____

_____

_____

_____

_____

_____

_____

Scoring Guide

SCORE	1	2
Content and Organization	– lacks introductory and concluding sentences – no logical organization – no transitions between ideas	– may lack an introductory and/or concluding sentence – organization is attempted – one or two transitions between ideas
Usage	– no apparent control over word choice	– little control over word choice
Sentence Construction	– far too many fragments and/or run-ons; choppy sentences	– much greater sentence variety needed – choppy sentences
Mechanics	– numerous serious errors prevent understanding	– numerous serious errors detract from understanding

SCORE	3	4
Content and Organization	– may lack introductory and/or concluding sentence – few transitions between ideas – some details in logical order	– may lack introductory and/or concluding sentence – several transitions between ideas – many details in logical order
Usage	– no contractions used appropriately – few vivid verbs or sensory words	– some contractions used appropriately – some vivid verbs and sensory words
Sentence Construction	– frequent fragments and run-on sentences affect understanding	– a few run-ons and/or fragments that do not take away meaning
Mechanics	– spelling and punctuation errors are obvious	– some errors but they don't take away from meaning

SCORE	5	6
Content and Organization	– usually has introductory and concluding paragraphs – topic is well developed with most details in logical order – several transitions	– has interesting introductory and concluding sentences – well-organized and developed with all details in logical order – numerous transitions
Usage	– an occasional error	– very few errors (if any)
Sentence Construction	– some variety of simple, compound, and complex sentences	– excellent variety of simple, compound, and complex sentences
Mechanics	– few errors	– very few errors (if any)

PRACTICE TEST: WRITING INFORMATIVE ESSAYS *(Continued)*
Student Samples

ESSAY A
How to Make Chocolate Cream Pie

Who doesn't love chocolate pudding? It's everyone's favorite! Chocolate cream pie is mostly chocolate pudding, but it's poured into a crispy pie crust and has sugary whipped cream on top. Here's how to make this easy dessert. (Make sure an adult helps with the stove, though.)

The first step is to prepare a pie crust. You can make one out of flour and butter, but it's easier to use a crust bought in the supermarket. Follow the directions on the package. Once your oven reaches 400 degrees, you'll need to bake the crust for about ten minutes at 400 degrees.

Next, get one package of chocolate pudding mix. Place the mix in a saucepan. Stir in two cups of milk. Heat this at medium heat and stir slowly with a spoon every so often. When the mixture starts to bubble, take it off the stove, and let it cool down for five minutes.

Then pour the chocolate pudding into the baked pie crust. Let it cool off in the refrigerator for a couple of hours. Add some whipped cream to it just before you serve it.

Now you'll have a delicious dessert and you'll know that you made it all by yourself!

Score _____

ESSAY B
How to Tie Shoes

Yes, you can learn to tie your shoes. Here's how you'll do it. First, you'll gently pull both laces up in the air away from the shoe. Then you'll hold both laces and slip the left lace under the right one. Now you'll pull both laces in separate directions. One to the left and the other to the right. Make sure you've tied the knot snugly, but not too tight. At this point you'll pull both laces up again as you did before. Then make two circles (some call them bunny ears). One with the left lace and one with the right lace. Here take one of the laced circles and slip it under the other one. Finally, pull both circles apart from each other.

Guess what? You've just tied your shoes! Good job!

Score _____

WRITING PERSUASIVE ESSAYS

Standardized Testing Information

Students in grade 4 are often asked to write persuasive essays on state assessment tests. The National Assessment of Educational Progress (NAEP) defines a persuasive essay as a type of writing that "seeks to influence the reader to take action or bring about change. It may contain factual information, such as reasons, examples, or comparisons; however, its main purpose is to persuade."

The NAEP guidelines go on to say, "In all persuasive writing, authors must choose the approach they will use. They may, for instance, use emotional or logical appeals or an accommodating or demanding tone. Regardless of the situation or approach, persuasive writers must be concerned with having a particular desired effect upon their readers, beyond merely adding to knowledge of the topic." The NAEP offers the following guidelines for scoring persuasive essays:

- **Excellent**—Takes a clear position and develops support with well-chosen details, reasons, or examples across the response. Is well organized, maintains focus. Sustains varied sentence structure and exhibits specific word choices. Exhibits control over sentence boundaries; errors in grammar, spelling, and mechanics do not interfere with understanding.

- **Skillful**—Takes a clear position and develops support with some specific details, reasons, or examples. Provides some organization of ideas by, for example, using contrast or building to a point. Exhibits some variety in sentence structure and exhibits some specific word choices. Generally exhibits control over sentence boundaries; errors in grammar, spelling, and mechanics do not interfere with understanding.

- **Sufficient**—Takes a clear position with support that is clear and generally related to the issue. Is generally organized. Generally has simple sentences and simple word choice; may exhibit uneven control over sentence boundaries. Has sentences that consist mostly of complete, clear, distinct thoughts; errors in grammar, spelling, and mechanics generally do not interfere with understanding.

- **Uneven**—Characterized by one or more of the following: Takes a position and offers limited or incomplete support; some reasons may not be clear or related to the issue. Is disorganized OR provides a disjointed sequence of information. Exhibits uneven control over sentence boundaries and may have some inaccurate word choices. Errors in grammar, spelling, and mechanics sometimes interfere with understanding.

- **Insufficient**—Characterized by one or more of the following: Takes a position, but provides only minimal support OR attempts to take a position but the position is unclear. Is very disorganized or too brief to detect organization. May exhibit little control over sentence boundaries and sentence formation; word choice is inaccurate in much of the response.

This scoring guide is typical of those in many states. The classroom teacher should keep these goals in mind when leading students through the exercises in this section.

It is of the utmost importance that students fully understand the nature and purpose of a persuasive essay and what is expected of them. It can help bring the purpose of this type of writing down to a fourth-grade perspective if the teacher poses one or more of the following questions:

How do you convince your parents to buy you something you want?

How would you talk your teacher out of giving the class a scheduled test?

How do you get a friend to play a game *you* wish to play instead of the one the friend wants?

Teacher Preparation and Lessons

Each activity in this section has three parts: (1) Prewriting; (2) First draft; and (3) Revising and writing a final copy. The directions for each activity are presented clearly; however, they should be read aloud and discussed. It would be helpful if students share their *prewriting activities* by reading them aloud or exchanging papers with their classmates. *First drafts* should be revised by the writer in accordance with the suggestions on the worksheet, and then by exchanging papers with another student and/or by the teacher. You may wish to review the proofreading marks on page 343, and encourage students to use them to make their revisions. Students should think of their *final copies* as their best work.

Practice Test: Writing Persuasive Essays

The sample student essays A and B on page 241 are given a rating of 2 and 5, respectively.

Essay A needs much improvement. It is almost incomprehensible. There are some reasons given for rejecting the proposed change, but they are unclear due to serious problems in mechanics and usage as well as sentence construction that detract from comprehension. Though some may disagree, this essay scored a 2 since there is an attempt at focus and organization.

Essay B's opening and concluding paragraphs are direct and clearly state the author's position. The three paragraphs that follow offer good reasons and examples. Within the text are a good variety of sentence types. The slang word *stuck*, the misspelling of *vacations*, the missing question mark, and the single run-on do not seriously mar a very orderly and convincing argument. Some vivid action verbs and strong adjectives could have added interest. This essay scored a 5.

Name _____   Date _____

7–1. SHOULD CHILDREN WATCH TV ON SCHOOL NIGHTS?
(PREWRITING)

Do you watch TV on school nights? Some parents allow their children to do this. Other parents permit TV-watching only on nights when there is no school the next day. What do you think?

A. DIRECTIONS: You are going to write an essay about this subject, trying to convince the reader that your opinion is the correct one. It will be easy to do if you first prepare a **brainstorming list.** In the first column, list three reasons for your opinion. In the second column, next to each reason, write specific details. (For example, if you list *homework* as a reason for not watching TV, then under details, you might list *not finishing homework* and *not concentrating on homework.*

BRAINSTORMING LIST	
Reasons	**Details**

B. DIRECTIONS: Write a **first sentence** for your essay on the back of this sheet. A question at the beginning of an essay can often grab the reader's attention, for example, *Aren't some of your favorite TV programs on during the week?* Can you think of a question for your first sentence?

7–2. SHOULD CHILDREN WATCH TV ON SCHOOL NIGHTS?
(FIRST DRAFT)

Are you ready to convince the reader (and your parents) that you are right about TV on school nights? Your brainstorming list will be a big help when you are writing your first draft of a three-paragraph essay. Don't worry about spelling or grammar when writing a draft. Concentrate on getting your thoughts down on paper.

- The first paragraph (*at least two sentences*) introduces the topic in an interesting way. Did you write an interesting question in your prewriting? Use that as the first sentence of your essay.

- The second paragraph (*at least four sentences*) develops the topic. Use the three reasons for your opinion that are on your brainstorming list. Give some details for each reason.

- The third paragraph (*at least two sentences*) restates and sums up the topic, as in this example: "I'm glad that my parents don't let me watch TV on school nights. I don't miss it at all, and it is one of the reasons that I've been able to keep up my grades."

DIRECTIONS: Begin your first draft below and continue on the back of this sheet. Write a title for your essay on the first line. Indent at the beginning of each paragraph.

_____

_____

_____

_____

_____

_____

_____

_____

_____

_____

7–3. SHOULD CHILDREN WATCH TV ON SCHOOL NIGHTS?
(FINAL COPY)

A. DIRECTIONS: Correct and revise your first draft.

---

1. Do you use a question in the first paragraph to introduce the topic and get the reader's interest?

2. Do you develop the topic with specific details in the second paragraph? Can you add anything else to persuade the reader that you are right?

3. Does your final paragraph restate and sum up the topic? Can you add or change anything that will make you sound more confident about your conclusion?

4. Are your sentences complete? Do subjects and verbs agree?

5. Are your words spelled correctly? Check with the dictionary.

6. Ask your teacher or another student to look at your first draft and make suggestions.

B. DIRECTIONS: Begin the final copy of your essay below and continue on the back of this sheet. Write the topic on the first line, and indent at the beginning of each paragraph.

_____

_____

_____

_____

_____

_____

_____

_____

_____

7–4. Convincing People to See a Show
(Prewriting)

The Drama Club in your school is putting on a show. They will be performing scenes from a favorite show. You are in charge of publicity. It is your job to write an article for the school newspaper about this event. Your aim is to convince people to come and see the show.

DIRECTIONS: Your article will be easy to write if you first organize your ideas with a **cluster.** Prepare your cluster in the large circle at the bottom of the page. Write STUDENT SHOW or the name of a specific show in the middle of the circle using large letters. In smaller print (or a different pencil color), write around the subject the reasons why people should attend this show. In even smaller print (or another color), write detailed words and phrases around each reason.

Here is an example of a cluster. ———→

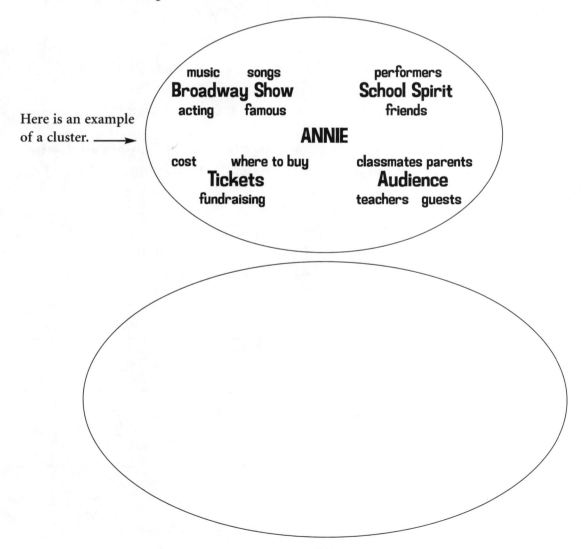

Name _____ **Date** _____

7–5. CONVINCING PEOPLE TO SEE A SHOW
(FIRST DRAFT)

DIRECTIONS: Write an article for your school newspaper to convince readers to run right out and buy tickets for your school production. The work you did on your cluster will help. (This is just a first draft, so don't worry about perfection—just concentrate on getting your thoughts on paper.)

First Paragraph: The first paragraph introduces the topic in an exciting way, as in this example: "Don't miss it! Here is your chance to see a hit Broadway musical right in our own school! The Drama Club's wonderful performance of *Annie* will take place in the auditorium on Wednesday evening, December 2." Write your first paragraph (*at least two sentences*) here or on another sheet of paper.

_____

_____

_____

Second Paragraph: The second paragraph gives exciting details about the performance. Use all the points you wrote on your cluster, arranged in a logical and convincing way. Write the second paragraph (*at least four sentences*) here or on the other sheet of paper.

_____

_____

_____

_____

Final Paragraph: The third paragraph restates and sums up the topic in a way that will be convincing to the reader, as in this example: "You don't want to be the only student in school who misses this exciting event. Hurry and get your tickets immediately before they are sold out." Write your third paragraph (*at least two sentences*) here or on the other sheet of paper.

_____

_____

_____

7–6. CONVINCING PEOPLE TO SEE A SHOW
(FINAL COPY)

A. DIRECTIONS: Correct and revise your first draft.

1. Does the first paragraph introduce the topic? Can you add any words to make it more interesting and exciting?

2. Does the second paragraph develop the topic? Can you add or change anything that will convince a reader to see the production? Use words like *eye-popping, amazing, stupendous, fantastic, incredible, joyful,* and so on.

3. Does the third paragraph sum up the topic in a way that will make the reader want to buy tickets? Can you change or add anything else to make it even more convincing?

4. Are your sentences complete? Do subjects and verbs agree?

5. Use a dictionary to check your spelling.

6. Ask your teacher or another student to look at your first draft and make suggestions.

B. DIRECTIONS: Begin the final copy of your article below and continue on the back of this sheet. Put an interesting title on the first line, and indent at the beginning of each paragraph.

_____

_____

_____

_____

_____

_____

_____

_____

© 2002 by The Center for Applied Research in Education

7–7. SHOULD ALL CHILDREN GET AN ALLOWANCE?
(PREWRITING)

Do you get an allowance? Most kids do. Do you think you get enough? How much allowance should kids get? Should they have to perform chores to get it? What should they be expected to buy with their allowances? Here is your chance to express your opinion on this subject that is of interest to kids and parents alike.

A. DIRECTIONS: First, prepare a **brainstorming list** that will help you get ready to write this essay. In the first column, write words and phrases that can be used to discuss allowances in general, such as amount, rules, age differences, differences among families, and so on. In the second column, write words and phrases to describe how you use your allowance and/or how you think most kids use it. In the third column, write words and phrases that express your feelings about allowances and their rules, and ideas about change.

BRAINSTORMING LIST—"ALLOWANCES"		
General Information	**Uses**	**Feelings and Ideas for Change**

B. DIRECTIONS: Getting started is often the hardest part of writing. This essay will be easy if you first decide upon an **opening sentence.** Sometimes an anecdote or story at the beginning grabs the reader's interest, for example: *When I was eight years old, I was the only kid in third grade who did not get an allowance.* Write your opening sentence on the back of this sheet.

© 2002 by The Center for Applied Research in Education

Name _____ Date _____

7–8. SHOULD ALL CHILDREN GET AN ALLOWANCE?
(FIRST DRAFT)

Can you write a convincing three-paragraph essay on your ideas about allowances? Your brainstorming list will be a big help as you follow these directions.

- The first paragraph (*at least two sentences*) introduces the topic in an interesting way. Can you begin with an amusing story? Use the opening sentence from your brainstorming list.

- The second paragraph (*at least four sentences*) develops the topic. Use words and ideas to convince the reader that your opinion is correct. Organize your thoughts logically and clearly using the three columns of the brainstorming list.

- The third paragraph (*at least two sentences*) restates and sums up the topic convincingly, as in this example: "My parents finally accepted the fact that children need allowances. Everyone would like to have more money, but it is important to use the amount you have wisely."

DIRECTIONS: Begin your first draft below and continue on the back of this sheet. This is just a rough copy, so don't worry about spelling and grammar. Concentrate on getting your thoughts down on paper as clearly as possible. Decide upon a title (such as "Allowances") and write it on the first line. Indent at the beginning of each paragraph.

_____

_____

_____

_____

_____

_____

_____

_____

_____

_____

7–9. SHOULD ALL CHILDREN GET AN ALLOWANCE?
(FINAL COPY)

A. DIRECTIONS: Correct and revise your first draft.

> 1. Does the first paragraph introduce the topic in an interesting way? Can you add or change anything to make it more exciting?
>
> 2. Does the second paragraph develop the topic? Can you add or change anything to make it more convincing?
>
> 3. Does the final paragraph restate and sum up the topic? Are you as convincing as you can be?
>
> 4. Are your sentences complete? Do subjects and verbs agree?
>
> 5. Use a dictionary to check your spelling.
>
> 6. Ask your teacher or another student to look at your first draft and make suggestions.

B. DIRECTIONS: Begin the final copy of your essay below and continue on the back of this sheet. Write the title on the first line. Indent at the beginning of each paragraph.

_____

_____

_____

_____

_____

_____

_____

_____

_____

7–10. SEE A MOVIE . . . READ A BOOK (PREWRITING)

How would you like to be a critic? Do you ever read reviews of movies, TV shows, books, or videos in newspapers or magazines? This is your chance to become a critic and to convince your readers whether or not they should look at the movie, TV show, book, or video you are writing about.

A. DIRECTIONS: Decide what you are going to review. On this line, write the name and type of review. (Example: <u>Chicken Run</u>— Movie).

_____

B. DIRECTIONS: Prepare a **brainstorming list** that will help you organize your review. In the first column, write words and phrases that describe the subject's general type, such as *comedy, drama, cartoon, funny, serious, musical,* and so on. In the second column, write words and phrases that describe the characters and the story. In the third column, list words and phrases that describe your feelings about the subject and why you would or would not recommend it.

BRAINSTORMING LIST—"REVIEW"		
Type and Description	**Characters and Plot**	**Recommendation**

C: DIRECTIONS: Beginning your review with a question and an amusing comment will often attract the reader's interest, as in this example: *Have you had a really good laugh lately? If not, be sure to watch the newest hit sitcom on TV, and you'll be rolling on the floor.* Write your **opening sentence(s)** on the back of this sheet.

Name _____   Date _____

7–11. SEE A MOVIE . . . READ A BOOK (FIRST DRAFT)

It is fun to write a review. Your brainstorming list will help you write a three-paragraph review. On this first draft, don't be concerned with grammar or spelling. Concentrate on getting your thoughts down on paper.

- The first paragraph (*at least two sentences*) begins your review with an interesting opening sentence (or sentences). Use the sentence from your prewriting activity.

- The second paragraph (*at least four sentences*) develops the topic. The three columns of your brainstorming list will help you do this clearly and logically. First, tell what type of movie, book, etc., you are reviewing. Then describe the characters and plot. Finally, tell your feelings and recommendations.

- The final paragraph (*at least two sentences*) restates and sums up your topic. If possible, it is helpful to refer back to your opening paragraph. For example: "This is truly the funniest new show on TV. It is sure to keep your whole family entertained and in a good mood for the rest of the day."

DIRECTIONS: Begin your first draft below and continue on the back of this sheet. Write the title on the first line, and indent at the beginning of each paragraph.

_____

_____

_____

_____

_____

_____

_____

_____

_____

_____

_____

Name _____ **Date** _____

7–12. SEE A MOVIE . . . READ A BOOK (FINAL COPY)

A. DIRECTIONS: Correct and revise your first draft.

> 1. Does your first paragraph introduce the topic? Can you think of anything to add or change to make it more interesting?
>
> 2. Does the second paragraph develop the topic? Do you describe interesting details? Is your recommendation clear? Do you give good reasons for it?
>
> 3. Does the final paragraph restate and sum up the topic? Can you change or add anything to make it more fun and interesting to the reader?
>
> 4. Are your sentences complete? Do subjects and verbs agree?
>
> 5. Do you always use the best word? Check your spelling with the dictionary.
>
> 6. Ask your teacher or another student to look at your first draft and make suggestions.

B. DIRECTIONS: Begin the final copy of your review below and continue on the back of this sheet. Write the subject on the first line, and indent at the beginning of each paragraph.

_____

_____

_____

_____

_____

_____

_____

© 2002 by The Center for Applied Research in Education

Name _____ Date_____

7–13. I CAN BE A TEACHER FOR A DAY! (PREWRITING)

How would you like to be "Teacher for a Day"? If you could be the teacher in your classroom, what would you change? What would you keep the same? Why? Here is your chance to explain what you would do as "Teacher for a Day" and convince your readers that you have good ideas.

A. DIRECTIONS: Place a check in the box next to the day you would choose to be "Teacher for a Day."

❏ A particular day of the week (which day?_____)

❏ A special day of the year (which date? _____)

❏ A particular season of the year (which season? _____)

❏ Any day

B. DIRECTIONS: If you have chosen a particular day or season, explain your reasons here. _____

_____

C. DIRECTIONS: Prepare a **brainstorming list.** In the first column, list three things that you would change. (You don't need complete sentences—words and phrases are enough.) In the second column, next to each item you would change, list reasons for doing so. (Use words and phrases.) In the third column, list three things you would *not* change. (Use words and phrases.) In the fourth column, next to each item you would not change, list reasons.

Here is a sample format for you to follow. Write your brainstorming list on another sheet of paper.

BRAINSTORMING LIST			
Things to Change	**Reasons**	**Things Not to Change**	**Reasons**
1.		1.	
2.		2.	
3.		3.	

7–14. I Can Be a Teacher for a Day! (first draft)

DIRECTIONS: Are you ready to be "Teacher for a Day" (at least in this essay)? Are you ready to convince the reader that certain things should be changed, and others should be kept the same? Write a four-paragraph essay about this. Use your brainstorming list as a guide. This is just a first draft, so don't worry about spelling or grammar at this point.

First Paragraph: Introduce the topic in an interesting way, as in this example: "Oh, how I wish I could be the teacher of this class for one day! What a great job I would do!" Write your first paragraph (*at least two sentences*) here or on another sheet of paper.

_____

_____

Second Paragraph: Begin to develop the topic. Discuss three things you would change and your reasons. Write your second paragraph (*at least four sentences*) here or on the other sheet of paper.

_____

_____

_____

Third Paragraph: Continue to develop the topic. Discuss three things you would not change and your reasons. Write your third paragraph *(at least four sentences)* here or on the other sheet of paper.

_____

_____

_____

Final Paragraph: Restate and sum up the topic in a convincing way, as in this example: "These are the things I would do if I were teacher for a day. Don't you agree that it would be a terrific day in our classroom?" Write your final paragraph (*at least two sentences*) here or on the other sheet of paper.

_____

_____

© 2002 by The Center for Applied Research in Education

Name _____ Date_____

7–15. I Can Be a Teacher for a Day! (final copy)

A. DIRECTIONS: Correct and revise your first draft.

1. Do you introduce the topic in the first paragraph? Can you change or add anything to make it more exciting?

2. Do you begin to develop the topic in the second paragraph? Do you clearly describe the *changes* you would make and give good reasons for them? Can you make any of these statements stronger and more convincing?

3. Do you continue to develop the topic in the third paragraph? Do you clearly describe three things you would **not** change and give good reasons? Can you make any of these statements stronger and more convincing?

4. Does the final paragraph restate and sum up the topic? Can you think of any other words or phrases that are stronger and more convincing?

5. Check each sentence carefully. Are all sentences complete? Do subjects and verbs agree?

6. Check your spelling with a dictionary.

7. Ask your teacher or another student to look at your first draft and make suggestions.

B. DIRECTIONS: Begin the final copy of your essay below and continue on the back of this sheet. Be sure to add the title, and indent at the beginning of each paragraph.

_____

_____

_____

_____

_____

_____

_____

7–16. What Makes a Good Neighbor? (Prewriting)

Do you have nice neighbors? Are there any who are not so nice? You are going to write an essay describing the qualities you think make a good neighbor.

A. DIRECTIONS: Complete the following **brainstorming list.** In the first column, list three qualities you think a good neighbor should have. In the second column, list words and phrases next to each item that describe this quality. In the third column, write the name of someone who has this quality.

BRAINSTORMING LIST—"GOOD NEIGHBORS"		
Qualities	Description	Example
1.		
2.		
3.		

B. DIRECTIONS: Begin your essay with an **opening sentence** that grabs the reader's interest, as in this example: *Someone once said, "Fences make good neighbors," but I don't agree.* Write your opening sentence on the back of this sheet.

7-17. WHAT MAKES A GOOD NEIGHBOR? (FIRST DRAFT)

DIRECTIONS: Write a three-paragraph essay called "Good Neighbors." Think about the people who live near you, especially those neighbors whom you really like. (This is a first draft, so don't worry about spelling or grammar—just concentrate on getting down your thoughts.)

First Paragraph: The first paragraph introduces the topic. Use the opening sentence you wrote below your brainstorming list and write your first paragraph (*at least two sentences*) here or on the other sheet of paper.

_____

_____

_____

Second Paragraph: The second paragraph develops the topic. Describe the three good-neighbor qualities you listed in your brainstorming list and give at least one example of a good neighbor. Write the second paragraph (*at least four sentences*) here or on the other sheet of paper.

_____

_____

_____

_____

Final Paragraph: The final paragraph restates and sums up the topic in a way that will convince the reader, as in this example: "Wouldn't it be wonderful if all neighbors had these good qualities? Then the world would surely be a much better place." Write your third paragraph (*at least two sentences*) here or on the other sheet of paper.

_____

_____

_____

7–18. WHAT MAKES A GOOD NEIGHBOR? (FIRST DRAFT)

A. DIRECTIONS: Correct and revise your first draft.

1. Do you introduce the topic in the first paragraph? Can you change or add anything to make it more interesting?

2. Do you develop the topic in the second paragraph? Are your reasons and examples clear and convincing? Can you add a simile (such as, *She is as sweet as a chocolate bar*) to make your writing more vivid?

3. Does the final paragraph restate and sum up the topic? Can you make it more convincing?

4. Check each sentence carefully. Are all sentences complete? Do subjects and verbs agree?

5. Check your spelling with a dictionary.

6. Ask your teacher or another student to look at your first draft and make suggestions.

B. DIRECTIONS: Begin the final copy of your essay below and continue on the back of this sheet. Write a title on the first line, and indent at the beginning of each paragraph.

_____

_____

_____

_____

_____

_____

_____

_____

_____

7–19. LARGE OR SMALL FAMILY—WHICH IS BETTER?
(PREWRITING)

Which of the following statements do you think is true? Check the one with which you agree.

❏ Large families are better than small ones.

❏ Small families are better than large ones.

A. DIRECTIONS: You are going to write an essay about this subject. It will be easy to do if you first prepare a **brainstorming list.** In the first column, list three reasons to support your opinion. In the second column, write all the words and phrases you can think of that might be used when you explain each reason.

BRAINSTORMING LIST—"FAMILIES"	
Reasons	**Words and Phrases**
1.	
2.	
3.	

B. DIRECTIONS: Write an interesting **opening sentence** for your essay, as in this example: "I could give you a million reasons why large families are better." Write your opening sentence on the back of this sheet.

Name _____ Date _____

7–20. LARGE OR SMALL FAMILY—WHICH IS BETTER?
(FIRST DRAFT)

You are going to write a first draft for a three-paragraph essay, telling whether you think a large family or a small family is better. This will be easy if you keep your brainstorming list in front of you. This is just a first draft, so don't be concerned about spelling or grammar. Concentrate on getting your thoughts on paper.

- The first paragraph (*at least two sentences*) introduces the topic. Begin this paragraph with the opening statement you wrote under your brainstorming list.

- The second paragraph (*at least four sentences*) develops the topic. Explain the three reasons you listed on your brainstorming list. Use the most exciting and vivid words from your list of words and phrases to describe each reason.

- The final paragraph (*at least two sentences*) restates and sums up the topic, as in this example: "Everyone knows that large families have more fun. They are surely the best kind to have."

DIRECTIONS: Begin your first draft below and continue on the back of this sheet. Write the word LARGE OR SMALL at the beginning of the title, and indent at the beginning of each paragraph.

_____ **Families Are Better!**

_____

_____

_____

_____

_____

_____

_____

_____

_____

© 2002 by The Center for Applied Research in Education

7–21. Large or Small Family—Which Is Better?
(final copy)

A. DIRECTIONS: Correct and revise your first draft.

> 1. Do you introduce the topic in the first paragraph? Can you add anything else to make it more interesting?
>
> 2. Do you develop the topic in the second paragraph? Do you list the reasons for your opinion and explain them clearly and convincingly? Have you used a vivid simile to make your writing more interesting?
>
> 3. Does the final paragraph restate and sum up the topic?
>
> 4. Check each sentence carefully. Are all sentences complete? Do subjects and verbs agree?
>
> 5. Check your spelling with a dictionary.
>
> 6. Ask your teacher or another student to look at your first draft and make suggestions.

B. DIRECTIONS: Begin the final copy of your essay below, and continue on the back of this sheet. Write the title on the first line, and indent at the beginning of each paragraph.

_____

_____

_____

_____

_____

_____

_____

_____

_____

7–22. WHAT IS THE BEST PET TO HAVE? (PREWRITING)

Do you have a pet? Many families have some kind of pet. Sometimes, it can be an unusual one such as a hamster, ferret, snake, goldfish, or rabbit. You are going to write about what you think is the best pet to have. It can be one you already own, or one you would like to get.

DIRECTIONS: It will be easy to write this essay if you first organize your ideas in a **cluster**. Prepare your cluster in the large circle at the bottom of the page. Write the pet you have chosen (dog, cat, fish, etc.) in the middle of the circle using large letters. In smaller print (or different pencil color), write the following subjects around the large name: *looks, actions, care, qualities*. In even smaller print (or another color), write detailed words and phrases around each subject that describe those points about your pet.

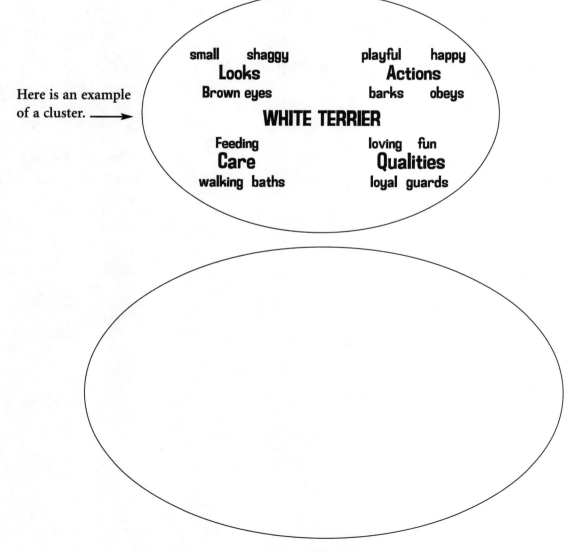

Here is an example of a cluster. ──▶

small   shaggy   playful   happy
Looks   **Actions**
Brown eyes   barks   obeys

WHITE TERRIER

Feeding   loving   fun
Care   **Qualities**
walking baths   loyal guards

7–23. What Is the Best Pet to Have? (first draft)

You are going to write a first draft for a three-paragraph essay telling why your choice of a pet is the best choice. Keep your cluster in front of you as a guide. This is just a first draft so don't be concerned about spelling or grammar. Concentrate on getting your thoughts on paper.

- The first paragraph (*at least two sentences*) introduces the topic in an interesting way. Sometimes a quote will grab the reader's attention, as in this example: "You're not going to write about a turtle, are you?" asked my friend staring in amazement. "Do you really think that is a pet?" I nodded. "My turtle is a great pet!" I told him.

- The second paragraph (*at least four sentences*) develops the topic. Write about the main points in your cluster and give examples of each.

- The final paragraph (*at least two sentences*) restates and sums up the topic, as in this example: "Don't you agree that the best pet is one you don't have to walk and will never run away? My turtle fits that description exactly, and I would never trade it in for a different pet."

DIRECTIONS: Begin your first draft below and continue on the back of this sheet. Remember to indent at the beginning of each paragraph.

The Best Pet

_____

_____

_____

_____

_____

_____

_____

_____

_____

7–24. What Is the Best Pet to Have? (final copy)

A. DIRECTIONS: Correct and revise the first draft of your essay about the best pet.

1. Do you introduce the topic in the first paragraph? Do you use a quote to grab the reader's attention? Can you think of a different quote that is more exciting?

2. Do you develop the topic in the second paragraph? Do you describe the pet and explain why it is the best? Can you add any more convincing details?

3. Does the final paragraph restate and sum up the topic? Can you add a strong statement or question to make it more convincing?

4. Check each sentence carefully. Are all sentences complete? Do subjects and verbs agree?

5. Check your spelling with a dictionary.

6. Ask your teacher or another student to look at your first draft and make suggestions.

B. DIRECTIONS: Begin the final copy of your essay below and continue on the back of this sheet. Write the title on the first line, and indent at the beginning of each paragraph.

_____

_____

_____

_____

_____

_____

_____

_____

_____

© 2002 by The Center for Applied Research in Education

FOURTH-GRADE LEVEL

WRITING PERSUASIVE ESSAYS

PRACTICE TEST

PRACTICE TEST: WRITING PERSUASIVE ESSAYS

DIRECTIONS: You have just found out that your school might be closed during January and February and open during July and August. The school board members would like you to write an essay of three or more paragraphs telling them how you feel about this proposed change. Try to convince the members to agree with you.

CHECKLIST

Make sure to:

_____ 1. Write an introductory paragraph that clearly states your position.

_____ 2. Capture the reader's attention with an interesting topic sentence.

_____ 3. Develop your argument convincingly with at least three reasons or examples.

_____ 4. Stay on the subject and sum up in the last paragraph.

_____ 5. Choose words that show you are positive and believe strongly in what you're saying.

_____ 6. Write the essay's title above the first line.

_____ 7. Indent the first line of each paragraph.

Follow these four steps to write your essay:

- FIRST, on the page labeled PREWRITING, brainstorm some ideas for your essay. Then organize your ideas in a logical way.

- SECOND, on a separate sheet of paper, write the first draft.

- THIRD, revise and edit your first draft. Make sure you have written complete sentences, spelled all the words correctly, and used verb tense consistently.

- FOURTH, on a separate sheet of paper, write the final draft of your essay.

PRACTICE TEST: WRITING PERSUASIVE ESSAYS *(Continued)*

Prewriting

On the lines below, brainstorm ideas to make your persuasive essay strong and convincing. Jot down any ideas that come to mind about the topic. Then, in the space, organize your ideas logically in a list, a cluster, or an outline.

_____

_____

_____

_____

_____

_____

_____

_____

Scoring Guide

SCORE	1	2
Content and Organization	– lacks introductory and concluding paragraphs – position statement is missing – reasons and examples missing	– may lack an introductory and/or concluding paragraph – a position statement is attempted – reasons and examples unfocused
Usage	– no control over word choice	– little control over word choice
Sentence Construction	– far too many fragments and/or run-ons	– greater sentence variety needed – too many run-ons and/or fragments
Mechanics	– numerous serious errors and misspellings prevent understanding	– numerous serious errors take away from understanding

SCORE	3	4
Content and Organization	– may lack an introductory or concluding paragraph – position is unclear	– attempt is made at an introductory and/or concluding paragraph – position is more focused
Usage	– several pronouns, verbs, adjectives, and adverbs used incorrectly	– some pronouns, verbs, adjectives, and adverbs used incorrectly
Sentence Construction	– frequent run-ons and/or fragments distract from the topic's focus	– a few run-ons and/or fragments do not really affect meaning
Mechanics	– spelling and punctuation errors are obvious	– some errors but they don't affect meaning

SCORE	5	6
Content and Organization	– usually has introductory and concluding paragraphs – position is clear and direct – good reasons and details	– has effective introductory and/or concluding paragraphs – position is strong and well-developed – excellent supporting reasons
Usage	– a few errors	– very few errors (if any)
Sentence Construction	– variety and order of sentences has merit	– excellent variety of sentence types in logical sequence
Mechanics	– few errors	– very few errors (if any)

Name _____   Date _____

PRACTICE TEST: WRITING PERSUASIVE ESSAYS *(Continued)*
Student Samples

DIRECTIONS: Read the sample student essays below. Rate each paragraph with a score from 1 (lowest) to 6 (highest). Use the information in the scoring guide to help you.

ESSAY A

The skool shuld stay closed in July and Agust. Because I wasnt going their if its to hot than same with my frends. Thay wasn't going to skool to. Plus teaches wont want to be in skool in hot rooms. With no body in them than.

We can all be their in Junury and Febrary when no body gose out side cause it is too cold than? It is more cold and boring you don't want to go anywheres than. Heat is not espnsive and dosesn't costed lots of money. But to cool room does.

So the idear is no good no one will be their. Or learn. So please no changeing the skool months. Its no good for any body who is in school.

Score _____

ESSAY A
Close School During Summer Months

The school board would like to have our school open during the months of July and August and closed during the months of January and February. They say this will save money on heating bills. I disagree.

First, where we live, it is too hot to go to school during the months of July and August. The students will not want to learn and won't learn if it is too hot in the rooms. They will want cool rooms. Who will pay for those rooms. Can the school board pay for that if they can't pay for the heat?

Next, students want to play in July and August. Then the weather is nice to play outside. They swim and play sports at that time some go on vactions with their family. They do not like to go to school when they can be doing other more fun things.

Finally, the parents will also be upset. They want to go on vactions too. Does the school board want to get the parents mad at them? Plus, parents do not want to have their kids stuck in the house during January and February. It would make everybody mad.

These three reasons show why I feel the idea will not work. Keep school as it is now. This change is bad.

Score _____

WRITING NARRATIVE/ DESCRIPTIVE ESSAYS

Standardized Testing Information

The National Assessment of Educational Progress (NAEP) describes **narrative writing** as the type of writing that "involves the production of stories or personal essays. It encourages writers to use their creativity and power of observation to develop stories that can capture a reader's imagination." Although many state tests also require students to do informative and persuasive writing, the type of writing that is usually emphasized in fourth or fifth grade is narrative/descriptive. Possibly, this is because students of this age respond best and feel most comfortable in the narrative form.

NOTE: The terms *narrative writing* and *descriptive writing* are used interchangeably in the guidelines below. Also, this section covers personal narrative and descriptive writing. Imaginative writing (stories) is covered in Section 10.

Knowledge of how personal narrative writing samples are scored will help prepare students effectively. Here is one example of a state's scoring guide for narrative/descriptive writing. The Illinois ISAT writing assessment is scored on five features:

- **Focus:** the clarity with which a paper presents and maintains a clear main idea, point of view, theme or unifying event.

- **Support/Elaboration:** the degree to which the main point is explained by specific details and reasons.

- **Organization:** the clarity of the logical flow of ideas and the explicitness of the text structure or plan.

- **Conventions:** the use of standard written English.

- **Integration:** the global judgment of how effectively the paper as a whole uses the basic features to address the assignment.

At the fifth-grade level, the points listed above are scored as follows for narrative writing:

Exceeds Standards (top score)
- **Focus:** "Introduces and maintains a clear subject and unifying event and has an effective closing."
- **Support/Elaboration:** "Demonstrates all major episodes/reactions and they are developed by specific detail, but may not be even or balanced. Word choice enhances specificity. Development of depth is clearly evident."

- **Organization:** "The narrative structure is clear and the episodes move through time without noticeable gaps. Paragraphing is appropriate. Coherence and cohesion are demonstrated with effective devices: varied sentence structure . . ."
- **Conventions:** "The writing shows mastery of sentence construction, some invented spelling of uncommon words, and some understanding of basic grammar. Few major errors are present in proportion to the amount written."
- **Integration:** "The fully developed paper has a clear and purposeful Focus; in-depth, balanced Elaboration; and a sequence of episodes that is coherently and cohesively developed throughout the paper."

Meets Standards

- **Focus:** "Establishes and maintains a clear subject and unifying event. . . . Writing at this level will contain reactions that are mostly relevant as well as a consistent closing."
- **Support/Elaboration:** "Elaboration of major episodes. . . . Most episodes/reactions are developed by specific detail with evidence of some depth. Word choice may be used to enhance specificity."
- **Organization:** "Narrative structure that moves episodes through time with few gaps. . . . Most major episodes are appropriately paragraphed. . . . Some varied sentence structures and/or word choices."
- **Conventions:** "Mastery of sentence construction, some invented spelling of uncommon words and some understanding of basic grammar."
- **Integration:** "Well developed for grade level, but all features may not be evenly developed. Less sophisticated writing will show bare-bones development for grade level . . . and limited depth."

Below Standards

- **Focus:** "Writing . . . may lack sufficiency to demonstrate a developed focus and does not serve the narrative purpose . . . subjects and events that lack clarity . . . ideas may be unrelated or drift from the focus."
- **Organization:** "Insufficient to sustain organization . . . inappropriate paragraphing and/or transitions . . . significant gaps or major digressions . . . little evidence of appropriate paragraphing."
- **Conventions:** "May lack mastery of sentence construction, basic subject/verb agreement and/or basic punctuation/capitalization . . . many invented spellings and major errors."
- **Integration:** "Only rudiments of Focus, Support, and Organization . . . lack narrative structure . . . some confusion or disjointedness."

Most scoring guidelines are similar to this example. The challenge, therefore, is to guide students into a better understanding of organizing an essay, staying on the subject, presenting major points and details in a clear and logical way, understanding and using correct sentence and paragraph structure, and having a grade-appropriate grasp of language usage.

Many states offer helpful directions to students taking the test. For example, the Pennsylvania PSSA Writing Assessment, which is completed in two 40-minute sessions over a two-day period, includes these instructions given to the students:

During Session 1:

- Think about what you want to say,

- make notes,

- and write a draft of your paper.

During Session 2:

- Reread the prompt,

- read your draft,

- make any changes in your draft you feel are necessary, and

- when you are satisfied with what you have written, copy it onto the FINAL COPY pages.

In addition, the PSSA Writing Assessment offers this reminder when prompting for a narrative/imaginative assignment:

- Describe what happened.

- Give details that are specific and relevant to this experience.

- Present your ideas clearly and logically.

- Use words and well-constructed sentences effectively.

- Correct any errors in spelling, punctuation, and capitalization.

These elements are stressed again and again in the pages of this resource. Students who complete these activities satisfactorily will be well-prepared for any state or national writing assessment test.

Here are some specific suggestions for working with the activities in this section.

Teacher Preparation and Lessons

1. Students should complete all parts of each activity. Prewriting, writing a first draft, and revising are all essential components of the writing process. Although the activities are written and presented clearly enough for students to work on their own, the teacher is strongly urged to go over the directions for each worksheet carefully with the class, making sure that students understand what they are expected to do.

2. It can be valuable experience (and fun for the students) occasionally to work on the **prewriting** activity as an entire class and in small or large discussion groups.

3. After the student has **revised** the **first draft,** but before writing a **final copy,** the paper should be reviewed by someone other than the writer. Sometimes, it can be the teacher. Other times, it should be another student or students. Critiquing of other students' material can be a valuable learning experience both for the writer and the one who is critiquing. Even experienced writers are not able to be completely objective about their own work. It is easier to see the flaws in someone else's writing than in one's own, and one can thereby learn to recognize those same mistakes in one's own work. Both the writer and the reader, therefore, benefit from this type of exercise. Students may find it helpful to use the proofreading marks on page 343 when they are revising their own writing or reviewing a classmate's paper.

Narrative/descriptive writing gives students the opportunity to use their creativity and imagination. It offers them an opportunity to "play with words" and discover the richness and excitement of written language.

Practice Test: Writing Narrative/Descriptive Essays

Sample student essays A and B on page 275 were rated 5 and 3, respectively.

Essay A: The opening sentence and paragraph are clear and direct. The three body paragraphs are well constructed with sensory examples and details. There is even a simile! An adequate summary paragraph is present. A fragment, an inconsistency in verb tense (*will throw*), and incorrect use of *it's* should not distract from an otherwise fine piece of writing. The content of paragraphs 2 and 4 are arguably the same topic. This narrative scored a 5.

Essay B: Choppy is the word here. The first paragraph becomes monotonous due to the lack of sentence variety and sentence length. Simple sentences abound! The student also has some problems with fragments, run-ons, and inconsistent verb tense. On the positive side, there are sensory words, descriptions (*giggly* noise, *dark* basement, and *steep* stairs), a somewhat interesting opening line, and an attempt at describing people's feelings. This two-paragraph narrative was rated a 3.

Name _____ Date _____

8–1. MY EARLIEST MEMORY (PREWRITING)

It can be fun to think about wonderful, or funny, or even unpleasant things that happened in the past. Some people have better memories than others, but most of us have had experiences that we never forget. An author named Ray Bradbury once claimed that he remembered the moment he was born.

Choose an event in your past that you remember clearly, and write about it. It will be easy if you first prepare a **brainstorming list.**

A. DIRECTIONS: Complete this brainstorming list.

1. Write the year and month (or exact date, if you know it) here.

   _____

2. What was your age at the time? _____

3. What was the event? _____

   _____

4. Who was present? _____

5. On the lines below, write as many words and phrases you can think of that describe what happened.

   _____

   _____

   _____

6. Write words and phrases to describe your feelings about what was happening.

   _____

   _____

7. Why do you think you remember this event? _____

   _____

B. DIRECTIONS: On the back of this sheet, write an **opening sentence** for your essay that will grab the reader's interest.

Name _____ Date _____

8–2. MY EARLIEST MEMORY (FIRST DRAFT)

You are going to write about an event that you remember and have already outlined in your brainstorming list. Try to use words and phrases that will help the reader see what you are remembering. Active verbs, such as *run* or *leap* instead of *go*, and *grab* or *snatch* for *take*, make your writing more vivid. Try to use sensory words that appeal to the senses of *touch, sight, smell, sound,* and *taste* to bring the scene to life. This will be just a first draft, so don't worry about spelling or grammar yet.

- The first paragraph (*at least two sentences*) introduces the topic in an interesting way. Use the opening sentence you wrote for the brainstorming list. Briefly name the event you remember. Tell when and where it happened, and your age at the time.

- The second paragraph (*at least four sentences*) develops the topic. Describe what happened, who was there, and how you felt about it. You should have this already written down on your brainstorming list. (If this is very long, you might want to describe your feelings in another paragraph.)

- The final paragraph (*at least two sentences*) restates and sums up the topic, as in this example: "This is one of my strongest and deepest memories. I'll never forget that day even if I live to be one hundred."

DIRECTIONS: Begin your first draft below and continue on the back of this sheet. Write a title on the first line (such as "My Most Unforgettable Day"), and indent at the beginning of each paragraph.

_____

_____

_____

_____

_____

_____

_____

_____

8–3. My Earliest Memory (final copy)

A. DIRECTIONS: Correct and revise the first draft of your essay about a memory.

1. Do you introduce the topic in the first paragraph? Can you change or add anything else to grab the reader's interest?

2. Do you develop the topic in the second (and possibly third) paragraph? Do you describe the event clearly just as it happened? Do you describe your feelings at the time? Can you add any active verbs or sensory words to help the reader see it more vividly?

3. Does the final paragraph restate and sum up the topic? Can you make it stronger with an active verb or sensory word?

4. Check each sentence carefully. Are all sentences complete? Do subjects and verbs agree?

5. Check your spelling with a dictionary.

6. Ask your teacher or another student to look at your first draft and make suggestions.

B. DIRECTIONS: Begin the final copy of your essay below and continue on the back of this sheet. Write the title on the first line, and indent at the beginning of each paragraph.

_____

_____

_____

_____

_____

_____

_____

_____

8–4. A DAY IN SOMEONE ELSE'S LIFE (PREWRITING)

You are going to pretend you are someone else, and write about a day in **that person's** life. The "someone else" can be either real or fictional. It can be a character in a book or your best friend. It might be someone in your family or a teacher. You might even choose to be a famous person (living or dead). Try to imagine yourself inside this person's head, thinking and feeling the way that person does.

A. DIRECTIONS: First prepare a **brainstorming list.** Write the name of your subject and where he or she lives. In the left-hand column below, list all the things your subject does from morning until night. In the right-hand column next to each activity, write words and phrases that describe the thoughts and feelings of the subject about that activity.

BRAINSTORMING LIST	
Name of Subject	**Where Subject Lives**
Activity	**Thoughts and Feelings**

B. DIRECTIONS: On the back of this sheet, write an interesting **opening sentence** for your essay (such as "My name is Mickey and I live in Walt Disney World").

© 2002 by The Center for Applied Research in Education

Name _____ Date _____

8–5. A DAY IN SOMEONE ELSE'S LIFE (FIRST DRAFT)

Pretend you are someone else and write a description of a day in your life, as though you were that person. It will be easy to do if you have already completed a brainstorming list and opening sentence. This is just a first draft, so don't be concerned about spelling or grammar. Concentrate on getting your thoughts on paper.

- The first paragraph (*at least two sentences*) introduces the topic. Tell who you are and where you live. Use the opening sentence from your brainstorming list.

- The second (or more) paragraphs describe a day in the life of the person you are pretending to be. Describe what happens from morning until night. (These details can be real or imagined!) Be sure to include your thoughts and feelings as that character.

- The final paragraph (*at least two sentences*) restates and sums up the topic.

DIRECTIONS: Begin your first draft below and continue on the back of this sheet. Write a title on the first line (such as "A Day in My Life"), and indent at the beginning of each paragraph.

8–6. A Day in Someone Else's Life (final copy)

A. DIRECTIONS: Correct and revise the first draft of your essay about a day in the life of someone you are pretending to be.

---

1. Do you introduce the topic in the first paragraph in an interesting way? Can you change or add anything else to grab the reader's interest?

2. Do you develop the topic in the second (or more) paragraphs? Is it organized clearly? Do you list the day's activities from morning until night? Do you describe the subject's thoughts and feelings while each thing is happening? Can you make it more vivid with active verbs and sensory words?

3. Does the final paragraph restate and sum up the topic?

4. Check each sentence carefully. Are all sentences complete? Do subjects and verbs agree?

5. Check your spelling with a dictionary.

6. Ask your teacher or another student to look at your first draft and make suggestions.

B. DIRECTIONS: Begin the final copy below and continue on the back of this sheet. Write the title on the first line, and indent at the beginning of each paragraph.

8–7. MY SPECIAL PLACE (PREWRITING)

Do you have a special place—a place where you like to be—a place where you feel good? It might be anywhere—a room in your house, your porch, the home of your grandmother or another relative. It could be a ball field, a park, a place where you went on vacation. You are going to describe your special place and explain why it feels special.

A. DIRECTIONS: Your essay will be easy to write if you first prepare a **brainstorming list**. In the left-hand column, write a list of words and phrases to describe your special place and where it is. In the right-hand column, write words and phrases to describe how you feel in your special place.

BRAINSTORMING LIST FOR "MY SPECIAL PLACE"	
Description of "My Special Place"	**My Feelings About It**

B. DIRECTIONS: On the back of this sheet, write one or two **opening sentences** for your essay, "My Special Place," as in this example: "No matter how hard you look, you will never find my special place. It belongs only to me."

8–8. MY SPECIAL PLACE (FIRST DRAFT)

Write the first draft of a three-paragraph essay describing your special place. It will be easy to do if you use your brainstorming list as a guide. Try to use interesting adjectives in your description. Use at least one simile to make your writing interesting, such as: *as quiet as the morning of a deep snowfall,* or *as familiar and comfortable as a well-worn sneaker.* In this first draft, don't worry about spelling or grammar. Concentrate on getting your thoughts on paper.

- The first paragraph introduces the topic in an interesting way. Use the opening sentences in your brainstorming list.

- The second paragraph develops the topic. Describe your special place so clearly that the reader can see it. Explain your feelings about it and why it is important to you.

- The final paragraph restates and sums up the topic, as in this example: "I feel better about everything when I am in my special place. I hope it will always be there for me to enjoy."

DIRECTIONS: Begin your first draft below and continue on the back of this sheet. Write a title on the first line, and indent at the beginning of each paragraph.

_____

_____

© 2002 by The Center for Applied Research in Education

8–9. MY SPECIAL PLACE (FINAL COPY)

A. DIRECTIONS: Correct and revise the first draft of your essay about a special place.

1. Do you introduce the topic in the first paragraph in an interesting way? Can you add any words and phrases to make it more exciting?

2. Do you develop the topic in the second paragraph? Do you describe the place clearly? Do you tell about the people and things that are there? Would a reader understand why it is important to you?

3. Do you restate and sum up the topic in the final paragraph?

4. Do you use colorful adjectives to describe your special place? Can you add two more adjectives to make your writing more vivid?

5. Do you use at least one interesting simile? Can you add one more?

6. Are your sentences complete? Do subjects and verbs agree?

7. Check your spelling with a dictionary.

8. Ask your teacher or another student to look at your first draft and make suggestions.

B. DIRECTIONS: Begin the final copy below and continue on the back of this sheet. Write a title on the first line, and indent at the beginning of each paragraph.

_____

_____

_____

_____

_____

_____

_____

_____

_____

_____

8–10. SOMEONE I ADMIRE (PREWRITING)

Is there anyone you admire a lot? Perhaps a parent or relative? How about a teacher or another student? Maybe you look up to someone famous like a performer or a world leader (living or dead)? What about a fictional character from a movie, book, or TV show?

Before writing about the person you admire, it will help to prepare an **idea tree**. You've probably heard of "family trees," which are diagrams of family members that cover many generations. Like trees, they have branches that go off in many directions, and these branches grow branches of their own. The **idea tree** begins with a **subject**. Branches lead to **main points**, which then grow branches of their own, as in this example:

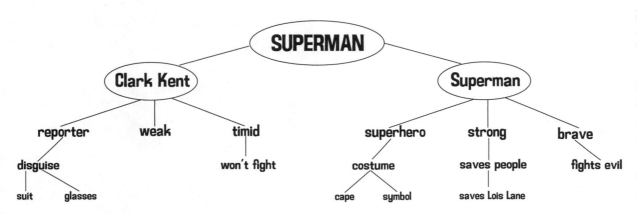

DIRECTIONS: Make your own idea tree on another sheet of paper. Write the name of the person you admire at the top in the middle, and circle it. Write several main points, circle them, and attach them to the subject with a line. Write descriptive words and phrases for each main point, and circle and attach them to the main point with a line.

8–11. Someone I Admire (first draft)

Your idea tree will help you organize your essay about the person you admire. Try to use descriptive adjectives and strong, active verbs to help the reader vividly see the person you are describing. In this first draft of a three-paragraph essay, don't worry about spelling or grammar. Concentrate on getting your thoughts on paper.

- The first paragraph (*at least two sentences*) introduces the topic in an interesting way, as in this example: "Superman is my hero. I try to be as much like him as I can."

- The second paragraph (*at least four sentences*) develops the topic. Organize your thoughts with the idea tree. Use details to support each main point.

- The final paragraph (*at least two sentences*) restates and sums up the topic, as in this example: "No human can hope to be as brave and noble as Superman. If more people tried to fight evil, however, wouldn't it be a better world?"

DIRECTIONS: Begin your first draft below and continue on the back of this sheet. Write a title on the first line, and indent at the beginning of each paragraph.

_____

_____

_____

_____

_____

_____

_____

_____

_____

_____

_____

_____

8–12. SOMEONE I ADMIRE (FINAL COPY)

A. DIRECTIONS: Correct and revise the first draft of your essay about the person you admire.

1. Does your first paragraph introduce the topic in an interesting way? Can you add or change any words to grab the reader's interest?

2. Does the second paragraph develop the topic? Are your thoughts clearly organized? Do you state the main points and support each with details and descriptive words and phrases?

3. Does the final paragraph restate and sum up the topic? Can you add anything to make the ending more satisfying and interesting to the reader?

4. Can you insert at least one interesting simile?

5. Do you use colorful adjectives and active verbs to bring your subject to life?

6. Are your sentences complete? Do subjects and verbs agree?

7. Check your spelling with a dictionary.

8. Ask your teacher or another student to read your first draft and make suggestions.

B. DIRECTIONS: Begin the final copy below and continue on the back of this sheet. Write a title on the first line, and indent at the beginning of each paragraph.

_____

_____

_____

_____

_____

_____

_____

© 2002 by The Center for Applied Research in Education

8–13. A VISIT TO THE DOCTOR OR DENTIST (PREWRITING)

All kids visit a doctor, dentist, or other health professional at times. Each of us is unique, however, so we experience these events differently. Now you will have a chance to describe one of your visits and then compare it with those of your classmates.

DIRECTIONS: Organize your thoughts and memories by completing this **brainstorming list**.

1. Check the box next to the type of visit you plan to describe. (If you check "Other," write the name [or profession] on the line.)

   ❏ Doctor   ❏ Hospital

   ❏ Dentist   ❏ Other (_____)

2. Name the person (or persons) who went with you. _____

3. List any tasks you had to do to prepare for this visit. (You don't need complete sentences to answer these questions—words and phrases are enough.) _____

   _____

4. How did you get to this place? What did you see along the way? (words and phrases) _____

   _____

5. Did you first wait in a waiting room? List words and phrases to describe the room and the people in it. _____

   _____

6. List words or phrases to describe the doctor, dentist, or other professional you saw, and his or her office. _____

   _____

7. List words and phrases to describe what happened to you there. _____

   _____

8. Write words and phrases that describe your feelings while you were there. _____

   _____

9. What happened after you left? (words and phrases) _____

   _____

8–14. A VISIT TO THE DOCTOR OR DENTIST
(FIRST DRAFT)

The notes you made on your brainstorming list will make it easy to write a five-paragraph essay about your visit to the doctor, dentist, or other health professional. This is just a first draft, so don't be concerned about spelling or grammar. Concentrate on getting your thoughts on paper.

- The first paragraph (*at least two sentences*) introduces the topic. Sometimes a question can make the beginning more interesting, as in this example: "Does anybody really want to go to the doctor?"

- The second paragraph (*at least three sentences*) uses your brainstorming page to describe what you did to prepare for this visit, the people who went with you, and your trip there.

- The third paragraph (*at least three sentences*) describes the waiting room and the office (and the people in it).

- The fourth paragraph (*at least three sentences*) describes what happened to you there, your feelings about it, and what occurred after you left.

- The final paragraph (*at least two sentences*) restates and sums up the topic, as in this example: "Was my visit to the doctor bad? Not really! In fact, it was a lot better than I expected. Still, I hope I don't have to go again for a long time."

DIRECTIONS: Begin your first draft here and continue on another sheet of paper. Fill in the title "A Visit to the _____" on the first line, and indent at the beginning of each paragraph.

A Visit to the _____

_____

_____

_____

_____

_____

_____

© 2002 by The Center for Applied Research in Education

8–15.   A Visit to the Doctor or Dentist
(final copy)

A. DIRECTIONS: Correct and revise the first draft of your essay about visiting a doctor, dentist, or other health worker.

1. Does your first paragraph introduce the topic? Can you make it more interesting?

2. Do the second, third, and fourth paragraphs develop the topic clearly and logically? Can the reader easily follow each step of your visit? Are these steps in order from beginning to end? Should any sentences be rearranged to make it clearer *what* is happening *when*?

3. Does the final paragraph restate and sum up the topic in an interesting way (serious or humorous)?

4. Can you add colorful adjectives and active verbs to make the writing more vivid?

5. Are your sentences complete? Do subjects and verbs agree?

6. Use a dictionary to check your spelling.

7. Ask the teacher or another student to read your first draft and make suggestions.

B. DIRECTIONS: Write the final copy on another sheet of paper. Fill in the title ("A Visit to the _____") on the first line, and indent at the beginning of each paragraph.

8–16. SOMETHING I DID FOR THE VERY FIRST TIME
(PREWRITING)

A. DIRECTIONS: Isn't it exciting to do (or see) something for the *very first time*? Can you remember the first time you did one of these things? Choose one of these "firsts" to write about. Check the box next to your choice.

❑ played in a Little League game

❑ met the person who is now your best friend

❑ saw your baby brother or sister

❑ saw a concert or stage show

❑ attended a new school

❑ received a report card with all A's

❑ played your favorite game

❑ flew in an airplane

❑ saw a circus

B. DIRECTIONS: Complete the **brainstorming list** below. In the left-hand column, write dates, words, and phrases to describe where and when this "first" took place. In the middle column, list words and phrases you can use to describe what happened during this "first." In the third column, list words and phrases to describe your feelings about this "first."

BRAINSTORMING LIST FOR "A 'FIRST' TO REMEMBER"		
Where and When	**Details of What Happened**	**My Feelings**

C. DIRECTIONS: Write an **opening sentence (or sentences)** for your essay on another sheet of paper. A strong statement, like this one, can be interesting: "Some 'firsts' will always be special! For example, I will never forget the day I met my best friend, Eric."

8–17. SOMETHING I DID FOR THE VERY FIRST TIME
(FIRST DRAFT)

DIRECTIONS: Write a three-paragraph essay about the first time you did something. It will be easy if you use your brainstorming list. This is just a first draft, so don't be concerned about spelling or grammar. Concentrate on getting your thoughts on paper.

First Paragraph: Introduce the topic in an interesting way. Begin with the strong statement you wrote on your brainstorming list. Write your first paragraph (*at least two sentences*) here or on another sheet of paper.

_____

_____

_____

Second Paragraph: Develop the topic. Use the words and phrases on your brainstorming list to tell details of this "first." Give the time and place, and include your own feelings about the event. Write your second paragraph (*at least four sentences*) here or on the other sheet of paper.

_____

_____

_____

_____

_____

_____

Final Paragraph: Restate and sum up the topic, as in this example: "Meeting a best friend is a great event. That is why I will never forget that first day of school in September 2001." Write your final paragraph (*at least two sentences*) here or on the other sheet of paper.

_____

_____

_____

© 2002 by The Center for Applied Research in Education

Name _____ Date _____

8–18. SOMETHING I DID FOR THE VERY FIRST TIME
(FIRST DRAFT)

A. DIRECTIONS: Correct and revise the first draft of your essay about a "first time."

1. Does your first paragraph introduce the topic? How can you make it more interesting?

2. Does the second paragraph develop the topic? Do you show clearly what this event was? Do you show where and when it happened? Do you use vivid details to describe exactly what happened and your feelings about it?

3. Does the final paragraph restate and sum up the topic? Is it a satisfying ending?

4. Can you add colorful adjectives and active verbs to make your writing stronger?

5. Are your sentences complete? Do subjects and verbs agree?

6. Check the dictionary for spelling.

7. Ask the teacher or another student to read your first draft and make suggestions.

B. DIRECTIONS: Begin the final copy below and continue on the back of this sheet. Write an interesting title on the first line, and indent at the beginning of each paragraph.

8–19. A Special Trip (Prewriting)

Did you ever take a trip? Did you ever travel to another city or state? Maybe your family went on vacation to a beach or a lake. Lots of people go to amusement and theme parks such as Walt Disney World.

DIRECTIONS: Write about a trip you have taken. Try to remember all the details by first preparing a **brainstorming list**.

1. On the lines below, write words and phrases to describe the events and your feelings **just before** this trip. Examples: *map of Florida, airplane tickets, shopping for clothes, packing, suitcases, tote bags, excitement, arguments.*

   _____

   _____

   _____

2. On the lines below, write words and phrases to describe traveling there and your feelings about it. Examples: *packing up car, forgetting earphones, rushing back, parking at airport, crowded, noisy, people rushing and shoving, like a zoo, hurrying to make the plane, nervous.*

   _____

   _____

   _____

3. On the lines below, write words and phrases to describe the place where you stayed and your feelings there. Examples: *hot, sunny, wide beach, high, foamy waves, swimming, diving, water-skiing, hotel, big room with balcony, fun, happy, sunburn, fast-food restaurants, pizza, burgers, relaxed.*

   _____

   _____

   _____

4. Write an **opening sentence or sentences** on the back of this sheet. Make it interesting with a question or strong statement, such as: "Can you imagine being on a hot, sunny beach in February? That's where I ended up during school vacation."

8–20. A Special Trip (first draft)

Write a three-paragraph essay about your trip. This is a first draft so don't be concerned about spelling or grammar. Concentrate on getting your thoughts on paper. Use your brainstorming list as a guide.

- The first paragraph (*at least two sentences*) introduces the topic with the interesting question or statement that you wrote on your brainstorming list.

- The second paragraph (*at least five sentences*) develops the topic by describing your trip from before you left until you returned. Tell what happened in logical order. Your brainstorming list will help you.

- The final paragraph (*at least two sentences*) restates and sums up the topic in a satisfying way, as in this example: "It was hard to come back to freezing temperatures after our week of fun in sunny Florida. I'll never forget what a wonderful time we had, and can hardly wait until next year."

DIRECTIONS: Begin your first draft below and continue on the back of this sheet. Complete the title on the first line, and indent at the beginning of each paragraph.

My Trip to _____

_____

_____

_____

_____

_____

_____

_____

_____

_____

_____

_____

_____

Name _____   Date_____

8–21. A SPECIAL TRIP (FINAL COPY)

A. DIRECTIONS: Correct and revise the first draft of your essay about a trip.

1. Does your first paragraph introduce the topic? Does it tell where you went and when you went there? Can you make it more interesting with a question or strong (or humorous) statement?

2. Does the second paragraph develop the topic? Do you describe events clearly and logically, in the order in which they happened? Make your writing more vivid by adding colorful adjectives and sensory words wherever possible.

3. Does the final paragraph restate and sum up the topic? Is there anything you can change or add to make it more interesting?

4. Are your sentences complete? Do subjects and verbs agree?

5. Check spelling with a dictionary.

6. Ask the teacher or another student to read your first draft and make suggestions.

B. DIRECTIONS: Begin the final copy below and continue on the back of this sheet. Write the title on the first line, and indent at the beginning of each paragraph.

_____

_____

_____

_____

_____

_____

_____

_____

_____

Name _____ Date_____

8–22. ME, MYSELF, AND I (PREWRITING)

DIRECTIONS: You are going to write an essay called "Me, Myself, and I." Can you guess what it will be about? That's right! It will be about *you*! You are going to write a description of yourself. This will be easy if you first prepare a **brainstorming list**.

1. In the box below, write words and phrases that can be used to describe your appearance, such as *hazel eyes, blonde hair, nine years old, tall for my age, skinny, strong,* and so on.

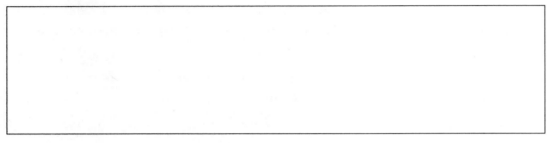

2. In the box below, write words and phrases to describe your personality, such as *friendly, average intelligence, talkative, easy-going, happy,* and so on.

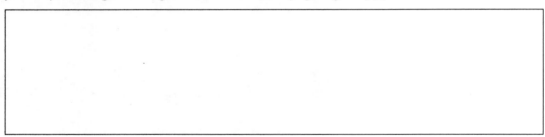

3. In the box below, write words and phrases to describe your activities and your feelings about them, such as *loves Little League, swimming, and bicycling; likes to play piano but hates practicing; spends hours playing computer games; friends always around,* and so on.

4. Write an **opening sentence or sentences** on the back of this sheet. Can you make it unusual or humorous, as "I just looked into a mirror, and guess what I saw? There in the looking glass was the real me, whoever that might be!"

Name _____ Date _____

8–23. ME, MYSELF, AND I (FIRST DRAFT)

Write a five-paragraph essay about *yourself*. Use your brainstorming list as a guide. Remember, this is only a first draft!

- The first paragraph (*at least two sentences*) introduces the topic with the unusual or humorous opening you wrote for the brainstorming list.

- The second paragraph (*at least three sentences*) develops the topic. In this paragraph, describe your appearance. Use the words and phrases on your brainstorming list.

- The third paragraph (*at least three sentences*) develops the topic further. Describe your personality. Use words and phrases from the brainstorming list.

- The fourth paragraph (*at least three sentences*) develops the topic by describing your activities. Use words and phrases from the brainstorming list.

- The final paragraph (*at least two sentences*) restates and sums up the topic in an unusual or humorous way, as in this example: "This is what I see in the mirror. I wonder if you see the same person when you look at me."

DIRECTIONS: Write your first draft on another sheet of paper. Fill in the title "Me, Myself, and I," and indent at the beginning of each paragraph.

8–24. ME, MYSELF, AND I (FINAL COPY)

A. DIRECTIONS: Correct and revise the first draft of your essay "Me, Myself, and I."

> 1. Does your first paragraph introduce the topic? Can you make it more unusual or humorous?
>
> 2. Does the second paragraph develop the topic by describing your appearance? Can you add anything unusual like *a tiny birthmark on my right foot*?
>
> 3. Does the third paragraph continue to develop the topic by describing your personality? Can you add an interesting simile, such as "My mom says that I am as active as the Energizer bunny"?
>
> 4. Does the fourth paragraph continue to develop the topic by describing your activities? Can you add a few strong, active verbs?
>
> 5. Does the final paragraph restate and sum up the topic? Can you add or change anything to make it unusual or humorous?
>
> 6. Use a dictionary to check your spelling.
>
> 7. Ask the teacher or another student to read your first draft and make suggestions.

B. DIRECTIONS: Write your final copy on another sheet of paper. Fill in the title "Me, Myself, and I," and indent at the beginning of each paragraph.

FOURTH-GRADE LEVEL

WRITING NARRATIVE/DESCRIPTIVE ESSAYS

PRACTICE TEST

Name _____   Date_____

PRACTICE TEST: WRITING NARRATIVE/DESCRIPTIVE ESSAYS

DIRECTIONS: In an essay of three to five paragraphs, tell about a place *or* a time you remember vividly. The place can be a vacation spot, a local amusement park, or any other location. The time can be a birthday party, a trip, or any other occasion that you recall.

CHECKLIST

Make sure to:

_____ 1. Begin with an interesting opening paragraph.

_____ 2. Develop your topic by giving reasons why it's memorable.

_____ 3. Include a description of what the person, event, or place is like.

_____ 4. Use sensory words, vivid verbs, and a simile.

_____ 5. Describe your thoughts and feelings.

_____ 6. Sum up with a strong last paragraph and last line.

_____ 7. Check for capitalization, subject–verb agreement, and consistent verb tense.

_____ 8. Write the essay's title above the first sentence and indent the first word of each paragraph.

Use the following four steps to complete your essay:

• FIRST, on the page labeled PREWRITING, brainstorm some ideas for your essay. Then organize your words and phrases in a way that is workable for you.

• SECOND, write the first draft of your essay. Use colorful adjectives, sensory words, and a simile. Make sure your essay has a beginning, a middle, and an end.

• THIRD, revise and edit your first draft. Check to see that you have written complete sentences. Make sure your sentences are organized logically to tell a story about what happened in that place or time.

• FOURTH, on a separate sheet of paper, write the final draft of your paragraph.

PRACTICE TEST: WRITING NARRATIVE/DESCRIPTIVE ESSAYS

(Continued)

Prewriting

Use the lines below to brainstorm some ideas for a topic. Jot down as many ideas as possible. Select one event or time to write about. In the space, organize details and examples to show the reader what happened. Use a list, a cluster, or an outline.

_____

_____

_____

_____

_____

_____

_____

Scoring Guide

SCORE	1	2
Content and Organization	– lacks introductory and concluding paragraphs – details lack clarity and focus – no logical flow of events or ideas	– may lack introductory and/or concluding paragraph(s) – most details lack clarity and focus – attempts a logical flow of events/ideas
Usage	– no control over word choice – far too many errors	– the many errors include verb tense and the incorrect use of modifiers
Sentence Construction	– far too many fragments and/or run-ons	– greater sentence variety needed – too many run-ons and/or fragments
Mechanics	– numerous serious errors and misspellings prevent comprehension	– numerous serious errors take away from comprehension

SCORE	3	4
Content and Organization	– may lack an introductory or concluding sentence – few sensory details but unclear focus – some logical flow of ideas	– attempt made at introductory and/or concluding paragraph – some sensory details and some focus – greater logical flow of ideas
Usage	– some errors in subject–verb agreement, verb tense, and comparison adjectives	– some errors but they don't take away from meaning
Sentence Construction	– frequent fragments and short, choppy sentences take away from meaning	– some fragments and choppy sentences but they don't detract from meaning
Mechanics	– spelling and punctuation errors are obvious	– some errors but they don't affect meaning

SCORE	5	6
Content and Organization	– usually has an introductory and/or concluding paragraph – focus is clear and direct – good sensory details that contribute to meaning	– has effective introductory and concluding paragraphs – well organized and developed with excellent sensory details that contribute meaning
Usage	– a few errors	– very few errors (if any)
Sentence Construction	– good sequence and variety of simple, compound, and complex sentences	– excellent sequence and variety of simple, compound, and complex sentences
Mechanics	– few errors	– very few errors (if any)

PRACTICE TEST: WRITING NARRATIVE/DESCRIPTIVE ESSAYS

(Continued)

Student Samples

DIRECTIONS: Rate the paragraphs below with a score from 1 (lowest) to 6 (highest). Use the information on the scoring guide to help you.

ESSAY A
At the Beach

There are many things about the beach in the summer that I like. The water, the food, and the activities I do are what I enjoy. It's fun being there with my friends and family, too.

Swimming and riding the waves with my dad or my mom are fun. When I see a huge wave rolling in, I get ready, and then I catch it. Body surf the wave as far as I can take it towards the beach. It's a great feeling, but not so great a feeling if the wave crashes you into the sand where you get scratched up pretty good.

Food at the beach is also good. I usually get a hot dog or a burger with some French fries. Then I get a big drink to wash it all down. Sometimes I even get ice cream if its real hot out there.

We keep active at the beach too. When I am at the beach, I will throw the Frisbee and play volleyball with some of my friends. We often throw a rubber ball to each other to see who can dive and catch it the best. Sprinting along with them near the water is fun too. We feel as fast as cheetahs when we run quickly there.

These are the many reasons why I like the beach in the summer so much. Wouldn't you?

Score _____

ESSAY B
My Party

Wow! What a party I had! It was a surprise. It was my ninth birthday. I come home to my house. It seems empty. I look all around, wondered where everyone was. Then I heard a noise. From the dark basement.

So I went down to the basement where the giggly noise was from. Then we I got to the boottom of the steep stairs, the lights went on. "Happy Birthday!" they shouted to me. I got lots of presents. A great birthday surprise it was the best I had ever had for a birthday party surprise!

Score _____

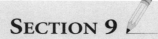

WRITING LETTERS

Standardized Testing Information

Standardized assessment tests sometimes call for writing samples in the form of letters. The National Association of Educational Progress (NAEP), for example, has asked fourth-grade students to write a letter to an imaginary friend offering advice on how to solve a problem. Other assessment tests have prompted students to write letters to a school principal or teacher suggesting a change in school policy.

Writing a letter is, in many ways, similar to an essay. Like essays, letters include the following: (1) a beginning identifying the subject of the letter; (2) a middle (one or more paragraphs) to develop the topic; and (3) an ending. There are aspects of letter writing, however, that differ from essay composition. These include:

- *Audience:* An essay is addressed to a general group of readers while a letter is addressed to one or more specific individuals.

- *Tone:* The tone of a letter is more personal and resembles one part of a dialog between two individuals.

- *Structure:* The structure of a letter, while having a beginning, middle and end, is somewhat looser and more flexible than in an essay.

Teacher Preparation and Lessons

The activities in this section cover two kinds of letters: **informative** and **persuasive**. Follow the following procedure to introduce each type of letter writing:

1. **Define the nature of an "informative" letter.** Write the word *informative* on the board. Discuss a definition of *informative* as "communicating information, sharing knowledge, or conveying instructions and ideas." Point out that the nature of letter writing is communication between the writer and his or her intended reader(s).

2. **Elicit examples of "informative" letters** such as *writing to a friend who has moved away to communicate news of interest, writing to a relative to express ideas for holiday and/or birthday gifts,* and so on. NOTE: Students may be used to referring to this type of informative letter as a *personal* letter.

3. **Demonstrate the form of an informative (personal) letter.** Display the diagram on the next page. **NOTE:** Most standardized tests for fourth grade do not call for formal letter structure, such as *return address, inside address,* and so on. Therefore, the letter format used in these activities will include only the use of a *date, greeting,* and *closing.*

```
                              Today's date
Dear (Name),
(Write message here.)

                           Closing,
                           Your name here
```

Point out the commas after the greeting and after the closing. Elicit some examples of closings, such as *Your friend, Your pal, Your student, Your daughter,* and so on.

4. **Define the nature of a "persuasive" letter.** Write the word *persuasive* on the board. Elicit a definition, such as "tries to influence the reader to take action or bring about change." Elicit examples of "persuasive" letters, such as *writing to a teacher or principal to bring about a change in school rules, writing to a parent to obtain a bigger allowance, writing to a friend to convince him or her to join your team,* and so on. Point out that the letter format for persuasive letters in the activities should be the same as the format for informative letters.

5. Explain to students that they may be asked to write an informative or a persuasive letter on standardized tests.

As with the activities for essays, each letter-writing activity in this section consists of three parts, as follows: **Prewriting; Writing a first draft;** and **Revising ≠Writing a final copy.** Here are some specific suggestions for working with the activities.

- Distribute **Prewriting.** First, read the instructions aloud and be sure the students understand them before proceeding. The prewriting activities can be done individually, in small groups, or as a class. Even when performed individually, it is a good idea for students to share their prewriting ideas with others whenever possible.

- Distribute **First Draft.** Read the instructions aloud. Discuss the nature of a *first draft* and encourage students to concentrate on getting their ideas on paper and not being too concerned about spelling and/or grammar.

- Distribute **Revising and Writing a Final Copy.** Read the directions aloud. Some of the revision instructions will be repeated in this part of each activity. Read them aloud *each time* to reinforce learning. Discuss any aspects of revising that are not clear to every student. You may wish to have students use the proofreading marks on page 343 to make revisions and corrections.

Practice Test: Writing Letters

The sample student letters on page 305 were scored a 5 and a 4, respectively.

Letter A: This letter is clear and direct. The writer presents an argument that is developed nicely with logical examples. An appeal to nature and recreation is apparent in the argument. The concluding paragraph sums up the writer's opinion effectively. Perhaps the letter could have included additional reasons and, therefore, been a bit longer. Yet, it does get the message across and appeals logically to common sense—at least from the writer's perspective. Letter format was followed. The letter scored a 5.

Letter B: The date is missing and there is only a one-word closing, but these errors do not take away from comprehension. The body includes mechanical errors (misspellings and capital letter problems) and a fragment. Yet, the message, to "leave it alone," is obvious to the owner. Could it be said in a more polished way? Absolutely! Considering that the writer's alternative plan is implicit, the members know what the writer desires. This letter scored a 4.

9–1. SHARING NEWS WITH A FRIEND (PREWRITING)

Do you know someone who has moved to a different neighborhood or to a different town? It's tough to be far away from familiar people and familiar things and not to know what is happening in the old hometown. You are going to write a letter to a friend who now lives far away and share interesting news with him or her.

If you do not have such a friend, you can make one up and even give this pretend friend a name. Write the name of your *real* or *pretend friend* here.

_____

DIRECTIONS: Organize your thoughts for this letter by preparing a **brainstorming list**. In the first column, list *three* recent events in your neighborhood or town. In the second column, next to each event, write words and phrases to describe that event. In the third column, list *three* recent events in your school. In the fourth column, next to each event, write words and phrases to describe that event.

BRAINSTORMING LIST			
Town Event	**Descriptive Words**	**School Event**	**Descriptive Words**
1.		1.	
2.		2.	
3.		3.	

© 2002 by The Center for Applied Research in Education

9–2. SHARING NEWS WITH A FRIEND
(FIRST DRAFT)

DIRECTIONS: It will be easy to write a first draft of a letter to a friend if you follow these directions and keep your brainstorming list in front of you.

1. **Date:** A letter always begins with the date. Write today's date here.

   _____

2. **Greeting:** The next part of a letter is the greeting, which is *Dear (Name of Person)*, followed by a *comma*, as in this example: *Dear Alex,*. Write your greeting here.

   _____

3. **Message (First Paragraph):** This letter will have four paragraphs. The first paragraph introduces the subject, as in this example: "You must be wondering what is happening now that you are so far away. I'm going to help you catch up with the latest news." Write your first paragraph (*at least one sentence*) on another sheet of paper.

4. **Message (Second Paragraph):** Tell about events in your neighborhood or town. Describe at least two of the events listed on your brainstorming list. Write your second paragraph (*at least three sentences*) on the other sheet of paper.

5. **Message (Third Paragraph):** Tell about events in your school. Describe at least two of the events from your brainstorming list. Write your third paragraph (*at least three sentences*) on the other sheet of paper.

6. **Message (Final Paragraph):** Say goodbye in the final paragraph, as in this example: "Everyone here really misses you. Please write soon." Write your final paragraph (*at least one sentence*) on the other sheet of paper.

7. **Closing:** This is the last part of a letter, and is followed by a comma, as in these examples: *Your friend, Miss you, Love,*. Write your closing here.

   _____

9–3. SHARING NEWS WITH A FRIEND (FINAL COPY)

A. DIRECTIONS: Revise and correct the first draft of your letter to a real or pretend friend.

1. Do you put a *comma* after the greeting?

2. Do you introduce the topic in the first paragraph in a friendly way?

3. Do you tell about events in your neighborhood or town in the second paragraph? Make your descriptions more vivid with colorful adjectives and active verbs.

4. Do you tell about events at school in the third paragraph? Can you add anything else interesting or exciting?

5. Do you say goodbye in the final paragraph in a friendly manner?

6. Do you put a *comma* after the closing?

7. Are your sentences complete? Do subjects and verbs agree?

8. Check your spelling with a dictionary.

B. DIRECTIONS: Write the final copy of your letter here and continue on the back of this sheet. Keep these points in mind:

- Write today's date in the upper right-hand corner.
- Write the greeting at the beginning of the next line, followed by a comma.
- Indent at the beginning of each paragraph of the message.
- Write your closing in the lower right-hand corner, followed by a comma.
- Sign your name under the closing.

_____

_____

_____

_____

_____

_____

_____

9–4. GIFT SUGGESTIONS FOR YOUR FAMILY MEMBERS (PREWRITING)

Pretend that your aunt has asked you to give her ideas for holiday or birthday presents for each member of your family. You are going to write a letter to your aunt telling her this information. It will be easy if you first prepare a brainstorming list.

A. DIRECTIONS: Fill out the **brainstorming list.** List the names of your family members in the left-hand column. (Put your name next to number 1.) In the middle column, next to each name, list several gift ideas for that person. In the right-hand column, write words and phrases that you can use to describe the gift and why it is right for each person.

BRAINSTORMING LIST		
Name	Gifts	Description
1.		
2.		
3.		
4.		
5.		
6.		

B. DIRECTIONS: On the back of this sheet, write a **greeting** and an **opening sentence** for your letter to your aunt. Make it interesting and funny, as in this example:

> Dear Aunt Linda,
>
> **This letter is going to make you feel like Santa Claus.**

9–5. GIFT SUGGESTIONS FOR YOUR FAMILY MEMBERS
(FIRST DRAFT)

Write a letter to your aunt (real or pretend) suggesting holiday or birthday gifts for the members of your family. Use your brainstorming list as a guide. This is just a first draft, so don't worry about spelling or grammar. Concentrate on getting your thoughts down on paper.

- Write today's date in the upper right corner.
- Write the greeting (followed by a comma) at the beginning of the next line.
- Copy the beginning you wrote on your brainstorming list.
- In your message, list one or more gifts for each person in your family. Describe each gift and why it would be good for that person. You can have a separate paragraph for each person, or write the whole message as one paragraph.
- Write a closing (followed by a comma), such as *Your loving nephew, Love,* etc.
- Sign your name below the closing.

DIRECTIONS: Begin your first draft here and continue on the back of this sheet.

_____

_____

_____

_____

_____

_____

_____

_____

_____

_____

_____

_____

_____

9–6. Gift Suggestions for Your Family Members
(final copy)

A. DIRECTIONS: Revise and correct the first draft of your letter to your aunt.

1. Do you begin with today's date?
2. Do you put a comma after the greeting?
3. Is your message clearly organized? Can you add some colorful adjectives to your descriptions of gifts?
4. Do you put a comma after the closing?
5. Are your sentences complete? Do subjects and verbs agree?
6. Check your spelling with a dictionary.

B. DIRECTIONS: Begin the final copy of your letter here and continue on the back of this sheet. Indent at the beginning of each paragraph, and sign your name at the end under the closing.

_____

_____

_____

_____

_____

_____

_____

_____

_____

_____

_____

_____

_____

Name _____ Date_____

9–7. Writing to a Pen Pal (prewriting)

A **pen pal** is someone with whom you exchange letters. You can get to know a person really well this way even if you never meet. Your pen pal might live in another city or state, or even in a different country. In this activity, you are going to write a first letter to a kid in another *country* who might become your pen pal. You will tell about yourself, your family and friends, and where you live.

DIRECTIONS: Prepare a **brainstorming list** to help you write this letter.

1. Write your age and grade here. _____

   _____

2. Write words and phrases that describe your appearance. _____

   _____

3. Write words and phrases that describe your personality. _____

   _____

4. Write words and phrases that describe things you like best. _____

   _____

5. Write words and phrases that describe what you dislike. _____

   _____

6. Write words and phrases that describe your family. _____

   _____

7. Write words and phrases that describe your school. _____

   _____

8. Write words and phrases that describe your friends._____

   _____

9. Write words and phrases that describe your town and country. _____

   _____

© 2002 by The Center for Applied Research in Education

Name _____ **Date**_____

9–8. WRITING TO A PEN PAL (FIRST DRAFT)

Write a letter introducing yourself to a pen pal who lives in another country. Use your brainstorming list as a guide. This is just a first draft, so don't be concerned about spelling or grammar.

- Write today's date at the end of the first line.
- Write a greeting at the beginning of the next line (followed by a comma), such as *Dear Pen Pal,*.
- Write an opening paragraph that will grab the reader's interest, such as "Wouldn't it be fun to have a far-away friend? I would like to be your pen pal and become good buddies across the miles."
- Write your message telling about yourself. You don't have to use *all* the information on your brainstorming list, just as much as you would like to put into this first letter to a pen pal. You can have just one paragraph, or several.
- Write a closing (followed by a comma), such as *Your pen pal,*.
- Sign your name below the closing.

DIRECTIONS: Begin your first draft here and continue on the back of this sheet.

_____

_____

_____

_____

_____

_____

_____

_____

_____

_____

_____

_____

_____

9–9. WRITING TO A PEN PAL (FINAL COPY)

A. DIRECTIONS: Revise and correct the first draft of your letter to a pen pal in another country.

> 1. Do you begin with today's date?
>
> 2. Do you put a comma after the greeting?
>
> 3. Is your opening paragraph interesting? Can you change anything to make it seem more exciting to a possible pen pal?
>
> 4. Is your message clearly organized? Do you paint a good word picture of who you are and where you live? Add some colorful adjectives and sensory words.
>
> 5. Do you put a comma after the closing?
>
> 6. Are your sentences complete? Do subjects and verbs agree?
>
> 7. Check your spelling with a dictionary.

B. DIRECTIONS: Begin the final copy of your letter here and continue on the back of this sheet. Indent at the beginning of each paragraph, and sign your name at the bottom under the closing.

_____

_____

_____

_____

_____

_____

_____

_____

_____

_____

9–10. NO DRESS CODE! (PREWRITING)

You just found out that your school is going to have a dress code. That means there will be rules telling you what you can and cannot wear to school. You don't agree with this. You are going to write a letter to the school principal trying to convince him or her to cancel this dress code. You must state your thoughts clearly and give good reasons for your opinion.

DIRECTIONS: Prepare a **brainstorming list** to help you write this letter.

1. Write a beginning paragraph for your letter that clearly tells why you are writing it, such as: "Is it true that we are going to have a dress code in our school? I think it is a terrible idea!" _____

   _____

   _____

2. State one reason for your opinion here. _____

   _____

   Write a list of words and phrases to explain this reason. _____

   _____

   _____

3. What is your second reason for this opinion? _____

   _____

   Write a list of words and phrases to explain this reason. _____

   _____

   _____

4. Write one more statement to support your opinion against a dress code.

   _____

   _____

   Write a list of words and phrases to explain this reason. _____

   _____

   _____

9–11. No Dress Code! (first draft)

Write a letter to the school principal disagreeing with the new dress code. Use the brainstorming list as a guide. This is just a first draft, so don't be concerned about spelling or grammar.

- Write today's date at the end of the first line.
- Write a greeting at the beginning of the next line (followed by a comma), such as *Dear Mr. Smith, Dear Ms. Adams,*.
- Copy your opening paragraph from the brainstorming list.
- Write the message. Give at least three reasons for your opinion. Use the words and phrases on your brainstorming list to explain each reason.
- Write a closing (followed by a comma), such as *Your student, Yours truly,* and so on.
- Sign your name below the closing.

DIRECTIONS: Begin your first draft here and continue on the back of this sheet.

_____

_____

_____

_____

_____

_____

_____

_____

_____

_____

_____

_____

_____

_____

© 2002 by The Center for Applied Research in Education

9–12. NO DRESS CODE! (FINAL COPY)

A. DIRECTIONS: Correct and revise the first draft of your letter to the principal disagreeing with the dress code.

---

1. Do you begin with today's date?
2. Do you place a comma after the greeting?
3. Is your opening paragraph interesting? Can you add anything else to make it grab the principal's interest?
4. Is your message clearly organized? Do you state and explain each reason convincingly? Would it be more effective if you used a separate paragraph for each of the three reasons?
5. Do you put a comma after the closing?
6. Are your sentences complete? Do subjects and verbs agree?
7. Check your spelling with a dictionary.
8. Ask your teacher or another student to look at your letter and make suggestions.

B. DIRECTIONS: Begin the final copy of your letter here and continue on the back of this sheet. Indent at the beginning of paragraphs, and sign your name at the end of the letter under the closing.

_____

_____

_____

_____

_____

_____

_____

_____

_____

9–13. TRYING OUT FOR A SPORT (PREWRITING)

You are planning to try out for your local Little League baseball team. You want your best friend to be on the team with you. He (or she) does not want to do it. You are going to write a letter to your friend that will convince him or her to try out for Little League. It will be easy to write if you first prepare a brainstorming list.

DIRECTIONS: Prepare a **brainstorming list** to help you write the letter.

1. Write your friend's name (real or pretend) here. _____

2. Write the greeting of the letter (Examples: *Dear Max, Dear Buddy, Dear Margie,*)
   here._____

3. Make notes for your letter in the box below. You don't need complete sentences here—words and phrases will be enough. In the left-hand column, list at least three reasons why your friend should join Little League. In the right-hand column (next to each reason), list words and phrases that explain that point in detail.

BRAINSTORMING LIST	
Reasons to Join	**Details**
1.	
2.	
3.	
4.	
5.	
6.	

© 2002 by The Center for Applied Research in Education

9–14. TRYING OUT FOR A SPORT (FIRST DRAFT)

Write a letter convincing your friend to join Little League. It will be easy if you use your brainstorming list as a guide. This is just a first draft, so don't be concerned about spelling or grammar. Concentrate on getting your thoughts on paper.

- Write today's date on the first line.
- Copy the greeting from your brainstorming list, followed by a comma.
- Write a beginning paragraph that will grab your friend's interest, such as: "How could you not want to join Little League? We could have the most fun of our lives there!"
- Write a message with at least three strong reasons. Write convincing details for each point.
- Write a closing and sign your name below.

DIRECTIONS: Begin your first draft here and continue on the back of this sheet.

_____
_____
_____
_____
_____
_____
_____
_____
_____
_____
_____
_____
_____

9–15. TRYING OUT FOR A SPORT (FINAL COPY)

A. DIRECTIONS: Correct and revise the first draft of your letter convincing a friend to join Little League.

1. Do you begin with today's date?

2. Do you place a comma after the greeting?

3. Can you make the beginning paragraph more exciting?

4. Is your message clearly organized? Can you add anything else to be more persuasive?

5. Do you put a comma after the closing?

6. Are your sentences complete? Do subjects and verbs agree?

7. Do you capitalize proper names and the beginning of sentences?

8. Check your spelling with a dictionary.

B. DIRECTIONS: Begin the final copy of your letter here and continue on the back of this sheet. Indent at the beginning of paragraphs, and sign your name at the end of the letter under the closing.

_____

_____

_____

_____

_____

_____

_____

_____

_____

_____

_____

9–16. SOMETHING I WISH FOR (PREWRITING)

Have you ever wished for something that your parents did not want you to have? Sometimes, it can be more convincing to put your ideas in writing. You are going to write a letter to one or both of your parents that will persuade them that your request is fair and good.

DIRECTIONS: Prepare a **brainstorming list** to help you write this letter.

1. Check the item you would like your parents to get. If you check *Pet*, indicate what pet you want. If you check *Other*, specify what it is.

   ❏ Pet _____   ❏ Musical instrument
   ❏ Your own TV   ❏ Basketball hoop
   ❏ Your own computer   ❏ Encyclopedia
   ❏ Video game   ❏ Other _____

2. In the left-hand column, list at least three reasons for your choice.

3. In the right-hand column (next to each reason), write words and phrases that will help to explain this point.

Reason	Details
1.	
2.	
3.	
4.	
5.	
6.	

9–17. SOMETHING I WISH FOR (FIRST DRAFT)

Write a letter to one or both of your parents convincing them to get something you want. Use your brainstorming list as a guide. This is just a first draft, so don't be concerned about spelling or grammar.

- Write today's date on the first line.
- Write a greeting, followed by a comma, such as *Dear Mom, Dear Dad, Dear Mother and Father,*.
- Write a beginning paragraph to get their attention, such as "Do you know how much I long to have a puppy? There are excellent reasons why our family should have a pet."
- Write a message with at least three good reasons for your point of view. Write convincing details for each reason.
- Write a closing, followed by a comma, such as *Your son, Your daughter, Your loving child,*.
- Sign your name under the closing.

DIRECTIONS: Begin your first draft here and continue on the back of this sheet.

_____

_____

_____

_____

_____

_____

_____

_____

_____

_____

_____

_____

9–18. SOMETHING I WISH FOR (FINAL COPY)

A. DIRECTIONS: Correct and revise the first draft of your letter convincing your parents to get something you desire.

1. Do you begin with today's date?

2. Do you place a comma after the greeting?

3. Is your beginning paragraph interesting? Can you add anything else to create interest?

4. Is your message clear and convincing? Do you give three good reasons for your opinion and support each one?

5. Are your sentences complete? Do subjects and verbs agree?

6. Do you capitalize proper names and the beginning of sentences?

7. Do you use correct punctuation (period, question mark, or exclamation point) to show the end of each sentence?

8. Check your spelling with a dictionary.

B. DIRECTIONS: Begin the final copy of your letter here and continue on the back of this sheet. Indent at the beginning of each paragraph, and sign your name at the end of the letter under the closing.

_____

_____

_____

_____

_____

_____

_____

_____

_____

_____

_____

9–19. WHY MY TOWN IS A GREAT PLACE TO LIVE
(PREWRITING)

Do you like the town or city in which you live? You have heard about a family named Green who is thinking of moving there. Write a letter convincing these people that they should move to your city or town.

A. DIRECTIONS: First, prepare a **brainstorming list.** In the left-hand column, write words and phrases that describe your town in general (size, location, region of country, appearance, buildings, people, etc.). In the middle column, write words and phrases describing things to do (parks, playgrounds, museums, ball fields, theaters, restaurants, pools, shopping, etc.). In the right-hand column, write words and phrases about your school (teachers, students, classes, computers, sports, clubs, bands, etc.).

BRAINSTORMING LIST		
Description	**Things to Do**	**School**

B. DIRECTIONS: Begin your letter in a positive and convincing way, as in this example: "So, you are planning to move! You could not find a better place to live than my home town, Macon Falls." Write your beginning paragraph on the back of this sheet.

9–20. WHY MY TOWN IS A GREAT PLACE TO LIVE
(FIRST DRAFT)

Write a letter to the Green family convincing them to move to your city or town. Use your brainstorming list as a guide. This is just a first draft, so concentrate on getting your thoughts on paper.

- Write today's date on the first line at the right.
- Write a greeting, such as *Dear Mr. and Mrs. Green,* or *Dear Green Family,*.
- Copy the first paragraph you wrote on your brainstorming list.
- Write a message that will persuade the Greens to move to your town. First, describe the town in general, then tell about things to do, and finally describe your school. Write a separate paragraph for each of these three main points, and give as many supporting details as you can.
- Write a closing, such as *Yours truly, Your soon-to-be neighbor, Your friend from Macon Falls,* and so on.
- Sign your name under the closing.

DIRECTIONS: Begin your first draft here and continue on the back of this sheet.

_____

_____

_____

_____

_____

_____

_____

_____

_____

_____

_____

9–21. WHY MY TOWN IS A GREAT PLACE TO LIVE
(FINAL COPY)

A. DIRECTIONS: Correct and revise the first draft of your letter convincing the Greens to move to your town.

1. Do you begin with today's date?
2. Do you put a comma after the greeting?
3. Is your beginning paragraph as interesting as you can make it?
4. Is your message clear? Do you use a separate paragraph for each of your three main points? Do you include supporting details in each paragraph? Can you add colorful adjectives or active verbs to make your writing more vivid?
5. Check each sentence to be sure it is complete. Do subjects and verbs agree?
6. Do you capitalize proper names (people, town, school, park, etc.)?
7. Check your spelling with a dictionary.

B. DIRECTIONS: Begin the final copy of your letter below and continue on the back of this sheet. Indent at the beginning of each paragraph, and sign your name at the end of the letter under the closing.

_____

_____

_____

_____

_____

_____

_____

_____

_____

_____

FOURTH-GRADE LEVEL

WRITING LETTERS
PRACTICE TEST

PRACTICE TEST: WRITING LETTERS

DIRECTIONS: For three years, you've gone to a wonderful summer camp in Colby County. Joe Pratt, the owner, is thinking of selling the camp. You just heard that the new owner might build a shopping mall on the land where the camp is located. Write a letter to Mr. Pratt explaining why you think he shouldn't sell the camp.

CHECKLIST

Make sure to:

_____ 1. Write today's date in the upper right-hand corner.

_____ 2. Write the greeting (followed by a comma) at the beginning of the next line.

_____ 3. Introduce the subject of your concern in the first paragraph.

_____ 4. Organize your message clearly, and present it in a convincing way.

_____ 5. Sum up your message in a strong concluding paragraph.

_____ 6. Indent at the beginning of each paragraph.

_____ 7. Write the closing (followed by a comma) in the lower right-hand corner and sign your name under the closing.

_____ 8. Check for capitalization, punctuation, misspellings, subject–verb agreement, and consistent verb tense.

Follow the four steps below to write your letter:

- FIRST, on the page labeled PREWRITING, brainstorm some ideas. Write down words and phrases to explain your position. Then organize your ideas the best way possible.

- SECOND, write the first draft of your letter. Your topic paragraph should be strong and state your message. Then use the reasons and examples from your brainstorming lists to support your opinion. Stay on the subject and remember to sum up at the end.

- THIRD, revise and edit your first draft. Make sure your sentences are organized logically and your argument is well developed.

- FOURTH, on a separate sheet of paper, write the final draft of your letter.

PRACTICE TEST: WRITING LETTERS *(Continued)*

Prewriting

On the lines below, brainstorm ideas for your letter. Jot down all the reasons that you can think of for why the camp should not be sold. Then, in the space, organize your ideas in a list, a cluster, or an outline.

_____

_____

_____

_____

_____

_____

_____

Scoring Guide

SCORE	1	2
Content and Organization	– no introductory or concluding paragraphs – details are unfocused and weak – does not follow letter format	– may be missing an introductory and/or concluding paragraph – focus and organization attempted – follows letter format slightly
Usage	– no control over word choice – verb tenses are inconsistent	– some control over word choice – many inconsistencies in verb tense
Sentence Construction	– far too many fragments and/or run-ons	– greater sentence variety needed – too many run-ons and/or fragments
Mechanics	– numerous serious errors and misspellings prevent understanding	– numerous serious errors and mispellings prevent understanding

SCORE	3	4
Content and Organization	– may lack an introductory and/or concluding sentence – focus could be stronger – has greeting and/or closing	– attempt made at introductory and/or concluding paragraph – focus is more convincing and direct – has date, greeting, and/or closing
Usage	– some errors in subject–verb agreement – some verb tense inconsistencies	– some errors, but they don't take away from meaning
Sentence Construction	– frequent fragments and short, choppy sentences take away from meaning	– some fragments and choppy sentences, but they do not take away from meaning
Mechanics	– spelling and punctuation errors are distracting	– some errors but they don't interfere with meaning of entire letter

SCORE	5	6
Content and Organization	– usually has an introductory and/or concluding paragraph – mostly organized and developed – follows letter format	– has strong and convincing introductory and concluding paragraphs – well organized and developed – follows letter format
Usage	– a few errors	– very few errors (if any)
Sentence Construction	– good logical sequence of ideas and variety of sentences	– excellent variety and sequence of sentences
Mechanics	– few errors	– very few errors (if any)

© 2002 by The Center for Applied Research in Education

PRACTICE TEST: WRITING LETTERS *(Continued)*
Student Samples

LETTER A

November 10, 2002

Dear Mr. Pratt,

There used to be a lot of trees and open land in Colby County. Most of it is now the site of shopping malls and houses. All that is left is Colby Camp. I do not want a shopping mall to be built where Colby Camp is now.

This camp is needed in Colby County. Kids from all over want a place to come in the summer that is safe. We also need the woods, the lake, and the plants of Colby Camp for their beauty.

Please don't sell off what little remains of our natural resources. We need to keep Colby Camp for our future and our children.

Your best camper,
Arthur Ransome

Score _____

LETTER B

Dear Mr. Pratt,

I hear that your going to sell Colby Camp and let them wreck it by built a mall there instead. This is not right at all. Because Colby Camp is pretty and has woods. Bike paths and a pool are there for us kids. What you should do is leave it alone. You could build the shoping mall some place other.

Thanks for reading this lettar. I hope you don't tear down Colby Camp.

Yours,
Stevie Ebertson

Score _____

WRITING STORIES

Standardized Testing Information

Imaginative narrative writing is often called for as a writing sample on standardized tests. The scoring standards for imaginative stories are the same as for other types of narrative writing. Here are excerpts from Idaho's scoring standard for narrative writing, which is typical of most state and national guidelines.

> A score of 3 (satisfactory) is achieved by a paper that "exhibits a basic understanding of the organization and development of ideas in narrative writing . . . may display errors in mechanics, usage or sentence structure . . . is satisfactory at grade level." A paper must exhibit most of the following traits to achieve this score:
>
> - Introduction and conclusion
> - Clear beginning, middle, and end
> - Logical progression of writing
> - Some elaboration of story elements: plot, setting, and characters
> - Clear connections with transitions
> - Relates thoughts and feelings throughout narrative
> - Limited figurative or descriptive language
> - Basic fourth-grade vocabulary
> - Word choices seldom surprise reader
> - Inconsistent expression of thoughts and feelings
> - Varied sentence lengths
> - Simple and complex sentences
> - Surface errors (spelling, punctuation, capitalization, and indentation) do not significantly interfere with readability
> - Correctly spells most high frequency words
> - Correctly capitalizes starts of sentences and place names
> - Correctly punctuates at ends of sentences
> - Attempts internal punctuation
> - Correctly indents at beginning of paragraphs
> - Evidence of proofreading

The highest score possible, 5, is achieved by a paper that "is an engaging piece of narrative writing. Demonstrating a clearly defined knowledge of narrative writing, the writer uses language which is above grade level to uniquely develop a clear and concise paper . . . demonstrates advanced proficiency for grade level." Papers must exhibit most of the following traits:

- Uniquely developed topic
- Effective (unique or exemplary) introduction and conclusion
- Details related to time, place, characters, and plot; elaboration of story elements, establishes context for reader
- Highly interesting to reader
- Figurative language: similes, metaphors, and/or personification
- Vibrant and consistent voice
- Unique, interesting, and above grade-level vocabulary
- Unique word choice may surprise, amuse, or move reader
- Descriptive language, adjectives, adverbs, and powerful verbs
- Specific, detailed description enhances story line
- Varied sentence length, structure, and beginnings
- Control of spelling, punctuation, and capitalization
- Correct general spelling as well as spelling of most unusual words
- Correct comma usage in the following: series, clauses, city/state
- Appropriate paragraphing facilitates readability

The Idaho scoring standard also provides guidelines for samples that fall between *satisfactory* and *excellent*, and also for writing that is less than satisfactory and is classified as *developing* or *minimal*. The examples given here, however, should provide the teacher with some insight into guidelines for scoring writing samples at the fourth-grade level.

Teacher Preparation and Lessons

Although the scoring standards are similar for narrative/descriptive writing and narrative/imaginative writing, the process and techniques used in producing the latter type of stories is significantly different. This entire section is devoted to offering students practice in the techniques and forms of imaginative story writing.

ACTIVITIES 10-1 through 10-3 introduce ways to find **story ideas from surroundings, from other people, and from books and other media.** Ask students if they believe that there are hundreds of story ideas that can be found right in their classroom. They will probably scoff at this idea. Ask them to look around the room carefully and point out objects, preferably things they have never noticed before. Offer an example of a story idea for the first few objects. For example, *if a student points out a vent in the ceiling, suggest that this might be a grid covering a pneumatic tube, through which materials and supplies are transported to the school from a central storage warehouse.* Another example: *a rolled-up paper in the corner could be a map that leads to a great treasure.* After the teacher has offered several possibilities, ask the students to come up with their own scenarios for various objects. There will be no shortage of ideas! Distribute **Activity 10-1 Getting Story Ideas from Surroundings.** Read the directions for each section of the page. Make sure they understand that they are not to write a complete story. When students have completed the exercises, have them share their answers with the class.

Next, discuss **getting story ideas from other people.** Point out a suitable article of clothing worn by a student or the teacher, and demonstrate how it could lead to a story idea. For example, *a T-shirt bearing the name of a theme park could lead to a story about a brother and sister accidentally locked inside the park overnight.* Another example: *a pair of red shoes might indicate a story about magical shoes that carry the wearer to far-off lands.* Point to several additional articles of clothing and ask students to volunteer story ideas. Distribute **Activity 10-2 Getting Story Ideas from Other People.** Make sure students understand the directions. When students have completed the page, have them share their answers with the class.

To introduce **getting ideas from books and other media,** ask students to name several of their favorite books, movies, and TV shows. Suggest ideas for further adventures with some of the characters in each one. Distribute **Activity 10-3 Getting Story Ideas from Books, Movies, and TV.** Read directions aloud. When students have completed the exercises, have them share their ideas with the class.

ACTIVITIES 10-4 through 10-6 cover **how to write a story's beginning, how to develop the plot, and how to create characters.** Tell students that a good beginning introduces the story characters (how they look and act) and the setting (where and when it takes place). On the board, list several of the story ideas generated by students as they complete Activities 10-1, 10-2, and 10-3. Ask several students to try beginning each story aloud (just a sentence or two). Discuss how successful each beginning is in introducing the characters and the setting. Distribute **Activity 10-4 Writing Story Beginnings**. Read directions aloud. When students have completed the exercises, share and discuss with the class.

To discuss **developing the plot** (the events that happen), ask students to offer oral suggestions for developing some of the stories in Activity 10-4. Discuss why some of their plot ideas seem to work while others do not. Distribute **Activity 10-5 Developing the Plot.** Have students follow the directions on the page for developing one of the plots from Activity 10-4. When students have completed the exercises, share and discuss them.

Discuss with students how to **develop a character**. Point out that this means that the story should tell what characters are like from a description of how they look, how they act, and what they say. Review several of the exercises from Activity 10-5. Discuss whether or not these stories, so far, show what the characters are like. Point out how this can be done. Distribute **Activity 10-6 Developing the Characters.** Read directions aloud. When students have completed the exercises, have students share and discuss them with the class. Focus on what the characters are like through their appearance, behavior, and what they say.

ACTIVITIES 10-7 through 10-9 cover **description.** Distribute **Activity 10-7 Using Place Description (Prewriting).** Complete part A together. Read aloud directions for Part B. Share and discuss student responses. Read aloud directions for part C. When students have completed all parts of **Activities 10-8 and 10-9,** share and discuss their papers.

The three types of imaginative narrative writing samples often called for on standardized assessment tests are the following: (1) realistic stories, (2) fantasy stories, and (3) mystery stories. Therefore, several activities are offered in this section for each of these categories. Every activity is divided into three parts—*prewriting, first draft, revising and writing a final copy.* Here are some specific suggestions for working with these activities.

ACTIVITIES 10-10 through 10-15 cover writing **realistic stories.** The directions for each activity are clear and specific. The teacher and students should read and discuss these to be certain that they are understood by every student. *Prewriting activities* should be shared and discussed before going on to the third part. Read and discuss directions for writing a *draft.* The suggestions in the third part for *correction and revision* should be examined and discussed carefully. When the student has completed this process, the paper should be examined by the teacher or another student before writing the *final copy.* Suggest students use the proofreading marks found on page 343 for revision. **ACTIVITIES 10-16 through 10- 21** cover writing **fantasy stories.** Follow the same procedures as above. **ACTIVITIES 10-22 through 10-27** cover writing **mystery stories.** Follow the same procedures as above.

Practice Test: Writing Stories

Sample student stories A and B on page 342 were rated 2 and 6, respectively.

Story A: There is an attempt to tell a story, but paragraphing and organization are lacking. There are serious problems writing complete sentences, since fragments and run-ons abound. Usage (*say he name; John wait his turn*) and spelling problems (*clappd, forth, skool, techr*) are numerous as well. Some plot and description is attempted. There are a few transitions (*Then* and *so*). The story is rated a 2.

Story B: This story has an interesting first sentence used to capture the reader's interest. It also has fine transitions, descriptions, and a clear beginning, middle, and end. Dialogue is even inserted. The reader is eagerly awaiting the story's climax, which the writer saves until the very last line. A fine variety of well-written sentences make the story even more enticing. This story is a 6.

10–1. GETTING STORY IDEAS FROM SURROUNDINGS

A. List **five** things that can be found in your room at home (examples: *bed, closet, baseball mitt, ballet slippers, library book, computer, etc.*).

❑ _____

❑ _____

❑ _____

❑ _____

❑ _____

B. Choose **one** of these things about which to make up a story. Put a check in front of the item you have chosen.

C. Write your story idea on the back of this sheet. DO NOT WRITE A COMPLETE STORY—just a few sentences to tell your story idea.

D. List **three** things that can be found **outside your house** or **on the street,** such as *garbage pail, garden, doghouse, basketball hoop, car, truck,* etc.

❑ _____

❑ _____

❑ _____

E. Put a check in front of **one** of the items above, and write a story idea for it on the lines below. DO NOT WRITE A COMPLETE STORY—just a few sentences to tell the story idea.

_____

_____

_____

_____

_____

_____

10–2. GETTING STORY IDEAS FROM OTHER PEOPLE

A. Check one of the following to use as a story idea:

❏ Someone you know who is very tall   ❏ A friendly neighbor

❏ Someone you know who is very small   ❏ An unfriendly neighbor

B. Write your story idea on the lines below. The story will **not** be about the actual person you chose. He or she will just suggest a story idea. DO NOT WRITE A COMPLETE STORY HERE—just a few sentences describing your story idea.

_____

_____

_____

_____

_____

_____

C. Check one of the following to use as a story idea:

❏ A stranger you recently saw near your school   ❏ Someone who wears stylish clothes

❏ Someone you like   ❏ Someone with unusual hair

❏ Someone you dislike

D. Write your story idea on the lines below. Your story will **not** be about the actual person. He or she will just suggest a story idea. DO NOT WRITE A COMPLETE STORY—just a few sentences describing your story idea.

_____

_____

_____

_____

_____

10–3. GETTING STORY IDEAS FROM BOOKS, MOVIES, AND TV

A. List the titles of three books you have read.

_____

_____

_____

B. Circle one of the books above. Write a story idea for a new book about the same characters. DO NOT WRITE A COMPLETE STORY HERE—just a few sentences describing your story idea.

_____

_____

_____

_____

_____

C. List three movies or TV shows you have seen.

_____

_____

_____

D. Circle one of the movies or TV shows above. Write a new story idea for the characters in that movie or show. DO NOT WRITE THE COMPLETE STORY—just a few sentences describing your idea.

_____

_____

_____

_____

_____

10–4. WRITING STORY BEGINNINGS

A. DIRECTIONS: Which story idea below do you like best? Put a check next to your choice.

❏ A child is on a family camping trip. The child gets separated from the rest and is lost in the woods. While wandering around, the child comes upon a deserted house.

❏ You and your best friend accidentally get locked in the school overnight.

❏ A child discovers that he or she has the ability to fly.

❏ You are a stowaway on the first spaceship to Mars.

❏ Two kids find a time machine and go back in time a hundred years or more.

❏ A mean bully is magically turned into a little bunny rabbit and discovers what it is like to be hunted by larger and stronger beasts.

B. DIRECTIONS: On the lines below or on the back of this sheet, write a **beginning** (*two to four sentences*) for the story you checked. A story beginning should introduce the main characters, and show the setting (where and when the story takes place). DO NOT WRITE A COMPLETE STORY—just the beginning (two to four sentences).

_____

_____

_____

_____

_____

_____

_____

_____

_____

_____

_____

_____

© 2002 by The Center for Applied Research in Education

10–5. DEVELOPING THE PLOT

A. DIRECTIONS: Carefully read the story beginning you wrote for Activity 10-4. Decide upon the **plot** you want, and make notes for it, as follows:

- List at least three things that will happen to the main character or characters. (These are just notes so you do not need complete sentences here.)

_____

_____

_____

- List any other characters who will appear in the story.

_____

_____

- Tell briefly how you plan to end the story.

_____

_____

B. DIRECTIONS: Continue the story from the point where you left off on Activity 10-4. (Use the back of this sheet if you need more room.)

_____

_____

_____

_____

_____

_____

_____

_____

_____

10–6. DEVELOPING THE CHARACTERS

A. DIRECTIONS: Using the story you wrote for Activity 10-5, write the names of two characters in the left-hand column below. In the right-hand column, next to each name, write words and phrases that describe that character, such as *huge, happy, mean, brave, frightened, tiny, timid, careless,* etc.

Name of Character	Description
1.	
2.	

B. DIRECTIONS: Rewrite your story below. Add description and action that show what the characters are like. (Use the back of this sheet if you need more room.)

_____

_____

_____

_____

_____

_____

_____

_____

_____

_____

_____

_____

_____

Name _____ Date _____

10–7. USING PLACE DESCRIPTION (PREWRITING)

A. DIRECTIONS: When you tell about a place in your story, the reader should be able to see and even feel what it looks like. The author used colorful adjectives, sensory words, and strong, active verbs to make this scene come to life.

> They began to run through the woods. It was growing darker by the minute. Only a dim glow flickered through the tree tops. Then they arrived at a section of the woods where the faint light disappeared. The blackness was total. The branches above were like gigantic black arms waiting to seize them.

- List three **sensory words** in this paragraph on the back of this sheet.

- List three **active verbs** in this paragraph on the back of this sheet.

- List three **colorful adjectives** in this paragraph on the back of this sheet.

B. DIRECTIONS: You are going to write a description about one of the following places. Place a check mark next to the one you have chosen.

❏ A scary place   ❏ Your classroom
❏ A place you have seen in a dream   ❏ Your room at home

C. DIRECTIONS: It will be easy to write your description if you first complete the **brainstorming list** below. In the left-hand column, list things that are seen in this place. In the middle column, write descriptive words about these things, using colorful adjectives, sensory words, and active verbs. In the right-hand column, list words and phrases to describe the way this place makes you feel.

Things	Descriptions	Feelings

Name _____ Date _____

10–8. Using Place Description (first draft)

You are going to write the first draft of a description of the place you have chosen. First, try to picture the place in your mind. Use colorful adjectives in your description. Use sensory words (sight, sound, touch, smell, taste). Use strong, active verbs such as *smash, run, leap, shout,* and so on.

DIRECTIONS: Begin your description below and continue on the back of this sheet. This is just a first draft so don't be concerned with spelling and grammar. Concentrate on getting your thoughts on paper. Write a title on the first line, such as "A Scary Place," "The Horrible House of My Dreams," "My Messy Room," etc.

_____

_____

_____

_____

_____

_____

_____

_____

_____

_____

_____

_____

_____

_____

_____

_____

_____

10–9. USING PLACE DESCRIPTION (FINAL COPY)

A. DIRECTIONS: Correct and revise your description of a place.

1. Do you use sensory words in your description? Can you add more?

2. Do you use colorful adjectives in your description? Can you add more?

3. Do you use strong, active verbs in your description? Can you add more?

4. Can you add more details so that the reader will see the place as clearly as you see it?

5. Are your sentences complete? Do subjects and verbs agree?

6. Check your spelling with a dictionary.

B. DIRECTIONS: Begin the final copy of your description below and continue on the back of this sheet. Write the title on the first line, and indent at the beginning of each paragraph.

_____

_____

_____

_____

_____

_____

_____

_____

_____

_____

_____

10–10. A REALISTIC STORY: MATT AND LUKE AT CAMP (PREWRITING)

Matt and his younger brother, Luke, are going to summer camp. Matt has been there before, but it is Luke's first time. Luke is nervous and wants to hang on to his big brother. Matt is annoyed and wishes he could get rid of Luke.

DIRECTIONS: Use your imagination to write a story about Matt and Luke and what happens to them at camp. It will be fun and easy to write if you first prepare a **brain-storming list.**

1. Write as many words and phrases you can think of to describe Matt. Include his appearance, personality, character, things he likes and dislikes, and so on.

   _____

   _____

   _____

   _____

2. Write words and phrases to describe Luke.

   _____

   _____

   _____

   _____

3. On the back of this sheet, list by name two or three more characters who will be in this story. Next to each name, tell who they are and what they are like. (Example: *Pete—counselor, strong, helpful, understanding*)

4. On the back of this sheet, list three or four events that will happen in this story.

5. On the back of this sheet, write a **beginning** for your story that will grab the reader's interest, such as: "Who needs a kid brother, thought Matt. He glanced with annoyance at his brother, Luke, who was sitting up close to him on the bus."

Name _____ Date _____

10–11. A Realistic Story: Matt and Luke at Camp
(first draft)

You are going to write a story about Matt and his younger brother, Luke, at camp.

- Make up a title for your story and write it on the first line.

- Copy the beginning from your brainstorming list. Try to make it even more exciting.

- Use your brainstorming list to tell what happens to Matt and Luke. Use strong, active verbs to show each event clearly.

- Use colorful adjectives and sensory words to describe Matt, Luke, and the other characters in the story.

- Describe the camp and what it looks like so the reader can see it.

- Stick to the point of the story—Luke's need to stick close to Matt, and Matt's wish to get rid of him.

- End the story with a solution to this problem.

DIRECTIONS: Begin the first draft of your story below and continue on the back of this sheet. This is just a draft, so don't worry about spelling and grammar.

_____

_____

_____

_____

_____

_____

_____

_____

10–12. A REALISTIC STORY: MATT AND LUKE AT CAMP
(FINAL COPY)

A. DIRECTIONS: Correct and revise the first draft of your story about Matt and Luke at summer camp.

---

1. Is your beginning as interesting as you can make it?
2. Can you add anything else to the description of the characters so they will seem more real to the reader?
3. Does your plot proceed logically? Cut anything that is boring or irrelevant.
4. Can you add more colorful adjectives and sensory words to your descriptions?
5. Can you use stronger, more active verbs for the action?
6. Does your ending solve the problem? Can you make it more satisfying to the reader?
7. Are your sentences complete? Do subjects and verbs agree?
8. Check your spelling with a dictionary.
9. Ask your teacher or another student to look at your story and make suggestions.

B. DIRECTIONS: Begin the final copy of your story here and continue on the back of this sheet. Write the title on the first line, and indent at the beginning of each paragraph.

_____

_____

_____

_____

_____

_____

_____

10–13. A REALISTIC STORY: A FALSE ACCUSATION
(PREWRITING)

How would you like to be accused of something you did not do? That is what is going to happen to the main character in your story. He (or she) will be accused of doing something wrong, such as *cheating on a test, hitting another kid, stealing from a classmate's locker, taking money from Mom's purse,* etc. He (or she) knows who really did it, but can't tell without being called a "rat" by the other kids.

DIRECTIONS: This story will be easy and fun to write if you first prepare a **brainstorming list** on another sheet of paper.

1. Give your main character a name and write a list of words to describe that person.

2. What is that person accused of doing?

3. Name the person who did it and list descriptive words and phrases.

4. Name one or two more characters and tell who they are.

5. List three or four events that will happen in this story.

6. List words and phrases to describe the main character's feelings.

7. Tell briefly how you think the story will end.

8. On the lines below or on the back of this sheet, write an exciting **beginning** for your story, such as: "How could this happen to me? Carlos wondered. He had not done anything wrong, but now everyone thought he was a thief."

_____

_____

_____

_____

_____

_____

_____

10–14. A REALISTIC STORY: A FALSE ACCUSATION
(FIRST DRAFT)

You are going to write a story about someone who has been unfairly accused.

- Make up a title for your story and write it on the first line.
- Copy the beginning from your brainstorming list. Can you add or change anything to make it even more exciting?
- Use the information on your brainstorming list to tell what happens next. Use strong, active verbs to show action.
- Use colorful adjectives and sensory words to describe the characters and how they feel.
- Describe the place where this is happening.
- End the story with a solution to the problem.

DIRECTIONS: Begin your story below and continue on the back of this sheet. This is just a first draft so don't be concerned about spelling or grammar. Concentrate on getting your thoughts on paper.

_____

_____

_____

_____

_____

_____

_____

_____

_____

_____

© 2002 by The Center for Applied Research in Education

10–15. A REALISTIC STORY: A FALSE ACCUSATION
(FINAL COPY)

A. DIRECTIONS: Correct and revise the first draft of your story about the person who has been unfairly accused.

1. Is your beginning as exciting as you can make it?
2. Can you add anything else to show what your main character looks like and feels?
3. Can you add anything else to the descriptions of the other characters?
4. Add something else to the description of the setting (where the story takes place) to make it clear to the reader.
5. Does the plot proceed logically? Should anything be added or cut to make it clearer?
6. Add at least one colorful adjective and one sensory word.
7. Does the ending solve the problem in a satisfying way?
8. Are your sentences complete? Do subjects and verbs agree?
9. Do you capitalize all proper names and sentence beginnings?
10. Check your spelling with a dictionary.
11. Ask your teacher or another student to look at your story and make suggestions.

B. DIRECTIONS: Begin the final copy of your story below and continue on the back of this sheet. Write the title on the first line, and indent at the beginning of each paragraph.

_____

_____

_____

_____

_____

_____

10–16. A FANTASY STORY: FALLING DOWN A HOLE
(PREWRITING)

You are walking in a park. Suddenly, you step into a hole and fall down, down, down. When you finally land at the bottom, you find yourself in a strange and different world. You are going to write a story telling what happens to you in this weird place.

DIRECTIONS: This story will be easy and fun to write if you first prepare a **brainstorming list** on another sheet of paper.

1. Write words and phrases to describe your feelings when falling down the hole.

2. What is the first thing you see when you reach bottom?

3. Write words and phrases to describe what this world looks like.

4. What is the name of this world?

5. Write at least three sensory words (sight, sound, taste, touch, and smell) that describe this world.

6. Write words and phrases to describe the people or creatures that live here.

7. Write at least three colorful adjectives that describe these people or creatures.

8. List three or four things that happen to you in this world.

9. List three active verbs you can use when describing your adventures here.

10. On the lines below or on the back of this sheet, write an exciting **beginning** for your story, as in this example: "Suddenly, the ground opened up. I was falling, falling, falling! I was too terrified to even scream."

_____

_____

_____

_____

_____

_____

© 2002 by The Center for Applied Research in Education

Name _____ Date _____

10–17. A Fantasy Story: Falling Down a Hole
(first draft)

You are going to write a story about falling through the ground into a different world.

- Make up a title for your story and write it on the first line.
- Copy the beginning from your brainstorming list. Can you add or change anything to make it more exciting?
- Use the information on your brainstorming list to tell what happens next. Use strong, active verbs to show action.
- Use colorful adjectives and sensory words to describe this world and the creatures that live there.
- End the story in a satisfying way.

DIRECTIONS: Begin your story below and continue on the back of this sheet. This is just a first draft so don't be concerned about spelling or grammar. Concentrate on getting your thoughts on paper.

10–18. A Fantasy Story: Falling Down a Hole
(final copy)

A. DIRECTIONS: Correct and revise the first draft of your story about falling through the ground into a different world.

1. Is your beginning as exciting as you can make it?

2. Can you add colorful adjectives and sensory words to your description of this world and the creatures that live there?

3. Can you add anything else to show your feelings more strongly?

4. Do you tell what happens in a clear and logical way? Should anything be added or cut?

5. Are your sentences complete? Do subjects and verbs agree?

6. Do you capitalize all proper names and sentence beginnings?

7. Check your spelling with a dictionary.

8. Ask your teacher or another student to look at your story and make suggestions.

B. DIRECTIONS: Begin the final copy of your story below and continue on the back of this sheet. Write the title on the first line, and indent at the beginning of each paragraph.

_____

_____

_____

_____

_____

_____

_____

_____

© 2002 by The Center for Applied Research in Education

10–19. A FANTASY STORY: WHAT IF? (PREWRITING)

An easy way to get a story idea is to say "What if . . . ?" as in these examples:

❑ What if you woke up one day and found yourself in a land of fairies and wizards?

❑ What if you discovered that aliens from a distant planet were living in the house next door?

❑ What if you discovered that you were really a royal prince or princess?

A. DIRECTIONS: Choose one of these "what if's" to write a story about. Place a check in the box next to the one you have chosen.

B. DIRECTIONS: Get ready to write your story by first preparing a **brainstorming list.**

Name	Description

1. List the names of three or four characters in your story. Next to each name, write words and phrases describing that character.

2. On the back of this sheet, write four or five colorful adjectives to describe the setting where the story takes place.

3. On the back of this sheet, write four or five sensory words to describe the setting (place).

4. On the back of this sheet, list at least four events that will happen in the story.

5. On the back of this sheet, write an exciting **beginning** for your story, as in this example: "In my heart, I always knew that I was different from other people. So, I was not really surprised when those people came and told me that I was a royal princess."

10–20. A Fantasy Story: What If? (first draft)

You are going to write a first draft of the story you chose in the prewriting part of this activity.

- Make up a title for your story and write it on the first line.
- Copy the beginning from your brainstorming list.
- Use the information from your brainstorming list to tell what happens next.
- Describe each character that comes into the story.
- Use colorful adjectives and sensory words to make your story vivid.
- End the story in a satisfying way.

DIRECTIONS: Begin your story below and continue on the back of this sheet. Since this is a first draft, don't worry about spelling or grammar. Concentrate on getting your thoughts on paper.

_____

_____

_____

_____

_____

_____

_____

_____

_____

_____

_____

_____

_____

_____

Name _____ Date _____

10–21. A Fantasy Story: What If? (final copy)

A. DIRECTIONS: Correct and revise the first draft of your "what if . . . ?" story.

1. Can you change or add anything to the beginning to make it more exciting?
2. Do you relate the events of the story in a clear and logical way? Is there anything unnecessary that should be cut?
3. Add at least two colorful adjectives and two sensory words to your descriptions of characters and setting.
4. Is your ending satisfactory? Does it seem right for the story?
5. Are your sentences complete? Do subjects and verbs agree?
6. Do you capitalize all proper names and sentence beginnings?
7. Check your spelling with the dictionary.
8. Ask your teacher or another student to read your story and make suggestions.

B. DIRECTIONS: Begin the final copy of your story below and continue on the back of this sheet. Write the title on the first line, and indent at the beginning of each paragraph.

_____

_____

_____

_____

_____

_____

_____

_____

10–22. A MYSTERY STORY: THE DISAPPEARING HAMSTER (PREWRITING)

Everyone loves to read a mystery. It is fun to write one, too. This story is going to be about the disappearance of a hamster from his cage in a classroom.

DIRECTIONS: It will be easy to write this mystery story if you first complete the following **brainstorming list.** Use another sheet of paper for your answers.

1. List two kids in the class who will work together to solve the mystery. These will be the main characters. You can use real names or pretend ones. Next to each name, write words and phrases describing that character.

2. List two or three characters who will be suspected of taking the hamster. Next to each name, write words and phrases describing who they are and what they are like.

3. Write words and phrases that describe the setting (the classroom).

4. List at least three things your "detectives" will do to try to solve the mystery.

5. How do you think the story will end? What happened to the hamster?

6. On the lines below or on the back of this sheet, write a **beginning** that will grab the reader's attention, such as: "Jenna walked over to the corner of the classroom to feed the hamster. To her horror, the cage was empty!"

_____

_____

_____

_____

_____

_____

_____

_____

© 2002 by The Center for Applied Research in Education

10–23. A MYSTERY STORY: THE DISAPPEARING HAMSTER
(FIRST DRAFT)

You are going to write a first draft of your story about the disappearance of the class hamster.

- Make up a title (such as "The Case of the Missing Hamster"). Write it on the first line.

- Copy the beginning from your brainstorming list.

- Describe your two main characters, using colorful adjectives and sensory words.

- Describe in logical order exactly what happens when the two main characters investigate the mystery. Make it exciting with strong, active verbs.

- Describe how the mystery is solved and show the feelings of all the characters.

DIRECTIONS: Begin your story below and continue on the back of this sheet. Since this is a first draft, don't be concerned with spelling or grammar. Just have fun getting your ideas on paper.

10–24. A MYSTERY STORY: THE DISAPPEARING HAMSTER
(FINAL COPY)

A. DIRECTIONS: Correct and revise the first draft of your mystery story about the missing hamster.

1. Can you change anything in the beginning to make it more exciting?
2. Can you add anything else to your descriptions of the main characters to make them seem like real people?
3. Can you add anything else to your description of the setting to make it seem like a real classroom?
4. Do the main characters go about solving the mystery logically? Can you add anything to make their adventures more exciting?
5. Is the ending satisfactory? Do you show the feelings of all the characters about it?
6. Be sure all your sentences are complete. Do subjects and verbs agree?
7. Do you capitalize all proper names and sentence beginnings?
8. Check your spelling with a dictionary.
9. Ask your teacher or another student to read your story and make suggestions.

B. DIRECTIONS: Begin the final copy of your story below and continue on the back of this sheet. Write the title on the first line, and indent at the beginning of each paragraph.

_____

_____

_____

_____

_____

_____

_____

10–25. A MYSTERY STORY: THE MISSING NEIGHBORS
(PREWRITING)

You are going to write a mystery story where *you* are the detective. Someone new has moved into the house next door to you. Sometimes you see lights and hear voices inside, but *no one has ever seen the new neighbors*! You will investigate and find out who they are.

DIRECTIONS: Prepare a **brainstorming list.** Use another sheet of paper for your answers.

1. Write words and phrases to describe the houses on your street.

2. Name several characters who will be in your story. Next to each name, write words and phrases to describe them.

3. What is the first thing you will do in your investigation?

4. List the next three things you will do. (You don't need complete sentences—words and phrases are enough.)

5. Make a list of strong, active verbs and colorful adjectives that can be used to describe your adventures.

6. Make a list of sensory words that can be used to describe your feelings during these adventures.

7. Describe briefly (words and phrases) who and what you are going to find in that house.

8. On the lines below or on the back of this sheet, write an exciting **beginning** for your mystery story, such as: "It was the weirdest thing! Lights flashed on and off and voices could be heard, but nobody had ever seen our new neighbors."

_____

_____

_____

_____

_____

_____

10–26. A MYSTERY STORY: THE MISSING NEIGHBORS
(FIRST DRAFT)

You are going to write a first draft of your story about the mysterious new neighbors.

- Make up a title (such as "The Invisible Neighbors"). Write it on the first line.

- Copy the beginning from your brainstorming list.

- Describe the houses and the people who live on your street, using colorful adjectives.

- Explain why *you* decide to investigate. Do you tell anyone else what you are doing? If so, who?

- Write exciting details of your investigation and what happens. Use strong, active verbs. Describe your *feelings* in each situation.

- Make up an exciting ending.

DIRECTIONS: Begin your story below and continue on the back of this sheet. This is just a first draft, so don't worry about spelling or grammar.

_____

_____

_____

_____

_____

_____

_____

_____

_____

_____

_____

_____

© 2002 by The Center for Applied Research in Education

Name _____   Date_____

10–27. A MYSTERY STORY: THE MISSING NEIGHBORS
(FINAL COPY)

A. DIRECTIONS: Correct and revise the first draft of your story about mysterious new neighbors.

1. Can you add anything else to the beginning to make it more exciting?

2. Can you add more colorful adjectives and strong, active verbs to make your writing more vivid?

3. Does your story progress logically? Is there anything unnecessary or irrelevant that should be cut?

4. Is the ending satisfying? Does it make sense?

5. Are your sentences complete? Do subjects and verbs agree?

6. Do you capitalize all proper names and sentence beginnings?

7. Check your spelling with a dictionary.

8. Ask your teacher or another student to read your story and make suggestions.

B. DIRECTIONS: Begin the final copy of the story below and continue on the back of this sheet. Write the title on the first line, and indent at the beginning of each paragraph.

_____

_____

_____

_____

_____

_____

_____

_____

FOURTH-GRADE LEVEL

WRITING STORIES

PRACTICE TEST

PRACTICE TEST: WRITING STORIES

DIRECTIONS: Your teacher has just shown you a picture of a boy about your age. He is standing in front of his classroom and seems to be speaking to his classmates. Make up a story of at least three paragraphs based on this description of the picture. Be as interesting and imaginative as you can be.

CHECKLIST

Make sure to:

_____ 1. Write an interesting beginning.

_____ 2. Describe the setting (where and when) and the character(s).

_____ 3. Tell how the character(s) is/are feeling.

_____ 4. Develop the plot by writing a clear beginning, a middle, and an end.

_____ 5. Include sensory words, vivid verbs, and colorful adjectives.

_____ 6. Vary sentence lengths and use effective transitions.

_____ 7. Write the story's title above the first sentence and indent each paragraph.

_____ 8. Check for complete sentences, misspellings, capitalization, subject–verb agreement, and consistent verb tense.

Follow these four steps to complete your story:

- FIRST, on the page labeled PREWRITING, brainstorm some ideas. Then rewrite them in a workable form to help you develop your story's plot and characters.

- SECOND, write the first draft of your story. Your opening sentence should capture the reader's interest. Write an interesting conclusion to satisfy the reader.

- THIRD, revise and edit your first draft. Make sure your story is well developed. Check to see that you have written complete sentences, spelled all the words correctly, and used verb tense consistently.

- FOURTH, on a separate sheet of paper, write the final draft of your story.

© 2002 by The Center for Applied Research in Education

PRACTICE TEST: WRITING STORIES *(Continued)*

Prewriting

On the lines brainstorm words and phrases about the plot, setting, and character(s) for your story. Then, in the space, organize your ideas in a cluster, a list, or an outline.

_____

_____

_____

_____

_____

_____

Scoring Guide

© 2002 by The Center for Applied Research in Education

SCORE	1	2
Content and Organization	– lacks beginning, middle, end – no organization of details – no evidence of setting – no plot/character development	– may lack beginning, middle, end – organization of details is attempted – some evidence of a setting – unclear plot/character development
Usage	– no control over word choice	– little control over word choice
Sentence Construction	– far too many sentence fragments and/or run-on sentences	– too many sentence fragments and run-on sentences affect understanding
Mechanics	– numerous serious errors prevent comprehension	– numerous serious errors affect understanding

SCORE	3	4
Content and Organization	– may lack beginning and ending – some organization is evident – setting is unclear – little plot/character development	– lacks clear beginning or ending – organization is more focused – setting is clear – plot/characters developed
Usage	– some errors affect understanding – few sensory or descriptive details	– errors do not affect understanding – some sensory and descriptive details
Sentence Construction	– frequent fragments and short, choppy sentences affect meaning	– some fragments and short, choppy sentences but do not affect meaning
Mechanics	– spelling and punctuation errors are distracting	– some errors but they don't take away from meaning

SCORE	5	6
Content and Organization	– usually has an effective beginning, middle, and ending – good details show time and place – good plot/character development	– has a very effective beginning, middle, and ending – excellent details show time and place – excellent plot/character development
Usage	– a few errors	– very few errors (if any)
Sentence Construction	– good variety of simple, compound, and complex sentences	– excellent variety of simple, compound, and complex sentences
Mechanics	– few errors	– very few errors (if any)

PRACTICE TEST: WRITING STORIES *(Continued)*

Student Samples

DIRECTIONS: Rate the stories below with a score from 1 (lowest) to 6 (highest). Use the information on the scoring guide to help you.

STORY A

John was boy forth grade, he walked up at class. Then say he name. So they clappd. Loud. Then he smiles. John wait his turn. John was happy be in forth grade. His friend in this new skool to. His techr say "sit down." So John sit down. He feel good inside. His first day in my class at skool. This be fun and nice techr to me this year?

Score _____

STORY B

It's Your Turn, Jose

Jose knew he had to do it. Why? Everyone else in his fourth grade class had already done it at least once this year. Plus, all the kids in the other fourth grade class across the hall did too. Now it was Jose's turn.

The big day finally arrived. The tall young teacher, Ms. Cauley, called Jose's name and told him to come up to the front of the room. The shy Jose nervously went to get up from his seat. He had a little sick feeling inside of him. As Jose went towards the teacher's desk, the other students stared at Jose. He could not really look back at them because he was so scared.

Ms. Cauley asked, "Are you ready, Jose?" He softly said, "I guess so." Then, feeling like the whole world was watching him, Jose cleared his throat and then started to do what all the other fourth graders had already done.

In less than a minute, it was over. Jose felt very relieved as he heard the students laugh and then clap. He had done it! Jose had told a joke in front of his teacher and classmates!

Score _____

Proofreading Marks

Mark	Meaning
⌐H	indent first line of paragraph
≡	capitalize
∧ or ∨	add
ℓ	remove
⊙	add a period
/	make lowercase
↺	move
∼	transpose

APPENDIX

PREPARING YOUR STUDENTS FOR STANDARDIZED PROFICIENCY TESTS

Even as the debate over the value and fairness of standardized tests continues, standardized tests are an annual event for millions of students. In most school districts the results of the tests are vitally important. Scores may be used to determine if students are meeting district or state guidelines, they may be used as a means of comparing the scores of the district's students to local or national norms, or they may be used to decide a student's placement in advanced or remedial classes. No matter how individual scores are used in your school, students deserve the chance to do well. They deserve to be prepared.

By providing students with practice in answering the kinds of questions they will face on a standardized test, an effective program of preparation can familiarize students with testing formats, refresh skills, build confidence, and reduce anxiety, all critical factors that can affect scores as much as basic knowledge. Just like the members of an orchestra rehearse to get ready for a concert, the dancer trains for the big show, and the pianist practices for weeks before the grand recital, preparing students for standardized tests is essential.

To be most effective a test-preparation program should be comprehensive, based on skills your students need to know, and enlist the support of parents. Because students often assume the attitudes of their parents regarding tests—for example, nervous parents frequently make their children anxious—you should seek as much parental involvement in your test preparations as possible. Students who are encouraged by their parents and prepared for tests by their teachers invariably do better than those who come to the testing session with little preparation and support.

What Parents Need to Know About Standardized Tests

While most parents will agree it is important for their children to do well on standardized tests, many feel there is little they can do to help the outcome. Consequently, aside from encouraging their children to "try your best," they feel there is nothing more for them to do. Much of this feeling arises from parents not fully understanding the testing process.

To provide the parents of your students with information about testing, consider sending home copies of the following reproducibles:

- ✏ The Uses of Standardized Tests
- ✏ Test Terms
- ✏ Common Types of Standardized Tests
- ✏ Preparing Your Child for Standardized Tests

You may wish to send these home in a packet with a cover letter (a sample of which is included) announcing the upcoming standardized tests.

The Uses of Standardized Tests

Schools administer standardized tests for a variety of purposes. It is likely that your child's school utilizes the scores of standardized tests in at least some of the following ways.

- Identify strengths and weaknesses in academic skills.

- Identify areas of high interest, ability, or aptitude. Likewise identify areas of average or low ability or aptitude.

- Compare the scores of students within the district to each other as well as to students of other districts. This can be done class to class, school to school, or district to district. Such comparisons help school systems to evaluate their curriculums and plan instruction and programs.

- Provide a basis for comparison of report card grades to national standards.

- Identify students who might benefit from advanced or remedial classes.

- Certify student achievement, for example, in regard to receiving awards.

- Provide reports on student progress.

Test Terms

Although standardized tests come in different forms and may be designed to measure different skills, most share many common terms. Understanding these "test terms" is the first step to understanding the tests.

- ✒ **Achievement tests** measure how much students have learned in a particular subject area. They concentrate on knowledge of subject matter.

- ✒ **Aptitude tests** are designed to predict how well students will do in learning new subject matter in the future. They generally measure a broad range of skills associated with success. Note that the line between aptitude and achievement tests is often indistinct.

- ✒ **Battery** refers to a group of tests that are administered during the same testing session. For example, separate tests for vocabulary, language, reading, spelling, and mathematics that comprise an achievement test are known as the *test battery*.

- ✒ **Correlation coefficient** is a measure of the strength and direction of the relationship between two items. It can be a positive or negative number.

- ✒ **Diagnostic tests** are designed to identify the strengths and weaknesses of students in specific subject areas. They are usually given only to students who show exceptional ability or serious weakness in an area.

- ✒ **Grade equivalent scores** are a translation of the score attained on the test to an approximate grade level. Thus, a student whose score translates to a grade level of 4.5 is working at roughly the midyear point of fourth grade. One whose score equals a grade level of 8.0 is able to successfully complete work typically given at the beginning of eighth grade.

- ✒ **Individual student profiles** (also referred to as *reports*) display detailed test results for a particular student. Some of these can be so precise that the answer to every question is shown.

- ✒ **Item** is a specific question on a test.

- ✒ **Mean** is the average of a group of scores.

- ✒ **Median** is the middle score in a group of scores.

- ✒ **Mode** is the score achieved most by a specific group of test takers.

- ✒ **Normal distribution** is a distribution of test scores in which the scores are distributed around the mean and where the mean, median, and mode are the same. A normal distribution, when displayed, appears bell-shaped.

- ✒ **Norming population** is the group of students (usually quite large) to whom the test was given and on whose results performance standards for various age or grade levels are based. *Local norms* refer to distributions based on a particular school or school district. *National norms* refer to distributions based on students from around the country.

- ✒ **Norm-referenced tests** are tests in which the results of the test may be compared with other norming populations.

Test Terms *(Continued)*

✎ *Percentile rank* is a comparison of a student's raw score with the raw scores of others who took the test. The comparison is most often made with members of the norming population. Percentile rank enables a test taker to see where his or her scores rank among others who take the same test. A percentile rank of 90, for example, means that the test taker scored better than 90% of those who took the test. A percentile rank of 60 means the test taker scored better than 60% of those who took the test. A percentile rank of 30 means he or she scored better than only 30% of those who took the test, and that 70% of the test takers had higher scores.

✎ *Raw score* is the score of a test based on the number correct. On some tests the raw score may include a correction for guessing.

✎ *Reliability* is a measure of the degree to which a test measures what it is designed to measure. A test's reliability may be expressed as a reliability coefficient that typically ranges from 0 to 1. Highly reliable tests have reliability coefficients of 0.90 or higher. Reliability coefficients may take several forms. For example, parallel-form reliability correlates the performance on two different forms of a test; split-half reliability correlates two halves of the same test; and test-retest reliability correlates test scores of the same test given at two different times. The producers of standardized tests strive to make them as reliable as possible. Although there are always cases of bright students not doing well on a standardized test and some students who do surprisingly well, most tests are quite reliable and provide accurate results.

✎ *Score* is the number of correct answers displayed in some form. Sometimes the score is expressed as a *scaled score*, which means that the score provided by the test is derived from the number of correct answers.

✎ *Standard deviation* is a measure of the variability of test scores. If most scores are near the mean score, the standard deviation will be small; if scores vary widely from the mean, the standard deviation will be large.

✎ *Standard error of measurement* is an estimate of the amount of possible measurement error in a test. It provides an estimate of how much a student's true test score may vary from the actual score he or she obtained on the test. Tests that have a large standard error of measurement may not accurately reflect a student's true ability. The standard error of measurement is usually small for well-designed tests.

✎ *Standardized tests* are tests that have been given to students under the same conditions. They are designed to measure the same skills and abilities for everyone who takes them.

✎ *Stanine scores* are scores expressed between the numbers 1 and 9 with 9 being high.

✎ *Validity* is the degree to which a test measures what it is supposed to measure. There are different kinds of validity. One, *content validity,* for example, refers to the degree to which the content of the test is valid for the purpose of the test. Another, *predictive validity,* refers to the extent to which predictions based on the test are later proven accurate by other evidence.

© 2002 by The Center for Applied Research in Education

Common Types of Standardized Tests

Most standardized tests are broken down into major sections that focus on specific subjects. Together these sections are referred to as a *battery.* The materials and skills tested are based on grade level. The following tests are common throughout the country; however, not all schools administer every test.

- ✆ *Analogy tests* measure a student's ability to understand relationships between words (ideas). Here is an example: Boy is to man as girl is to woman. The relationship, of course, is that a boy becomes a man and a girl becomes a woman. Not only does an analogy test the ability to recognize relationships, it tests vocabulary as well.

- ✆ *Vocabulary tests* determine whether students understand the meaning of certain words. They are most often based on the student's projected grade-level reading, comprehension, and spelling skills.

- ✆ *Reading comprehension tests* show how well students can understand reading passages. These tests appear in many different formats. In most, students are required to read a passage and then answer questions designed to measure reading ability.

- ✆ *Spelling tests* show spelling competence, based on grade-level appropriate words. The tests may require students to select a correctly spelled word from among misspelled words, or may require students to find the misspelled word among correctly spelled words.

- ✆ *Language mechanics tests* concentrate on capitalization and punctuation. Students may be required to find examples of incorrect capitalization and punctuation as well as examples of correct capitalization and punctuation in sentences and short paragraphs.

- ✆ *Language expression tests* focus on the ability of students to use words correctly according to the standards of conventional English. In many "expression" tests, effective structuring of ideas is also tested.

- ✆ *Writing tests* determine how effectively students write and can express their ideas. Usually a topic is given and students must express their ideas on the topic.

- ✆ *Mathematics problem-solving tests* are based on concepts and applications, and assess the ability of students to solve math problems. These tests often include sections on number theory, interpretation of data and graphs, and logical analysis.

- ✆ *Mathematics computation tests* measure how well students can add, subtract, multiply, and divide. While the difficulty of the material depends on grade level, these tests generally cover whole numbers, fractions, decimals, percents, and geometry.

- ✆ *Science tests* measure students' understanding of basic science facts and the methodology used by scientists in the development of theoretical models that explain natural phenomena.

- ✆ *Social studies tests* measure students' understanding of basic facts in social studies.

Preparing Your Child for Standardized Tests

As a parent, there is much you can do to help your son or daughter get ready for taking a standardized test.

During the weeks leading up to the test . . .

✏ Attend parent–teacher conferences and find out how you can help your child succeed in school.

✏ Assume an active role in school. Seeing your commitment to his or her school enhances the image of school in your child's eyes.

✏ Find out when standardized tests are given and plan accordingly. For example, avoid scheduling doctor or dentist appointments for your child during the testing dates. Students who take standardized tests with their class usually do better than students who make up tests because of absences.

✏ Monitor your child's progress in school. Make sure your child completes his or her homework and projects. Support good study habits and encourage your child to always do his or her best.

✏ Encourage your child's creativity and interests. Provide plenty of books, magazines, and educational opportunities.

✏ Whenever you speak of standardized tests, speak of them in a positive manner. Emphasize that while these tests are important, it is not the final score that counts, but that your child tries his or her best.

During the days immediately preceding the test . . .

✏ Once the test has been announced, discuss the test with your child to relieve apprehension. Encourage your son or daughter to take the test seriously, but avoid being overly anxious. (Sometimes parents are more nervous about their children's tests than the kids are.)

✏ Help your child with any materials his or her teacher sends home in preparation for the test.

✏ Make sure your child gets a good night's sleep each night before a testing day.

✏ On the morning of the test, make sure your child wakes up on time, eats a solid breakfast, and arrives at school on time.

✏ Remind your child to listen to the directions of the teacher carefully and to read directions carefully.

✏ Encourage your child to do his or her best.

Cover Letter to Parents
Announcing Standardized Tests

Use the following letter to inform the parents of your students about upcoming standardized tests in your school. Feel free to adjust the letter according to your needs.

Dear Parents/Guardians,

On _____ (dates) _____ , our class will be taking the _____ (name of test) _____ . During the next few weeks students will work on various practice tests to help prepare for the actual test.

You can help, too. Please read the attached materials and discuss the importance of the tests with your child. By supporting your child's efforts in preparation, you can help him or her attain the best possible scores.

Thank you.

Sincerely,

(Name)

What Students Need to Know About Standardized Tests

The mere thought of taking a standardized test frightens many students, causing a wide range of symptoms from mild apprehension to upset stomachs and panic attacks. Since even low levels of anxiety can distract students and undermine their achievement, you should attempt to lessen their concerns.

Apprehension, anxiety, and fear are common responses to situations that we perceive as being out of our control. When students are faced with a test on which they don't know what to expect, they may worry excessively that they won't do well. Such emotions, especially when intense, almost guarantee that they will make careless mistakes. When students are prepared properly for a test, they are more likely to know "what to expect." This reduces negative emotions and students are able to enter the testing situation with confidence, which almost always results in better scores.

The first step to preparing your students for standardized tests is to mention the upcoming tests well in advance—at least a few weeks ahead of time—and explain that in the days leading up to the test, the class will be preparing. Explain that while they will not be working with the actual test, the work they will be doing is designed to help them get ready. You may wish to use the analogy of a sports team practicing during the pre-season. Practices help players sharpen their skills, anticipate game situations, and build confidence. Practicing during the pre-season helps athletes perform better during the regular season.

You might find it useful to distribute copies of the following reproducibles:

✏ Test-taking Tips for Students

✏ Test Words You Should Know

Hand these out a few days before the testing session. Go over them with your students and suggest that they take them home and ask their parents to review the sheets with them on the night before the test.

TEST-TAKING TIPS FOR STUDENTS

1. Try your best.

2. Be confident and think positively. People who believe they will do well usually do better than those who are not confident.

3. Fill out the answer sheet correctly. Be careful that you darken all "circles." Be sure to use a number 2 pencil unless your teacher tells you otherwise.

4. Listen carefully to all directions and follow them exactly. If you don't understand something, ask your teacher.

5. Read all questions and their possible answers carefully. Sometimes an answer may at first seem right, but it isn't. Always read all answers before picking one.

6. Try to answer the questions in order, but don't waste too much time on hard questions. Go on to easier ones and then go back to the hard ones.

7. Don't be discouraged by hard questions. On most tests for every hard question there are many easy ones.

8. Try not to make careless mistakes.

9. Budget your time and work quickly.

10. Be sure to fill in the correct answer spaces on your answer sheet. Use a finger of your non-writing hand to keep your place on the answer space.

11. Look for clues and key words when answering questions.

12. If you become "stuck" on a question, eliminate any answers you know are wrong and then make your best guess of the remaining answers. (Do this only if there is no penalty for guessing. Check with your teacher about this.)

13. Don't leave any blanks. Guess if you are running out of time. (Only do this if unanswered questions are counted wrong. Check with your teacher.)

14. Double-check your work if time permits.

15. Erase completely any unnecessary marks on your answer sheet.

TEST WORDS YOU SHOULD KNOW

The words below are used in standardized tests. Understanding what each one means will help you when you take your test.

all	double-check	opposite
always	end	order
answer sheet	error	oval
best	example	part
blank	fill in	passage
booklet	finish	pick
bubble	following	punctuation
capitalization	go on	question
check	item	read
choose	language expression	reread
circle	language mechanics	right
column	mark	row
complete	match	same as
comprehension	missing	sample
continue	mistake	section
correct	name	select
definition	never	stop
details	none	topic
directions	not true	true
does not belong	number 2 pencil	vocabulary

Creating a Positive
Test-taking Environment

Little things really do matter when students take standardized tests. Students who are consistently encouraged to do their best throughout the year in the regular classroom generally achieve higher scores on standardized tests than students who maintain a careless attitude regarding their studies. Of course, motivating students to do their best is an easy thing to suggest, but not such an easy goal to accomplish.

There are, fortunately, some steps you can take to foster positive attitudes on the part of your students in regard to standardized tests. Start by discussing the test students will take, and explain how the results of standardized tests are used. When students understand the purpose of testing, they are more likely to take the tests seriously. Never speak of tests in a negative manner, for example, saying that students must work hard or they will do poorly. Instead, speak in positive terms: by working hard and trying their best they will achieve the best results.

To reduce students' concerns, assure them that the use of practice tests will improve their scores. Set up a thorough test-preparation schedule well in advance of the tests, based upon the needs and abilities of your students. Avoid cramming preparation into the last few days before the test. Cramming only burdens students with an increased workload and leads to anxiety and worry. A regular, methodical approach to preparation is best, because this enables you to check for weaknesses in skills and offer remediation.

The value of preparation for standardized tests cannot be understated. When your students feel that they are prepared for the tests, and that you have confidence in them, they will feel more confident and approach the tests with a positive frame of mind. Along with effective instruction throughout the year, a focused program of test preparation will help ensure that your students will have the chance to achieve their best scores on standardized tests.